UnderWords

UnderWords

Perspectives on Don DeLillo's
Underworld

Edited by Joseph Dewey,
Steven G. Kellman,
and Irving Malin

DELAWARE

Newark: University of Delaware Press
London: Associated University Presses

Associated University Presses
440 Forsgate Drive
Cranbury, NJ 08512

Associated University Presses
16 Barter Street
London WC1A 2AH, England

Associated University Presses
P.O. Box 338, Port Credit
Mississauga, Ontario
Canada L5G 4L8

The paper used in this publication meets the requirements of the American National Standard for Permanence of Paper for Printed Library Materials Z39.48-1984.

Library of Congress Cataloging-in-Publication Data

UnderWords : perspectives on Don DeLillo's Underworld / edited by
    Joseph Dewey, Steven G. Kellman, and Irving Malin.
        p.   cm.
    Includes bibliographical references and index.
    ISBN 0-87413-785-3 (alk. paper)
    1. DeLillo, Don. Underworld.   I. Dewey, Joseph, 1957–   .
II. Kellman, Steven G., 1947–   .   III. Malin, Irving.
PS3554.E4425 U5338   2002
813'.54—dc21   2002021769

Contents

5

Acknowledgments

WHEN WE FIRST ANNOUNCED PLANS FOR A BOOK DEVOTED EXCLUSIVELY to Don DeLillo's 1997 masterwork *Underworld*, we initially received more than one hundred queries, proposals, outlines, e-mail directives, and drafts. By deadline, we had received nearly that many submissions to consider. We very much want to thank those who forwarded their essays, not only for their interest in this project but for allowing us the opportunity to read their work. We would also like to thank our contributors whose gracious assistance and prompt help kept the project moving forward. We would also like to thank those at the Associated University Presses, specifically Julien Yoseloff and Christine Retz, and Donald C. Mell of the University of Delaware Press for seeing this project through into book form with care, interest, consummate professionalism, and efficient expertise. The editors are also grateful to Priscilla Stump and Julie Miller for their help in preparing the submissions into a single manuscript; to Mark Thomas for his computer savvy and know-how in preparing the computer work; and Carrie Lynn who worked methodically and carefully to proofread the manuscript with diligence and thought and who made sure every comma was honestly used, every semi-colon was in place, and every sentence kept its direction. Finally we would like to thank Scribner's for their help in this project; *The New York Times* for their permission to use the 4 October 1951 front page as the jacket subject; and Don DeLillo himself for conjuring a work so beautifully able to sustain this treatment.

A Gathering Under Words: An Introduction

JOSEPH DEWEY

THERE IS SURELY SOMETHING DEFIANT ABOUT A CONSTELLATION—NOT the secondhand act of locating one in the night sky, but rather the original work of fetching a convincing pattern from such forbidding vastness. It is a telling exercise—horrified over the irrevocable implication of our puniness, the ancients indulged a fondness for invented (hence, manageable) complication, the familiar love of control implicit in devising any system, the deep intoxication of controlled intricacy. Recovering such fragile configurations— chariots, swans, peacocks, even drinking cups—is, of course, the bravura act of the imagination. The night sky stays wonderfully free of our primitive need to map such an environment, the need we feel dwarfed by such architecture, fashioned by the free arm of chance, for the satisfying sense of grasping at least a bit of its formidable structure.

Readers of contemporary serious fiction are surely sympathetic with those ancient skymappers, there under the night sky. Such readers, necessarily enthralled by the intrigue of re-rereading a multidimensional text, appreciate the immense reach of such texts. They gather—under words, as it were—to devise readings, to connect the dots, to configure convincing patterns that satisfy the complicated need to understand. Surely, those who shape such eloquent systems share the initial awe of stepping within such formidable texts, the sheer vulnerability in engaging in the aesthetic enterprise with texts that since the heyday of Pynchon and Gaddis have sustained a generation of critical scrutiny.

Underworld, Don DeLillo's 1997 masterwork, surely belongs in such company. It invites terror and awe. It intimidates. It has the heft and forbidding feel of serious fiction—not merely the weight of its more than 800 pages, but its massively conceived trajectories of multiple plotlines sustained across an investigation of American culture that begins in the early frost of the Cold War and closes in the contemporary virtual wonderland of cyberspace. It is at turns elusive and inviting, difficult and mesmerizing, hopeful and despairing, enthralling and exasperating. Of course, masterworks in American experience have a way of barely disturbing the surface calm of their moment—published, they pass quickly into obscurity, thus privileging later generations with the right of excavation. *Underworld* is an exception to this. In its short life, barely four years at this writing, it has generated, apart from an expansive clutch of critical reviews, an impressive array of academic speculations that have completed the canonization of DeLillo. It would appear that we agree something unusual happened with this text, that here is something that will last.

Still, like the night sky, *Underworld* eludes each effort at definition. Indeed any definition is beset by yets. It is most obviously a cultural biography, a complex weave of fictional characters and historical personages, a wide-lens look at fifty years of the American experience that moves from the apocalyptic anxieties of the Cold War to the unearned giddiness following the stunningly quick collapse of the Soviet empire. Yet, if it is cultural in its reach, it as well a narrow look at the aesthetic enterprise, specifically an investigation into the evolution of the artist in the era of mass media. It is also a traditional realistic narrative, the going-into of a recognizable character, an exhaustive excavation into one man's life-long loss of vitality, a narrative that tracks backwards the difficult dynamic that man has maintained with his family, his education, his work, and his marriage.

It as well a fierce satire that examines with the glowering dissatisfaction of a savage Old Testament prophet the contemporary lurch into the wasteland, our terminal fascination with violence, the tentacled reach of domestic entertainment technologies, our deep faith in the propaganda of consumerism, our indulgence of fanaticism. Yet, if it despairs, it celebrates as well. *Underworld* is a daring religious novel that confirms as significant the need to touch a spiritual overlay amid the intricate circuitry of our physical nature—the narrative draws from the mystical energy of traditional Catholicism, the vocabulary of miracles, eerie New Age spirituality, even primitive numerology (particularly the number thirteen). Despite such ascent into the spiritual, the novel lovingly indulges the press and feel of the immediate; it is DeLillo's touching gesture at autobiography, his most intimate record of his own childhood in the Bronx.

But, if it generates such warmth, it is as well maddeningly cool, it is a self-reflexive exercise in language, a vast and enclosing playscape in which a writer manipulates voices to create a stunning jazz-like improv, and a collage of styles to direct our attention not on the events but on the implications of transcribing events into the virtual reality of words. Yet, despite such cerebral experimenting, *Underworld* is also a shamelessly sentimental jock novel, a sort of *Field of Dreams*-ish (melo)drama that speculates about how we coin our heroes (and our myths) from the unpromising stuff on the playing field and even plays on the missing-father/wounded-son tension critical to so much traditional sports fiction.

Or, perhaps it is more like a Gothic novel of sensation in which the plot accelerates toward the revelation of a stunning secret (the accidental shooting of a man and an affair between a teenager and an older married woman), a narrative in which duplicity yields ultimately to confession. Perhaps it is a comedy in the largest sense, a narrative that records the stunning freewheeling adlib of our contemporary moment to argue how we need only examine any moment to find the refulgent argument for design. Or, perhaps it is a cutting parody of such expectations that deliberately spins mock-webs of connection that turn the closing affirmation of peace and unexpected transcendence bitterly ironic.

That it is each of these is fascinating—that it manages to be all of them rewards the speculations gathered here, a clutch of constellation-makers who gather under the spell of words. But, we hope they are more than speculations—they are, as well, invitations that recognize the function of such a collection is to extend the round, to keep alive texts that promise to become defining works of their cultural moment. It is a matter of coincidence that *Underworld* appeared within weeks of another masterwork of the late-century American imagination, Thomas Pynchon's long-anticipated *Mason & Dixon*. Like *Underworld*, *Mason & Dixon* is large-scaled in its intention, a vast tale of the closing of the American Garden and our relaxation into technology. Like *Underworld*, it demands re-reading and invites speculations. The two monumental works vied, depending on critical disposition, for the title of Last Great Achievement of Modernism or the Long-Promised Summary-Text of Postmodernism or the First Great Work of Post-Post Modernism.

But, therein lies a dilemma. These two stunning achievements stand rather like the twin towers of the World Trade Center, whose construction figures in *Underworld* and whose unmistakable shapes stand fogbound in the Andre Kertesz photo on the jacket of the first hardcover edition. Like those twin towers, *Underworld* and *Mason & Dixon* can stand as sterile examples of the marvelous expenditure of design, simply towering monuments to our need for towering monuments, intricate complexes of parts and forces that coalesce into cold monuments to our need for bigness, our hunger for scale and design. After all, nothing was done in the World Trade Center that could not have been done in a dozen smaller office buildings. Thus such monuments eventually blend into the urban landscape, lost once we register our initial breathless appreciation for so vast an architectured structure. And similarly such formidable texts, after initial critical response, can settle too quickly into the tombdust of university library shelves, lost to a larger reading public that has long ago abandoned the stamina such texts require.

This collection recognizes that we have only begun the work of explicating this formidable text and that appreciation of its achievement cannot lapse into nostalgia. It is one of those rare texts that invites continued participation. Despite DeLillo's quite public assertion that he feels diminished by readers, this text compels. We venture into its labyrinth relentlessly aware of the search-ness of our search. *Underworld* is a book about connections, a book that is itself relentlessly aware of its fascination with coincidences, with patterns that go unsuspected amid the rolling ad-lib of the day to day. Thus, willing readers are intrigued, taunted, and impressed by the apparently inexhaustible strategies of connections deployed amid the vast narrative lines, a rococo exercise in coincidences that recovers, like those colored stones in a turning kaleidoscope tube, a stunning and satisfying sense of design. Like the night sky, the novel is a site that invites pattern-making and yet can stand apart from such expenditure of intuition and intellection. No essay here pretends completeness, or argues that, now, the novel is exhausted. Each is an eloquent act of clarity, a stunning recovery of a sustainable picture, like the longitude and latitude of a single constellation. But, like a constellation, each is designed to help orient those preparing to step under the vast spell of the text itself.

We have gathered 13—no surprise given the novel's obsession with the number—speculations that interrogate the text, conjure such speculations into manageable arguments, yet recognize the text untidily resists such tidiness. Recognizing the text's confirmation of our need to manage and organize, we begin with the tightest and most involved sort of critical explication, the focused reading. Irving Malin and Joseph Dewey collaborate to investigate a single such patterning, the intricate possibilities suggested by De-Lillo's curious use of three Edgars: FBI Director J. Edgar Hoover; the classroom tyrant Sister Alma Edgar; and the poet Edgar Allan Poe. Such speculations, of course, only hint at the design operating in even the smallest unit of the novel and invite, indeed demand, similar improvisations, similar explorations of other designs within the novel.

We move then into wider explorations, summary analyses that touch on the wider reach of the novel using two apparently different (yet strikingly consistent patterns) of argument: cubism and chaos theory. David Yetter finds the text a cubist experiment in narrative that manipulates language strategies to interrogate events simultaneously from multiple angles, to create, like a cubist canvas, a disconcerting anxiety. Using chaos theory, Robert McMinn maps out a text that coheres as a search for meaning mirrored by Nick's search for atonement, a book that pursues the design implicit in narrative by interrogating how multiple lines of related narratives can achieve coherence, like a fractal pattern, without the ham-fisted authorial intrusion associated with traditional linear narratives. David Cowart senses the uneasiness beneath such a freewheeling narrative and speaks to the terror we share over a contemporary world that appears to defy understanding and how DeLillo suggests that the exacting effort of language—the decision to open up through sharing and confession—endows this narrative with a profound intimacy, the record of a bitter character's search for his lost vitality.

We branch out then into broader patterns of meaning, the first an offering that locates *Underworld* within the ever-evolving complex of DeLillo's own canon and then three others that link the novel's considerable argument to other significant contemporary texts. Steven G. Kellman explores DeLillo's career-long fascination with the enterprise of conspiracy as a way to provide the satisfying bend and curve of plot to the otherwise hot-rush of unmediated events. Timothy L. Parrish and Carl Ostrowski use the coincidental publication of *Mason & Dixon* to shed light on how each writer has refined the midcentury fad-sensation of paranoia into a more compelling, even benevolent logic that empowers artists to provide what in another age the deity sustained: the defiant assurance that only the unexamined moment appears adrift within an unbounded chaos. Using *Underworld*'s manipulations of the epic, Bobby Thomson's shot as organizing strategy, Donald J. Greiner juxtaposes DeLillo's extensive Prologue with John Updike's classic essay on Ted Williams' last game to argue that both writers understand the religious dimension to sports, particularly how we have come to fashion our sustaining myths from those titanic athletic moments recorded not only within the freezeframe of media technologies but as well within the collective give-and-take of memory and retellings, a thesis all the more intriguing given the revelation in late 2000 that perhaps Thomson's Giants were stealing signals and that there was a bit of unsavory and decidedly unheroic duplicity in the melodrama at the Polo Grounds.

We then move into even broader branchings as a way to suggest that *Underworld* binds itself to larger traditions within the American imagination. Joanne Gass establishes critical ties between two Nicks—Nick Shay and Fitzgerald's Nick Carraway—to argue that DeLillo senses how we have trashed the Garden, how we have lost the powerful comforts of the natural realm and the moral innocence that went with such bindings, and how the estrangement forecast in the nostalgic closing lines of *Gatsby* is realized in the broad alienation and complete disconnection of the cyberspace frontier toward which DeLillo's narrative irrevocably moves. Paul Gleason shares the forbidding sense of the waste land and takes us through a close rendering of *Underworld* as a return to Eliot's crisis-poem to argue how DeLillo fashions his own sort of redemptive act, not via Eliot's mystical aestheticism, but rather by endorsing the power of language to recycle waste, that is random experience itself, into a usable order.

We close with three readings that usher us into the vast conspiracy of connectionism that makes a work such as *Underworld* an inviting text-site for speculating. Kathleen Fitzpatrick locates *Underworld* within the company of metafictional texts that track the process of making a plot and suggests that DeLillo's radical use of backwards trajectory—the lurch from 1951 in the Prologue to the 1990s and then backwards—is an exercise in untelling Nick's story, of peeling away the secrecy, that reinvigorates the premise of history even as it undermines any pretense to authenticity and absoluteness by underscoring the act of recycling events, the telling difference between events and the narratives we tell about them. Thomas Myers takes us to a far different frontier, dispensing with literary pedigrees entirely to explore the cinema (a critical influence reservoir in *Underworld*), specifically unexpected parallels between the disturbing visions of two kids from the same Bronx neighborhood, DeLillo and filmmaker Stanley Kubrick. Juxtaposing the comic terror that centers the Cold War sensibility of each, Myers places *Underworld* within the complex of post-Hiroshima thought shaped by artists who found themselves inextricably steeped in the techno-madness of nuclear logic. And we close with our collection's most far-reaching sensibility—Ira Nadel's speculations on *Underworld* as comedy, an ambitious configuration that begins with the hot improv chatter of Lenny Bruce and the prefab sitcom slickness of Jackie Gleason but reaches ultimately to the classic comic affirmation of Dante to suggest that DeLillo's deployment of comedy is as it has been since *The Divine Comedy* a strategy of resistance to mediocrity and conformity, a strike-force guerrilla strategy in which comedy separates itself from the annihilating force of group-thought.

Each essay, we hope, opens further speculation, about the novel's considerable interior architecture; about the novel's larger themes of spiritual transcendence, the mechanics of a culture's collective memory, the role of language, the need for secrecy, and psychology of violence; about the novel's position within DeLillo's long career and specifically how the novel, so massive in its scope and so daunting in its execution, segues into its spare and minimal successor, the haunting and haunted *The Body Artist*; how the novel fits among other fin-de-siècle/fin-de-millennium works of the American literary imagination; and ultimately how the novel places among the other massively-conceived and defining works of the American experience since *Moby-Dick*. Like *Underworld* itself, we offer a welter of voices, a juxtaposition of lightly choreographed speculations from the full range of academic backgrounds. Each essay invites us to turn text-ward and there to fetch original synchronicities, new convergences, unsuspected possibilities of patterning—a chance for each of us to touch the sweet author-ity of design that is at the heart of *Underworld*.

UnderWords

"What Beauty, What Power":
Speculations on the Third Edgar

IRVING MALIN AND JOSEPH DEWEY

Alone in her room [Sister Alma Edgar] wore a plain shift and read "The Raven." She read it many times, memorizing the lines. She wanted to recite the poem to her class when school reopened. Her namesake poet, yes, and the dark croaking poem that made her feel Edgarish again , contoured, shaped, bevoiced, in the absence of her boys and girls.

—*Underworld* (775)

Reality doesn't happen until you analyze the dots.

—Marvin Lundy

WHEN ALBERT BRONZINI LECTURES HIS HIGH SCHOOL GENERAL SCIENCE class, a gathering of the restless and the bored, he speaks (largely to the walls and windows, he acknowledges) of the sheer intrigue of observation, how "we can't see the world clearly until we understand how nature is organized. We need to count, measure and test." He goes on to enthuse, "This is the real power. How the mind operates. How the mind identifies, analyzes and represents. What beauty and power" (734–35). *Underworld* is supremely such an invitation to observe, to analyze, to count, measure, and test. In every chapter, in virtually every paragraph, passages intrigue, patterns of evidence appear to appear, suggestive links seem to manifest themselves. Readers moving through such a vast text, one so animated by the sheer suggestivity of possible designs, are encouraged—even compelled—to participate, in effect, to connect the dots. What beauty, indeed; what power!

What follows is one such speculation, one such patterning, a design suggested by DeLillo's curious doppelgängers—J. Edgar Hoover and Sister Alma Edgar—two characters who although they never meet (indeed, one is historical, the other fictional) neverthe-

19

less create and sustain a most intriguing contrapuntal design. Their linkage creates one of DeLillo's most curious doublings in a novel that, like the radical architecture of the World Trade Center whose on-going construction centers the narrative action in the 1970s, rests on the principle of pairing. This tension, however, is resolved ultimately by the subtle introduction of a third Edgar—Edgar Allan Poe—as DeLillo loads unmistakable allusions to Poe's most celebrated poem, "The Raven," into the narrative lines of the two other Edgars. It is this third Edgar who ultimately resolves what is otherwise a stubborn dichotomy generated by the not-entirely unlikely pairing of a nun and the FBI Director—after all, generations of Catholic schoolchildren would likely grin over any parallels struck between a classroom nun and the most (in)famous police-bully of the twentieth century. Indeed, in a curious aside, Sister Edgar even sees herself as a "junior G-man protecting laws" (249). Using Poe's poem, the reader can see how the cop and the nun ultimately depend on each for what DeLillo terms elsewhere "deep completion" (51).

We begin our speculation modestly: with the names. Amid a novel of more than 800 pages, we have two characters who together appear in perhaps only one-eighth of the novel's bulk. Hoover is in the stands of the Polo Grounds on the afternoon of Thomson's home run. Later, he is part of the in-crowd at Truman Capote's 1966 Black & White Ball at the Plaza in New York City. Sister Alma Edgar figures largely in the later portions of the novel, specifically as the terrifying authority figure in Matt and Nick Shay's parochial school education in the 1950s and then in the 1990s, shortly before her death, when she is part of the surging Bronx crowds that gather to observe the sensational appearance on the Minute Maid billboard of the spirit of the murdered child Esmeralda. Yet, what triggers, even demands this speculation is the odd naming echo—a Catholic nun named Edgar? Such a deliberate echo of the FBI Director's name demands attention—in fact, both characters are simply referred to as "Edgar." Immediately, we are to see the two as paired.

In rereading, we begin, as Bronzini instructs, to organize, to count, measure, and test (what beauty! what power!). There are the obvious character similarities. Both characters exist (literally and metaphorically) in a world of black and white: Hoover's black leather biker get-up for Capote's party is complemented by Sister Edgar who, years after Vatican Two, still retains the regimental white veil and black habit, itself offset by the bone-whiteness of her skin (her nickname is Sister Skelly Bone). But, apart from such costuming, both share a decidedly Manichean worldview that is sustained by the tension between identifiable evil and uncontestable good. Hoover himself thrives amid the Cold War logic of "us vs. them." His afternoon at the ballpark is energized by the news of the Soviet hydrogen bomb test that confirms what has compelled him since his earliest days tracking down syndicate bootleggers: the world is in perpetual conflict between forces of good and legions of evil. There is no middle ground, no compromise. It is surely a worldview echoed later in Sister Edgar's religion class with its grim recitation of the unrelenting Q-and-A format of the Baltimore Catechism with its implicit argument that the world's mysteries can be tidily resolved into a black-and-white world of angels and devils, heaven and hell, God and Satan—no middle ground, no compromise: as Sister Edgar acknowledges, the Catechism allows only for "[t]rue or false, yes or no, fill in the blanks" (244).

But, we observe more. Both characters are haunted by a sense of the world as seething with germs and disease. Both combat such bacterial invasions with constant cleaning and scrubbing. They are both obsessive handwashers, both are drawn to lavatories as refuges from such invasive pathogens, both believe in the protection of latex gloves. When we watch Sister Edgar meticulously scrubbing a series of brushes (each time to disinfect the brush she has just used to clean), we recall Hoover's obsessive fears of "germs, an all-pervading medium of pathogens, microbes, floating colonies of spirochetes that fuse and separate and elongate and spiral and engulf, whole trainloads of matter that people cough forth, rudimentary and deadly" (19).

But, there is more to this design. There is the matter of the characters' elective isolation. Despite professions that theoretically help people—law enforcement and teaching—both maintain tight spheres of distance around themselves, insulating zones that speak of their deep distrust of people. Both maintain a single sustaining same-gender relationship (he with Clyde Tolson, who for more than forty years served as his loyal alter-ego at the Bureau; and she with another nun, the long-suffering Gracie). And, despite lives given over to Spartan simplicity and to oft-spoken outrage over the culture's moral decline, both characters are curiously drawn to the world of glitz and celebrity. Hoover attends the ballgame with

Jackie Gleason and Toots Shor, relishing his proximity to celebrity: "Fame and secrecy are the high and low ends of the same fascination, the static crackle of some libidinous thing in the world, and Edgar responds to people who have access to this energy. He wants to be their dearly devoted friend provided their hidden lives are in his private files, all the rumors collected and indexed, the shadow facts made real" (17). Later, amid the garish spectacle of Capote's ball, he is enthralled, "damp with excitement" (570). And, Sister Edgar, who reprimands Matt Shay for wasting playground time huddled over glossy photos of Rita Hayworth and Lana Turner in a well-thumbed movie magazine, has in her own closet stacks of such magazines. "She knew a lot about the stars. Their favorite flavors and worst insect bites and their wallflower nights in high school. Their basic everydayness inside the cosmetic surgeries and tragic marriages" (720).

We begin to warm to Bronzini's argument. Encouraged, we observe more. Both characters are obsessively drawn to death: Hoover meditates on construction plans for his own elaborate lead-lined coffin, and for years he studies Bruegel's lurid painting *The Triumph of Death*, which he first sees when it lands on his shoulder amid the blizzard of magazine pages that confetti the Polo Grounds in the giddy celebration after Thomson's home run—a color reproduction of it is featured in that week's *Life* magazine in an article on the Prado. Sister Edgar, for her part, sees death everywhere about her in the impoverished Bronx neighborhoods where she ministers (she is certain, for instance, that Ismael Muñoz is dying from the AIDS virus). "She was not sentimental about fatal diseases. Dying was just an extended version of Ash Wednesday. She intended to meet her own end with senses intact, grasp it, know it finally, open herself to the mystery that others mistake for something freakish and unspeakable" (245). Thus, it not altogether surprising that both are unnervingly comfortable with the imminence of nuclear apocalypse—Hoover is haunted by the profound implications of the Soviet arms buildup and Sister Edgar calmly inspects her students' dog tags (which they wear so that their bodies can be identified after a nuclear strike) and conducts surprise civil defense drills calculated to terrify her students with the possibility of instantaneous annihilation.

We measure even more (what beauty! what power!).

Both characters are committed to asserting order amid a world they see as hopelessly chaotic. Hoover's vast system of files where

he says he keeps a tight overview on the collapse of American culture is surely complemented by Sister Edgar's own blueprint for
understanding that collapse: her Baltimore Catechism. Both characters, furthermore, believe in an intricate underworld of signs and
in the certainty that every person—every soul—masks hidden secrets, that confession alone will secure the sweet release of correction, an affirmation of the medieval process of presumed guilt
followed by grueling punishment. Both conceive of the world itself
in terms of conspiracy, of forces that operate without apparent
traces but whose immense impact is clearly felt. Within DeLillo's
matrix, both the FBI and the Catholic Church maintain their positions only by ruthlessly manipulating paranoia and preserving a
permanent atmosphere of crisis.

Yet, we count, measure, and test more. Both characters are case
studies in the tension between flesh and spirit, or specifically in in-
terdicting the expression of the flesh. Both are lifelong celibates.
Hoover's ambiguous homosexuality is kept under tight reign. De-
Lillo offers insight into the Director's forty-year non-relationship
with Clyde Tolson in which—like a nun in a nunnery—whatever
urges or desires he might have felt are kept deliberately unex-
pressed, unacted upon. At the Waldorf the evening of the ball,
Hoover is content to watch Tolson undress via an elaborate series
of hotel mirrors. Both characters are unnerved by a moment's bald
confrontation with their own bodies—both pause with some trepi-
dation, naked, in front of a mirror. Finally, and perhaps most insidious, both characters exert unreasonable authority based on a
calculated strategy to instill terror, both manipulate fear and intim-
idation as a strategy for control, whether Hoover's ruthless (and
largely illegal) pursuit/persecution of the counterculture or Sister
Edgar's verbal and physical assaults against her terrified students.

Thus, we have a most intriguing pairing, a deliberate (we assume) resonance between two characters who never actually share
narrative space, a suggestion perhaps of the larger game afoot in
DeLillo's intricate novel, specifically the participation of the reader
in unearthing such patterns that become, in their intricacy and subtlety, sustaining and self-validating. What beauty; what power!
Such patterning is clearly in the front of DeLillo's thematic concerns—he gives us so much material and invites us to examine
such material within the leisure of the reading experience and to
find to our surprise (and ultimate contentment) a reassuring network of echoes and patterns—like constellations drawn in the

night sky. J. Edgar Hoover and Sister Alma Edgar: we have snatched from amid the more than 800 pages that bombard us with data a reassuring, if slender, design, rather like snatching a single hummable tune amid a massive symphony.

But, we cannot be content. There is more to this design. These apparently complementary characters after all come to significantly different endings. They come to represent what is perhaps the dichotomy that most defines the dilemma of the human condition: specifically, the tension between the corrupt and fallible flesh/animal and the immaculate and untouchable spirit/soul. We last see Hoover more than 300 pages from the novel's end. In the late hours after the Black & White Ball, Hoover, isolated and withdrawn, drinks alone and contemplates the half-ton, lead-lined casket he has had specially designed to protect his corpse from invasion by bugs, nuclear radiation, germs, even terrorists. Even though his death is years off (it is only 1966) and he is not even sick, he broods (flanked by a party-goer costumed as a hooded executioner), death-soaked and earthbound, locked into the logic of eventual death and inevitable decomposition, unavailable to any higher plane of reality. Sister Edgar, however, comes to a much different close. Just pages from the novel's close, she becomes caught up in the neighborhood hysteria over the apparent manifestation of the spirit of the dead Esmeralda. She gathers under the billboard and, when the commuter train clacks past and casts its headlights onto the billboard, she believes she glimpses the vision. She is suddenly infused with certainty that a world she had begun to consign to chaos, had begun to doubt was in the control of any benevolent Creator, was in fact deeply, undeniably spiritual. The reader, of course, hesitates, but then anybody else's transcendent experience is potentially ironic to everyone else. But, it confirms Sister Edgar. "She feels something break upon her. An angelus of clearest joy" (822). In a burst of Christian open-heartedness, she casts off her rubber gloves and moves about the throng, shaking hands and embracing those she had avoided only moment earlier as diseased and threatening. More to the point, she is prepared now to die and does so peacefully and joyfully in her sleep. Unlike Hoover, who is more dead alive, Sister Edgar is more alive dead—she "awakes" into a cyberspace version of eternity and there finds her soul a part finally of a cosmic-wide webbing that confirms as the novel closes the premise of a transcendent reality beyond the logic of understanding and the iron grip of the flesh. Even as Hoover contemplates the indignities of feeding worms and the hermetic enclosure of his eventual coffin, Sister Edgar, or at least her soul, soars into a breathtaking openness that defies our niggling fears of mortality.

So, our patterning has taken a dramatic turn—one of the Edgars is left death-haunted, the other triumphant over its irresistible stroke. Are we then to choose? Do they stand like those formidable World Trade Center towers, apparently identical yet absolutely separate? If the two Edgars must stand apart, we are left with little reassurance. It is difficult to live within such a black-and-white, ei-ther-or worldview. After all, who wants to accept only the ghastly cellular holocaust of decomposition? Yet, who can sustain belief in transcendence and the triumph over death? It is as if both charac-ters move to the extreme position—so, which character are we to assume is the cartoon? Which character is intended as the exem-plum? Which vision receives DeLillo's authorial imprimatur?

To resolve this dilemma, DeLillo introduces a third Edgar, spe-cifically Edgar Allan Poe and "The Raven," to suggest that corrup-tion and transcendence are, finally, complementary processes, parts of the same vast enterprise. It is not a matter of choice. Like Ralph Branca and Bobby Thomson, flesh and spirit may appear to be on different "teams" but ultimately they are part of the same "game." We are as much flesh as we are spirit—we are not at war within ourselves (as the justice system and the Catholic Church argue and attempt to control) but rather our interior circuitry is more an intricate system of cooperation, expression, and interdic-tion. Applied to the two Edgars, we can see perhaps why in the ether of cyberspace into which Sister Edgar is finally propelled she meets there none other than J. Edgar himself, "fellow celibate and more or less kindred spirit but her biological opposite"—and to-gether they become "hyperlinked. . . . Sister and Brother. A fantasy in cyberspace and a way of seeing the other side" (826). It is only then that the narrative moves toward the valedictory word: the un-ironic offer of Peace.

Such a strategy of reconciliation is keyed to the third Edgar who is a shadow presence within both of the other Edgars' narratives. Consider how DeLillo introduces images of the raven into those narratives. As Hoover contemplates the photograph of the Bruegel painting by the arc lights of the Polo Grounds, he notes particularly the detail of a raven riding the rump of a white horse. Later at the Black & White Ball, Clyde Tolson dances with a mysterious and darkly erotic woman (we suspect she is one of the counterculture guerrillas crashing the party) who is dressed in the elaborate mask of a medieval raven. And, Sister Edgar, of course, methodically memorizes the text of "The Raven," anticipating the odd thrill of scaring her students on the first day of classes. As she recites each line, she claims she will actually become the poem (earlier she had admitted that she has a "raven's heart" [249], a metaphor for her lack of "nun-ly" compassion).

Thus, the contrapuntal design of the two Edgars must account for this third Edgar. Why the Poe references? Why the raven specifically? Consider the poem. It is at once one of the most harrowing works of literature ever conceived by the American imagination and yet a playful parody of that very terror. Which poem are we to read: the wrenching nightmare of a young student who, one stormy night, is haunted by the memory of a beautiful dead mistress; a man who is tortured by a wandering raven who has been, apparently, trained to speak a single word, "Nevermore"; a man who conducts a devastating interrogation of the bird, asking it questions for which that word will only cause him more grief. Or are we to enjoy with a smirk a poem that is in fact an exaggerated, contrived, deliberately constructed melodrama (consult "The Philosophy of Composition") that can be relished as a hokey (if brilliant) parody, one that delights in its own obsessive rhythms and manic rhymes and one that borders on the absurd (what is the likelihood that this bird's entire vocabulary would consist of a word that happens to rhyme with the name of the man's dead lover?) and the meaningless (after all, the bird does not know what it is saying)? Is the poem then a penetrating study in grief or a study in calculated poetic effect? Is it a case study in passionate, even obsessive melancholy or is that merely a pretext for the execution of a cold-blooded aesthetic contrivance? Is it then a nightmare or a joke?

It is, of course, necessarily both—and surely that qualifies it as seminal text for DeLillo's *Underworld*. Readers of Poe intent on the reader-ly business of gathering evidence can assemble and defend either reading—yet, a reading that does not acknowledge the viability of the other necessarily diminishes the text. And in attempting to convert *Underworld* into the neat formula of a consistent "reading" we are confronted by an assortment of deliberately contradictory evidence: a baseball that is and is not authentic, junk that is and is not waste, a religious apparition that is and is not real, a wandering garbage barge that is and is not real, a latter-day prophet who is and is not a nightclub comedian, a nun who does and does not believe in God, a Cold War that is and is not a war, subway graffiti that is and is not art, a shooting that is and is not accidental, etc. DeLillo's reader is then feeling decidedly Edgarish, left much like the young student in Poe's poem: sustained by a game of interrogation that is ultimately, even necessarily, ironic. Thus, the third Edgar cautions—and at the same time celebrates— that DeLillo's novel, like Poe's poem, is ultimately about that game itself—not its resolution. Like baseball, like chess, like *briscola*, hop- scotch, tag, jacks, pool, poker, *sett' e mezz*, indeed like any of the games that so frequently figure in the pages of *Underworld* (includ- ing the real-life war-games conducted in Cuba and in Vietnam and the theoretical war-games played out by the computer banks in the nuclear weapons facility where Matt Shay briefly works), reading itself is a game that means nothing—and yet, everything.

What beauty! What power!

Subjectifying the Objective:
Underworld as Mutable Narrative

DAVID YETTER

He speaks in your voice, American . . .

—*Underworld*

A KEY STRENGTH OF *UNDERWORLD* IS THE MUTABILITY OF ITS OBJECTIVE narration. Like deep-focus cinematography DeLillo's narrative lens captures in precise detail foreground figures—the subjective narrative—while simultaneously maintaining focus on the background—the objective narrative—and all gradients between. His dexterous narrative language adapts continually, allowing itself to be subsumed by the language of character and milieu, individual subject and historical context, blurring toward a formal point-of-view assumption, then waning back toward third-person omniscience. At times, these adaptations manifest themselves in a single character-specific word or idiom that shades and alters the course of the objective narration—a character's voice interjects itself into the narrative to express a point more clearly. At other times, the mutation is more intrusive—a character's language literally wrests control of the objective narration, heightening tension and deepening narrative association. Ultimately, this novel attunes its reader to detect the impact of a single word on a sentence, a single sentence on a chapter.

The Prologue opens in the second person, a recurrent motif that echoes across the novel in the god-like voice of Russ Hodges, serving as an overarching reminder, an ache from a more hopeful, innocent age. The scene is New York's Polo Grounds, the "you" is a collective you, a disparate assembly connected to the game and to itself by a common language: the folkloric narrative of Russ Hodges:

28

Somebody hands you a piece of paper filled with letters and numbers and you have to make a ball game out of it. You create the weather,
flesh out the players, you make them sweat and grouse and hitch up
their pants, and it is remarkable, thinks Russ, how much earthly disturbance, how much summer and dust the mind can manage to order up
from a single Latin letter lying flat.

"That's not a bush curve Maglie's throwing," he says into the mike.

When he was doing ghost games he liked to take the action into the
stands, inventing a kid chasing a foul ball, a carrot-topped boy with a
cowlick (shameless, ain't I) who retrieves the ball and holds it aloft, this
five-ounce sphere of cork, rubber, yarn, horsehide and spiral stitching,
a souvenir baseball, a priceless thing somehow, a thing that seems to
recapitulate the whole history of the game every time it is thrown or
hit or touched. (25–26)

The narrative is now in the present-tense third person. DeLillo's
use of Hodges's language without formal point-of-view assumption lends the scene a smooth intimacy, as though Hodges were
placing a hand over the microphone and leaning toward the
reader. The audience is no longer the invisible multitude, but suddenly, in mid-sentence, an informal partner, a buddy. By choosing
the colloquial "you" (instead of the formal "one") to describe his
character's memory, DeLillo enfolds the subjectivity of Hodges's
character into the narrative, thus deepening and characterizing it,
without formally taking on Hodges's point of view.

By using the present tense, DeLillo imbues the narrative with a
feeling of greater immediacy; the game's action seems to take place
just a beat faster than the reader's eyes can move across the page.
Why then does DeLillo risk losing this carefully constructed intimacy by appropriating Hodges's thoughts, thus drawing the
reader away from the action and toward the artifice of the narrative? By attributing the thought to Hodges and thereby drawing
the reader out of the perceived first-person point of view, DeLillo
creates a dialectic between the present-tense immediacy and the
relative distance of the narrated moment—a back and forth—that
places the reader in the moment of the action while simultaneously
allowing the reader to reflect on that moment and on its telling.

A similar pattern shows up later in the Prologue:

Thomson in his bent stance, chin tucked, waiting.
Russ says, "One out, last of the ninth."

He says, "Branca pitches, Thomson takes a strike called on the inside corner." (40)

The first sentence is told from an objective third-person point of view—or, is it? After reading the second and third sentences, the reader can see that the first sentence also bears the mark of character subjectivity. The lack of the positioning verb "is" creates another facet to the narration. Without "is," the narrative reads with much more immediacy; the story is not being narrated but relayed. By writing that first sentence in the idiom of Hodges, DeLillo introduces a tiered motif that at once heightens the suspense of Hodges's narration while at the same time drawing attention to it. The first tier begins with the unattributed lead-in; the second with: "Russ says . . ."; the third tier: "He says. . . ." Each tier suggests a different level of narrative identification. The first sentence of the triplet is the closest to Hodges: it takes on his language, is the most closely aligned with his voice. Interestingly, the sentence is the only one of the three not directly attributed. The action is described, but the reader is not fully placed into the scene. No frame of reference is provided; all the reader has to go on is Hodges's language. The second sentence identifies Hodges as the speaker. Where the first sentence allowed the reader back into the announcing booth, the second sentence begins pulling the reader away, drawing attention back to the story of the game rather than the game itself; and, by the third sentence, the objective narrative is fully restored.

Through language and idiom the narrative is deepened, given greater dimension, suggesting at once the announcer's play-by-play narration and the listener's anxiety; simultaneity of action and a multiplicity of view that encompasses speaker and distant listener, character and milieu.

The Prologue sets the rules of the narrative but also establishes their flexible nature. The narrative camera swoops all over the ballpark, cozies up to characters and takes on their language, and gives the reader a glimpse into their subjective response to the game. Take Cotter Martin out in the bleachers, hoping against hope that the Giants can pull one out:

Lucky seventh. Cotter needs a measly run to keep him from despairing—the cheapest eked-out run ever pushed across. Or he's ready to give up. You know that thing that happens when you give up before the end and then your team comes back to perform acts of valor and you feel queasy shame stealing over you like pond slick. (30)

Here the entrance into Cotter's subjectivity is signaled by individual word choice. "[C]heapest eked-out" and "measly" are Cotter's words, but "despairing" is not. In this "lucky seventh" the narrative allows the intrusion of Cotter's vernacular and so deepens the feeling of his profound adolescent yearning. In the same paragraph we move back into the language of tale-spinner Russ Hodges: "You know that thing that happens. . . ." By juxtaposing Cotter's language with that of Hodges, Cotter's yearning becomes part of a continuum, an essential element of the game's collective soul. Attached in this way to the language of baseball's myth, Cotter becomes a part of it, he is Hodges's imaginary carrot-top, part of that "thing that seems to recapitulate the whole history of the game" (26).

If the mutability of the narrative lends to the playoff game a feeling of intense public reverie, other scenes in the novel demonstrate how the same technique can infuse the narrative with a deep sense of public foreclosure.

Richard Henry Gilkey is featured in only one scene. He is nearly 42, and, clearly, too old to be still living with his parents. And, he's angry—the vague nature of which fuels his character—and, as the scene progresses, the reader learns that Richard is in fact the Texas Highway Killer, a character who haunts the novel's contemporary news-loops.

The narrative point of view used to describe Richard is a close third person, and from the outset it is infused with Richard's language, which contributes to the suspense of the scene, a suspense that differs in purpose and effect from the observations of the ballgame. Whereas the narrative of the Prologue suggested the collective excitement of a vast outdoor community—endless facets of a larger picture projecting different reactions toward the same event—similar narrative composition around Richard's character produces quite a different result, one that draws the narrative inward, toward that ultimately ineffable element in an everyday someone that drives that someone to murder randomly.

The description of Richard's actions lends suspense to the narrative by virtue of the banality of its content. Richard is a loner—always a bad sign in contemporary fiction. We are first introduced to him—unaware at this point that he is the killer, as he carefully assembles a sandwich: "He spread the mayonnaise. He spread the mayonnaise on the bread. Then he slapped the lunch meat down. He never spread the mayonnaise on the meat. He spread it on the bread. Then he slapped down the meat and watched the mayo seep around the edges" (262). Richard's character is defined by the manic nature of the narrative's observations. These observations cue the reader, without revealing that Richard is actually a murderer, that things are somehow not quite right, that the reader is on shaky ground. The language used to describe Richard is syntactically at odds with the rest of the book: the sentences have become simple, declarative, the observations regressive, drained of irony. Richard's voice has bled into the story and has shifted the delicate balance of DeLillo's narrative. By altering the diction within the framework of the third-person narrative, DeLillo involves the reader more directly, pushes the reader, by way of that diction, closer to the subjective viewpoint of his serial murderer.

Later in the scene Richard drives away from the family home, and DeLillo continues to shade his narrative with Richard's subjective responses to the world around him:

> He realized he'd forgotten to give his dad two glasses of water to take with the blue and yellow capsule despite the bold-faced reminder on the prescription bottle. These little failures ate away at his confidence even when he knew it was his father's fault for not managing his own intake or his mother's for not being around when she was needed. There were constant little wars of whose fault is it and okay I'm sorry and I wish he'd die and get it over with, all taking place in Richard's inner mind. (263)

The use of the word "dad" marks the narrative with Richard's subjectivity. The word choice of the narrator is established in the sentence that follows: the more formal "father" and "mother." The first sentence, with its use of "dad," suggests an unself-conscious moment, a crack, as the sentences that follow corroborate, both in Richard's armor and in the narrative's objectivity. And so "dad" when used in the midst of the third-person narrative can read as simultaneously intimate (another facet through which to view Richard) and as distancing, with the neurotic Richard singled out and emasculated by the objective third person.

Richard's guard is clearly signaled as down when the self-flagellation begins over the "bold-faced reminder" on the prescription bottle. The next sentence shows the way in which the language of the narrative creates tension: word choice itself hints at a child-like vindictiveness. Richard, with his "little failures" and petty assignations of blame, is established as an emotional child, and thus his threat becomes more pervasive by its childish lack of rationale.

The suspense is ratcheted still higher with Richard's forced takeover of the narration. "These were constant little wars of whose fault is it and okay I'm sorry and I wish he'd die and get it over with, all taking place in Richard's inner mind." Richard's menace—his capacity for slipping out of control—is conveyed as his language begins to overwhelm the narration. DeLillo begins the sentence in the language of the objective narrative then as the sentence gains momentum, as "the constant little wars" are brought to light, the narrative is seized by Richard's language and syntax. The breakdown in sentence structure, the fractured grammar, parallels the fragmentary nature of Richard's "inner mind."

Thus, the reader is prepared for the casual revelation of Richard's identity in the remarks that follow:

> If you fire out the window on the driver's side, which you have to do if you don't want to shoot across the width of your own car and the space between your car and the other car, you still face the problem of having to fire across the space between cars and the width of the other car because the other driver's side is the far side in relation to your position at the wheel. (267)

All the flat language used to describe making a sandwich and dispensing pills is now enriched, and the reader's vague anxieties are rewarded with a specific threat. Now the narrative reads as though a gun were jabbed into the narrator's back.

DeLillo, returning to the subject of the ballgame, picks it up decades later with the character of Marvin Lundy. Marvin has devoted his life to the pursuit of baseball memorabilia; the Bobby Thomson home run ball is his grail.

Previously, we saw how dropped quotation marks and inconsistent idiomatic phrasing lends a breathless quality to the Russ Hodges scenes, mirroring the excitement over the game's uncertain outcome: over who exactly was speaking and would it all be said in time. Syntax, grammar, and idiom set a different tone of suspense with Richard Henry Gilkey. Whereas the grammatical inconsistencies surrounding Hodges lends immediacy to the narrative, the inconsistencies surrounding Richard halt it.

In the scene that follows, Marvin, surrounded in his basement by elaborate mementos of the game, describes his quest for the Thomson ball to Brian Glassic. In this passage we find another aspect of DeLillo's mutable narrative as the prose moves from absent-minded verbal fumbling to high rhetoric and Marvin's character becomes a cipher for the novel's own social-theoretical agenda

> "This is major collectors looking for big history. Does that mean the objects in this room are total trivia? What's the word I'm looking for that sounds like you're getting injected with a vaccine in the fleshy part of your arm?"
> "Innocuous."
> "Innocuous. What am I, innocuous? This is history, back-page. From back to front. Happy, tragic, desperate." Marvin shifted his gaze. "In this trunk right here I have the one thing that my whole life for the past twenty-two years I was trying to collect. . . ."
> Marvin said morosely, "It's the Bobby Thomson home-run ball, which I traced it back starting with rumors in the business. It wasn't even a business back then, just a few interested parties with someone's telephone number or first name, the skimpiest kind of lead that I pursued with a fury. . . ."
> For the next three hours Marvin talked about his search for the baseball. He forgot some names and mangled others. He lost whole cities, placing them in the wrong time zones. He described how he followed false leads into remote places. He climbed the stairs to raftered upper rooms and looked in old trunks among the grandmother's linen and the photographs of the dead.
> "I said to myself a thousand times. Why do I want this thing? What does it mean? Who has it? . . ."
> "I looked at a million photographs because this is the dot theory of reality, that all knowledge is available if you analyze the dots. . . ."
> There was the photographic detailwork, the fineness of image, the what-do-you-call-it into littler units.
> "Resolution," Brian said . . . (174–75)

Throughout this passage, if we follow the thread of Marvin's dialogue (both attributed and unattributed), we see that both the quoted and unquoted dialogue begins to sound increasingly unlike Marvin, slipping further and further from his idiom and more toward that of the third-person narrator.

As the passage begins the dialogue reflects an old man searching for language: "What's the word I'm looking for that sounds like you're getting injected with a vaccine in the fleshy part of your arm" (174); to the same old man morosely describing his life's empty quest: "In this trunk right here I have the one thing that my whole life for the past twenty-two years I was trying to collect" (174); to an uncharacteristically rhetorical tone: "all knowledge is available if you analyze the dots" (175).

The narrative mechanism of Marvin's voice has brushed into contact with one of the novel's overarching themes—the yearning, backward glance in the face of a rapidly advancing age—and this theme speaks through him. Marvin is another lone man trying to impose himself on history. Yet history, in the form of this baseball game and, for Marvin, its maddeningly inconclusive outcome, imposes itself on him. Searching the pixels of the past is Marvin's attempt at reconciliation with the present; some answer contained within those photographs must justify all his years of searching. By defining Marvin through characterizing dialogue and then blurring that dialogue slowly into the language of the objective narrative, DeLillo pixelates Marvin's character into the novel's overarching thematic picture.

DeLillo boils down Marvin's dialogue gradually. The first sentence is all Marvin, is quoted as such, and contains his words, syntax, and mannerisms. Marvin's next quoted passage shows the narrator's first subtle intrusion: "This is history, back-page. From back to front. Happy, tragic, desperate" (174). This staccato observation is entirely outside of Marvin's diffuse diction. The proof is in the two sentences that surround it. The first begins: "What's the word I'm looking for," and the second reads, "In this trunk right here I have the one thing that my whole life for the past twenty-two years I was trying to collect" (174). Looking at the middle three sentences—clipped, sharp in tone—bookended by the two long, rambling sentences, we can easily see the difference. The narrator's voice has been foregrounded, and it comments on Marvin through Marvin. "This is history. . . . Happy, tragic, desperate." The next two sentences follow Marvin's meandering speech pattern. Then we are greeted with the "dot theory of reality." Slowly the diction has changed, the quotation marks soon fall away, and Marvin, the verbally challenged collector who places cities in entirely different time zones, suddenly channels the anxious grumblings of the media age.

By the next cited sentence the quotation marks have been abandoned and the narrator appears to have taken charge. This time, however, Marvin intrudes, "There was the photographic detail-work, the fineness of image, the what-do-you-call-it into littler units." To which Brian is attributed an answer: "Resolution" (175). But, in this sentence, there is no resolution. Like the faces in his minutely studied photographs, Marvin's dialogue blurs into the background. Marvin's words have become intertwined with the language of the third-person narrative—each intruding on the other—until the integrity of each point of view fades into the other, like those half-tone figures in Marvin's newspaper photographs.

All of DeLillo's novels explore this symbiotic relationship between the pixel and the broad American picture. His technique matches the dissonance of his age, a technique that allows the reader to detect the whispers of the individual while simultaneously absorbing the clamor of the crowd.

Underworld: Sin and Atonement

Robert McMinn

Transubstantiation

An irresistible impulse to connect overtakes the reader of
Underworld, a sacred text concerning sin, atonement, and the local
gods of the Underworld. This is because the subject matter of the
book explicitly includes the topics of connectivity and connection
and because the narrative itself consists of connected sections with
quasihypertextual anchors placed throughout, leading you from
one chapter to the next and back again. In this fashion the mind of
the reader becomes a slave to connection.

This does not necessarily make *Underworld* unique. This is surely
how any narrative or plot works: the reader connects characters
with events and with other characters, thus building up a picture
of the action within the novel. But, the combination of connection
as a subject in a novel with multiple plot threads, which intersect
randomly and arbitrarily, makes *Underworld* about connection
more than it is about anything else.

DeLillo's narrative trains the reader to read in a particular way.
We become accustomed to connection and coincidence, begin to
expect them and look out for them. Just as montage is now standard in cinema and on television (life would be strange indeed
without it), we do not read *Underworld* to see what happens next
but to see what happened *before* and how it connects. This message
is emphasized by the frequent repetition of some variant of the
phrase, "Everything is connected."

Much, for example, has been made of the baseball, collected by
Cotter Martin in the crush of the crowd at the baseball game, then
chased across the continent by Marvin Lundy, and finally pur-
chased by Nick Shay for "Thirty-four thousand five hundred dol-
lars" (132). Although this connecting thread was mentioned
frequently in the *Underworld* reviews, if you read the novel expect-

ing the ball to be some kind of strange attractor with the whole story circling around it, you will be disappointed. The ball fades in and out of the novel but in a half-hearted way, and the most you can say about it is that it is a device, like Hitchcock's MacGuffin, that allows DeLillo to play with certain ideas.

The character of Marvin Lundy, who chases after the ball and then traces its provenance as far back as the day after the game (when it came into the possession of Charles Wainwright, advertising executive), is more concerned in the end with the provenance than he is with the ball. It is the narrative he chases not the ball, not the physical object but something metaphysical, the connections themselves, and the links. So, when he ends up in San Francisco waiting for Chuckie Wainwright (Charles's son) to arrive on a ship, it is not the ball he is waiting for (he already has it) but the story. And what he finds in the harbor is neither Chuckie nor his story but the waste ship. And the reader should realize at this point that we are not in San Francisco for the ball, and not even just for the story of the ball, but for the smell of the ship.

Marvin's primary concern is with information. In his search for the ball he has minutely examined the photographic record, looking for data hidden in the grains of the film that would tell him who it was who carried the ball out of the stadium. But this is not a mystery DeLillo sets up and asks the reader to solve, nor even a mystery we enjoy as Marvin Lundy tries to solve it. We already have the solution. We have been told at the very beginning of the novel that Cotter Martin grabbed the ball. And the point about Cotter, the fact we learn on the opening page of the novel, is that he sneaked into the game (though "sneaking" hardly does justice): so there is no ticket, there can be no confirmation of block number, seat, and row, which means that Marvin will never get to the beginning of the story: "I looked at a million photographs because this is the dot theory of reality, that all knowledge is available if you analyze the dots" (175).

Of course, he is wrong, Marvin is, about the dots, and this is a point that DeLillo makes repeatedly in his works. You have to get to the stage where you acknowledge that your systems and your rationality can take you so far and no further, that they have limitations. The latest high technology is always defeated by the ever-present rat in the foundations: noise, static, the parasite.[1] There is no information in the photograph that is not in it, visible. Photographs can be enhanced by software, but in converting a photograph (which is made up of grains) to a digital image, data is already lost. Two guys sitting next to each other wearing the same colored shirt will become one object. A crowd bundled around a ball will just be a mass of dots with no clear edges.

For finding edges and the fear of edges is actually one of the themes of *Underworld*. The situation of the Epilogue, the indeterminate timing of it, indicates that we are living in a space between boundaries. After the end of one thing, before the beginning— before we can clearly see the beginning—of another. And in his heart Marvin knows this. He knows that analyzing dots will tell him nothing because there is always a parasite in the system:

> "I looked at a million photographs because this is the dot theory of reality, that all knowledge is available if you analyze the dots."
> There was a slight crackle in his voice that sounded like random radio noise produced by some disturbance of the signal. (175)

What is it called when the next sentence, or your own breath, carries the contradictory response to your statement? The random radio noise is always there, in the background, ready to undermine any attempt to rationalize the system. Marvin is a walking contradiction: a man who believes that the truth is both deeper and in plain view: on billboards and matchbooks, in the captured light of old photographs.

Montage and its relation to the subject of events concern DeLillo in this novel as they do in all his others. DeLillo's aim here is to narrate events, then renarrate them, to give one character's point of view, then another's; to juxtapose events, to double and mirror them, until we have seen or been reminded of the same thing many times. This again is something DeLillo has done repeatedly: shine a spotlight onto a scene, focus on it, seeking the "pixel in the data swarm" (118) that will explain the mystery of events. But, each new angle, each new shining of the light, casts new shadows and creates new mysteries.

The technique of montage immerses us in memory, where one thing reminds us of another, where each repetition makes the memory stronger. But, because DeLillo tells some of the story in reverse, we are sometimes reminded of something before it happened. Immediately after a conversation with his wife about the plumber and the shower and maps and great bodies, Nick wakes from a dream, "deep-breathing and clammy" (131), and sits in an

armchair in his bedroom holding the ball in his hand: "How the
hand works memories out of the baseball that have nothing to do
with games of the usual sort. Bad luck, Branca luck. From him to
me. The moment that makes the life" (131–32).

And, he sits remembering the conversation with Marian, and the
game, the radio commentary, the sound of the crowd, in two places
at once, remembering fragments of conversation, fragments of his
life, his reasons for doing certain things. The reader has been at the
game, has heard Russ Hodges repeat over and over *"The Giants win
the pennant,"* but does not know much more about Nick's life and
his secrets:

> I heard my mother in the next room getting up to go to the toilet. . . .
> I waited and listened, nearly breathless. I waited for the shuffle of slip-
> pers along the hall . . . and then I listened for the sound of water flush-
> ing—fully intent, listening in the fiercest kind of concentrated stillness
> until she was safely back in bed.
>
> I hefted the weapon and pointed it and saw an interested smile fall
> across his face, the slyest kind of shit-eating grin.
>
> Maybe that was the dream—I wasn't sure. (132)

The line about hefting the weapon and seeing the interested smile
occurs nearly 650 pages (in narrative time) before and 40 years (in
story time) after the event to which it refers:

> A little brightness entered George's eye. Rare in George. This bright-
> ness in the eye. And an interested look moved across his mouth. It was
> the slyest kind of shit-eating grin.
>
> "Is it loaded?"
>
> "No," George said. (780)

This singular event narrated more than once is the turning point
in Nick's life and a memory that haunts him. From the distance of
forty years he narrates it in the first person, bringing him closer to
it. But, the event itself is narrated in a more distant third-person
voice, a third person who watches the scene as if from above.
Which is "closer"?

Nick, the Italian-American with an Irish Catholic mother, has
been educated at a Catholic school and then reeducated by the Jesuits. No matter how old he gets, no matter how far west he moves,
he is not removed from this shaping event. As he holds the ball
in the armchair in Phoenix, he is transubstantiated into that third-

person Nick holding the sawed-off shotgun. He is in another place. The one shot, the Shot Heard 'Round the World, is transformed into another, the shot felt down the years. Thomson's homer takes Nick home to the Bronx.

Marvin Lundy also suffers a moment of transubstantiation (I use the term figuratively). As he stands in San Francisco harbor with his wife Eleanor, contemplating the waste ship, the smell of it takes him back to a trip to Europe they made in 1951, to look for Marvin's half brother. The smell of the ship in spring 1978 reminds him of the stomach problems he experienced in 1951 when his bowel movements grew heavy and strange as they moved farther east:

> He realized this was probably a part of every early marriage, smelling the other's smell, getting it over and done with so you can move ahead with your lives, have children, buy a little house, remember everybody's birthday, take a drive on the Blue Ridge Parkway, get sick and die. But in this case the husband had to take extreme precautions because the odor was shameful, it was intense and deeply personal and seemed to say something awful about the bearer.
>
> His smell was a secret he had to keep from his wife. (310)

Now, in 1978, he feels he has "to conceal the memory from her just as he'd once concealed the smell" (311). Marvin is silent about his uncleanness, just as Nick is silent about his crime. Both men keep a dark secret from their wives. How else to atone?

This is the meaning and purpose of ritual, some kind of transubstantiation or time-travel. As Nick's mother says her Hail Marys in bed before going to sleep, she cannot remember whether she last said them a few minutes ago or the night before because each Hail Mary is the same as the last and the one to follow. The past that is always here, "that never stops happening, and the passing minute, and what she feels when she scratches the back of her hand" (201).

BORDERS, EDGES, CATEGORIES

Nick and Marian recycle their household garbage on particular days for particular categories of waste. It is important that one kind of waste is not mixed in with another. It is all waste, and yet it is possible to contaminate it, for waste to be out of place even among waste. This scene mirrors that in *White Noise* when Jack Gladney sorts through the compacted household waste looking for Dylar.

Whereas the Gladneys threw everything in together, the Shays do their sorting before disposal:

> At home we separated our waste into glass and cans and paper products. Then we did clear glass versus colored glass. Then we did tin versus aluminum. We did plastic containers, without caps or lids, on Tuesdays only. Then we did yard waste. Then we did newspapers including glossy inserts but were careful not to tie the bundles in twine, which is always the temptation. (89)

This idea of not tying newspaper bundles with twine becomes a refrain: Nick repeats it over and over so that the recycling itself takes on the quality of a ritual with the point of the ritual being the delineation of categories. This idea is not unique, and could indeed have come straight from the pages of Mary Douglas' seminal work *Purity and Danger*.

According to Douglas, things that don't fit properly into categories are unclean, and we "chase dirt" in order to impose order upon our environment. Ideas of uncleanness are dominated by things being out of place. Douglas gives the examples of shoes on the table or food on clothes. Crucially, Douglas argues, "rituals of purity and impurity . . . are positive contributions to atonement" (2–3). She goes on to identify the interesting anthropological puzzle that sacred or holy things are simultaneously "sacred" and "defiled"; that the category of the sacred is sometimes indistinguishable from the category of the unclean (8). She argues that this is because "sacred" and "unclean" are relative rather than absolute categories. So the twine, though it is tempting to see it as somewhat similar to newspaper, does not belong in the same category. The (clean) twine with the (read) newspaper is unclean. Why is this important to *Underworld*? Douglas does suggest an answer, "Any given culture must confront events which seem to defy its assumptions. . . . This is why, I suggest, we find in any culture worthy of the name various provisions for dealing with ambiguous and anomalous events" (40).

Douglas identifies several ways of dealing with anomalies: they can be treated negatively or positively. To adjust a paradigm to fit the anomaly, as argued famously by Thomas S. Kuhn in his 1962 *The Structure of Scientific Revolution*, is to react positively. To ignore or condemn the anomaly is to be negative. One way of thinking about an anomaly is to use an ambiguous symbol in a ritual: like the twine and the newspaper. Nick's ritual of recycling forces him to think in certain ways, just as DeLillo's montage forces the reader to think about connections.

What happens if I try to reconcile to two ways of thinking? Nick's ritual involves only putting things together that belong together. It fits in with his matter-of-fact, antiparanoid view of the world, in which he believes "we could know what was happening to us" (82). But, the ritual of the montage encourages us to connect everything in the same way that contemporary scientific paradigms of uncertainty and chaos encourage us to take account of the observer at the scene and sensitive dependence on initial conditions. We forge so many connections that we begin to exist in a state that is radically between all categories, we are positively dissolving ourselves in connections or, like the Gladneys with their household waste, crushing and compacting everything into one solid lump: "All margins are dangerous. . . . Any structure of ideas is vulnerable at its margins. We should expect the orifices of the body to symbolise its specially vulnerable points. Matter issuing from them is marginal stuff of the most obvious kind" (Douglas 122).

They have exceeded the body's boundary: stuff that should be inside is outside. Stuff that should be private is public: recall Marvin Lundy trying to hide his bowel problem. Newspapers are public documents—they should be left open not tied with twine, which privatizes them. This is the problem of waste. It is a public concern that over the century has ended up in private hands. So, in *Underworld* we encounter the breakdown of public waste management in New York City in 1974, with the garbage strike leaving waste to pile up conspicuously in the streets. We see the privatization of waste disposal in the Bronx in 1951, with Antoine's car ferrying restaurant waste around the city. And the waste ship, endlessly touring the world with its unnamable cargo that belongs to everyone and no one.

The categories of public and private are important in *Underworld*, which is concerned with both momentous public events and the quotidian details of daily life. Fittingly, most of the (public) newspaper and magazine publicity surrounding *Underworld* on its publication spoke extensively about the Cold War, the nuclear threat, the collapse of the Soviet Union, and the other great public news events that feature in the novel. These events, however, are inextricably entwined with the everyday, the private and personal, so that a counterreading of the text is possible.

What DeLillo picks at throughout *Underworld* is the idea that we might be looking another way, might be in another place, when these momentous public events occur. He hints at it when Matt Shay gets up early on his camping trip with his girlfriend to watch the sunrise: "He sat in the dust with his eyes opened and realized the sun was rising behind him and he wondered what this meant. It meant he'd been facing in the wrong direction all along" (467). DeLillo has many characters sit watching the Texas Highway Killer videotape and points out that when the killer strikes again they play the old tape because it was the only one they had. But there is another point about the tape, which DeLillo describes at length, and it is that the girl holding the camera keeps it pointed at the victim and never points it at the killer. "Of course if she had panned to another car, the right car at the precise time, she would have caught the gunman as he fired" (157). But, she never does, and there is a sense that this almost always happens. And the novel looks at history in this way, not at the underside, the secret side, the paranoid undercurrents, but at the slightly oblique angle that denotes personal and private like the child's game with the camera.

Even Lenny Bruce refers to this in one of his fictive monologues about the Cuban Missile Crisis:

> "The Navy boarded a ship yesterday at the quarantine line. First ship boarded. Armed boarding party. Bet your ass it was tense, baby. Turns out the ship's not carrying missiles. Carrying truck parts and toilet paper. See, there it is, ordinary life trying to reassert itself. That's the secret meaning of this week. The secret history that never appears in the written accounts of the time or in the public statements of the men in power." (593–94)

It seems, in fact, that the most interesting aspects of the novel are in these quotidian details—that a point is being made throughout *Underworld* about individual experience as opposed to public history. I am not suggesting that the momentous public events be uncoupled from the private experience of them. But, I think it is possible to see these events not as forming the connecting threads of some paranoid metahistory, but as the anchors—as the hangers—upon which characters drape intense personal memories and feelings that have more to do with spirituality than with politics. This is how we feel at home with events. As DeLillo himself commented in "The Power of History": "Against the force of history, so powerful, visible and real, the novelist poses the idiosyncratic self. Here it is, sly, mazed, mercurial, scared half-crazy. It is also free and undivided, the only thing that can match the enormous dimensions of social reality."

The dark side of 1950s conspicuous consumption featured in Part 5 ("Better Things for Better Living through Chemistry") is the result of all that excess: waste, landfills and recycling plants, devastated landscapes, and the sense of something profoundly unholy building up within civil society. The Demings in their DuPont Utopia are doubled in *Underworld* by the Shays, a 1990s family concerned with recycling, who see products on supermarket shelves as always-already household waste, ready for the ritual of recycling. This again is a form of transubstantiation:

> Marian and I saw products as garbage even when they sat gleaming on store shelves, yet unbought. We didn't say, What kind of casserole will that make? We said, What kind of garbage will that make? Safe, clean, neat, easily disposed of? Can the package be recycled and come back as a tawny envelope that is difficult to lick closed? (121)

As pointed out above, according to Mary Douglas, "rituals of purity and impurity . . . are positive contributions to atonement" (2–3). Apart from the Texas Highway Killer, the other killer in the novel is Nick Shay, who spends 40 years atoning for the murder of George the Waiter. One form his atonement takes is silence on the subject of his crime, but at the end of the novel a change has overtaken him and he now talks to Marian about it, about "things she didn't know, or knew at an unlearned level" (805). This is an interesting puzzle. What changes Nick, or what changes for him?

One possible answer may be found within the anthropological puzzle of categories: or how the sacred shades into the profane. In *Underworld* the form this puzzle takes is the sacralization of waste. It seems inadequate to aver that this phenomenon results from sacred and profane being relative rather than absolute categories. Something else is at work.

DeLillo signals the importance of this theme by introducing it close to the beginning of the novel, in Part 1. Nick says, "The Jesuits taught me to examine things for second meanings and deeper connections. Were they thinking about waste? We were waste managers, waste giants, we processed universal waste. Waste has a solemn aura now, an aspect of untouchability" (88). Later, Nick connects his recycling ritual with the preparation of "a pharaoh for his death and burial" (119). The dead consumer object, no longer shining on the supermarket shelf, has to be prepared for its trip into the afterlife, the Underworld. The categories must be delineated, or the waste may end up in the wrong place. We are back with the *Egyptian Book of the Dead* when Brian Glassic visits New York to inspect Staten Island's Fresh Kills landfill, a real place named for the slaughterhouse that had previously stood on the site. Fresh Kills is an extraordinary name in this context, and Brian is overawed by the sight, in two places at once ("It was science fiction and prehistory . . . "): "He imagined he was watching the construction of the Great Pyramids at Giza—only this was twenty-five times bigger, with tanker trucks spraying perfumed water on the approach roads. He found the sight inspiring" (184).

The spraying of perfumed water again recalls rituals for preparation of the dead, and Brian is classically ambivalent, looking forward and backward at the same time, and deeply afraid of crossing boundaries. He is, in fact, afraid of crossing bridges: after a meeting with Marvin Lundy, "Brian asks about a way back to Manhattan that did not include the George Washington Bridge" (183) and after losing his way comes across Fresh Kills, by chance, though it was the primary reason for his visit. Why fear bridges? In Zoroastrianism there are three gods or demons who wait on the Cinvat Bridge to accost and judge the dead on their way to the Underworld: Astvihat, Frehzist, and Hihr.[2] Brian is afraid of being judged, perhaps because of his affair with Marian Shay.

Another way in which waste is transformed in the novel is through art. Klara Sax abandons the painting with oils of her formative years in the Bronx and becomes notorious for using objects that have been discarded. The apogee of this is her use of the decommissioned B-52s in the desert, the project she names *Long Tall Sally* after one of the planes there, the very one in which Chuckie Wainwright flies over Vietnam.

But Klara is preempted by one Sabato (a.k.a., Simon) Rodia, who built three towers of broken tiles, dishes, bottles, and seashells in the Watts area of Los Angeles over a 33-year period, finishing in 1954. And, when Nick Shay visits the towers in spring 1978, he thinks of his father Jimmy:

> When he finished the towers Sabato Rodia gave away the land and all the art that was on it. He left Watts and went away, he said, to die.

The work he did is a kind of swirling free-souled noise, a jazz cathedral, and the power of the thing, for me, the deep disturbance, was that my own ghost father was living in the walls. (277)

But, you wonder also if Rodia's story is not also Nick's. To spend over thirty years transforming simple household waste into something exalted, some higher form of garbage, and then to walk away from it, to give it away, smacks of the kind of self-effacing atonement that Nick is seeking. For there is always the danger with atonement of taking too much of the holy upon oneself, in starting to think of the self as untouchable because it is holy rather than because it is profane.

Rudolf Otto attempted in *The Idea of the Holy*, like Douglas, to tackle the problem of the confusion of categories between sacred and profane. For Otto, the problem begins with the idea that the sacred as a category is wholly (or holy) good. Otto points out that in addition to goodness, the category carries an "overplus" of meaning, and that, originally, this "overplus" was the only meaning of the holy (2). In extracting the idea of goodness from the holy, because it is a moral rationalization, Otto comes close to identifying the reason why one might treat a landfill like Fresh Kills as sacred. In encountering the sacred, the individual is overawed: "It is the emotion of a creature, submerged and overwhelmed by its own nothingness in contrast to that which is supreme above all creatures" (10).

Such a feeling will overtake the individual faced with something 25 times larger than one of the Seven Wonders of the Ancient World or even the Watts Towers. Another element of the holy identified by Otto is "absolute unapproachability" (19), which could apply to a great work of art or to a landfill; to the site of a former slaughterhouse or to nuclear waste. In Part 3 DeLillo introduces Jesse Detwiler, garbage archaeologist, who points out that civilization is built upon waste, that "Garbage comes first, then we build a system to deal with it" (288).

> "The more dangerous the waste, the more heroic it will become. Irradiated ground. The way the Indians venerate this terrain now, we'll come to see it as sacred in the next century. Plutonium National Park. The last haunt of the white gods. Tourists wearing respirator masks and protective suits." (289)

The precession of garbage creates an interesting puzzle. Referring back to Otto, if the "aweful majesty" of the sacred compares with the "dust and ashes" of the human subject, what is that subject to think when faced with the "aweful majesty" of literal dust and ashes? We are back with categories and exceeded boundaries because an excess of waste, the wastefulness of humanity, makes visible that which should be invisible. The landfill, which should be buried in the Underworld, becomes an all-too-visible reminder of our dust and ashes.

Waste reminds us that we are going to die.

And, what of sin; what of atonement? According to Otto, atonement is a form of protection not just for the subject but also for the holy itself. Individuals need to protect themselves from the power of the sacred object but might also endanger the object with their own profanity:

> Mere awe, mere need of shelter from the *tremendum*, has here been elevated to the feeling that man in his "profaneness" is not *worthy* to stand in the presence of the holy one, and that his own entire personal unworthiness might defile even holiness itself. (54 italics Otto's)

In order not to contaminate the holy, individuals must consecrate themselves in ritual by taking on some of the qualities of the holy. A moral transgression, according to Otto, creates two kinds of response: remorse (when guilt weighs upon us) and self-loathing, which leads to activities of washing and cleansing (55). The moral transgression that might create a sense of unworthiness, in Nick's case, is the shooting of George the Waiter. But, it takes Nick some years to get close enough to this event to feel remorse, to appreciate his own self-loathing, and to understand the necessity of washing and cleansing rituals.

Underworld then is the story of Nick Shay's spiritual journey from the wasteland of the Bronx to the empty space of Arizona and the waste disposal business; from wasted life to a life of waste. He atones for killing George the Waiter and abandoning his family by caring for his mother in her old age and supporting his younger brother at her funeral. Finally, he can make peace with himself and speak to his wife of the events years before, can speak the unspeakable. It is so much harder now to keep secrets. Information is spilling out all over. Ultimately, there is hope in all this: if we can share information, if we can be connected, we can be at peace. For this is the root meaning of peace: a pact, a contract, people with differences joining together; people joined together by differences and events; and this is why DeLillo finishes his longest novel in the endless connections of cyberspace and closes it with a one-syllable note of transcendence: Peace.

NOTES

1. See, for example, Michel Serres' 1982 *The Parasite.*
2. See Marjorie Leach, "Underworld Gods," in *Guide to the Gods,* ed. Michael Owen-Jones and Frances Cattermole-Tally (London: Gale Research, 1992): 490–95.

"Shall These Bones Live?"

David Cowart

UNDERWORLD IS IN LARGE MEASURE A STORY OF SPIRITUAL TRAVAIL.
Nick Shay, protagonist and sometime narrator, learns from Father
Paulus that he must master the names of things. Doing so over the
course of his life Nick engages with the mythic legacy of Adam,
the primal namer. Nick's lifelong alienation has its Adamic dimension as well, for his slaying of George Manza is a version of the Fall,
the primal transgression that can be fully expiated only in eternity.
Some such absolutist frame may account for a curiously Janus-
faced element in the narrative's unfolding affect. Throughout his
story (but with increasing insistence as he gets older) Nick presents
himself to the reader as a person who, though unable finally to
transcend his past and what it has done to him, seems nonetheless
to be moving toward a degree of equanimity. A pure product of
the Bronx, Nick lives now in Phoenix, the city that David Bell, in
Americana, never gets to in his odyssey through the American West.
Here, the city in the desert seems an appropriate home for a person
subject to late-Christian yearnings for some ultimate recycling of
what must otherwise rot in the rubbish pile of Gehenna.

DeLillo is unsparing in his depiction of Nick's residual disquiet,
which cannot be allayed by smoothing things out with Marian, by
becoming a grandfather, or by savoring his professional success.
One cannot, it seems, ever leave altogether behind the loss of a
father, the act of "criminal negligence" that resulted in a death, the
marital betraying and being betrayed. In a way Nick suffers the fate
of the child touched, in his brother Matt's fantasy, by "Sister Skelly
Bone" to become "*it* forever" (717). Profoundly suggestive, this
condition of being "it" also fascinates Albert Bronzini, who recognizes "[a] fearsome power in the term" that renders one not just
"separate from all the others" but "nameless" or "name-shorn"
(677). Himself shorn of the paternal surname, the son of Jimmy
Costanza seems to exemplify the pronouncement of Klara Sax re-

garding the disturbing connection between namelessness and waste ("something that eludes naming is automatically relegated ... to the status of shit" [77]).

"It" all his life, Nick may recognize an affinity with the children he sees in Kazakhstan. Always and irreversibly "it" in the games-manship of nuclear powers, these children play at versions of the amusements Albert Bronzini and Father Paulus reminisce about—amusements that have survived unchanged for centuries, as Father Paulus, recalling Bruegel's 1560 canvas *De Kinderspelen*, points out to Bronzini. But, when the latter mentions the painting to his wife Klara, she not only characterizes it as "unwholesome," "sinister," and filled with some nameless "menace" (682), she links it to Bruegel's terrifying apocalyptic canvas *The Triumph of Death* (ca. 1562). The discussions of Albert, Klara, and Father Paulus take place in the same historical moment—1951—as the author's previous introduction of Bruegel: J. Edgar Hoover's encounter with *The Triumph of Death* floating from the upper stands at a baseball field (of course, 600 pages have intervened, with temporal settings throughout the latter part of the century, including the 1966 of Truman Capote's Black & White Ball, at which Klara—in another life and on the arm of another husband—actually crosses paths with Hoover). But much comes together in this long delayed dropping of the second allusive shoe—especially when the subject of children's games recurs in the Kazakhstan sequence, where Nick observes a group of disfigured children "playing follow the leader. A boy falls down, gets up. They all fall down, get up" (802). This game and its cousin, blindman's buff, figure in *De Kinderspelen*, but as the Kazakh children stumble over each other, they momentarily act out another Bruegel painting, *The Parable of the Blind* (1568), which pictorializes the familiar biblical precept: "if the blind lead the blind, both shall fall into the ditch" (Matt. 15:14). In the mutual blindness of nuclear rivalry, a particularly fearsome ditch first yawned on that day in 1951 when, as the Soviets tested the bomb and as assorted innocents played a game—its antecedents also appear in Bruegel's 1560 painting—with stick and ball, the reproduction of that other Bruegel wafts earthward as gently as radioactive dew.

The Kazakh victims of radiation figure proleptically in DeLillo's imagined Sergei Eisenstein film *Unterwelt*, which supplies this novel's title with one of its important referents.[1] Thought to have been filmed in Kazakhstan some time in the 1930s, *Unterwelt* concerns the horribly mutilated and crippled victims of a crazed scientist, the embodiment of Faustian desire and its consequences. DeLillo represents this film as the anticipation of a cinematic subgenre that would flourish during the first decade of the Cold War. A kind of cross between Fritz Lang's *Metropolis* (a screening of which DeLillo once saw at Radio City Music Hall) and Wells's *The Island of Dr. Moreau*, *Unterwelt* parodies both "Japanese science fiction"[2] cinema (though less explicitly than Pynchon in *Vineland*) and the exercises in nuclear dread that proliferated in the 1950s—variously witting allegories of atom-bomb-engendered teratology and Communist infiltration (from *Them* to aliens-among-us films such as *Invasion of the Body Snatchers* and *Village of the Damned*). But, this element of droll pastiche proves unstable. With an irony that has its own half-life, like some radioactive isotope, DeLillo imagines *Unterwelt* as modulating toward more sober augury. A Bruegel for the twentieth century, its director prophecies the atrocities committed on the human form at Auschwitz, at Hiroshima, and at Minamata, as well as the horrors witnessed by Nick.

Simulacra and the Spiritual

The medium or interface between the personal and the historical is the single baseball that more than one character intuitively sees as the living vehicle of a whole culture's youth. Marvin Lundy understands, when he relinquishes the ball, that "[t]here's men in the coming years they'll pay fortunes. . . . They'll pay unbelievable. Because this is desperation speaking" (182). A postmodern refinement of the familiar twentieth-century angst, this desperation cloaks a hunger for authentic experience, for the historically unique event that binds whole nations. Such was the Bobby Thomson home run, a shot heard 'round the world by which ordinary people might experience a moment of shared historical intensity (unlike remote "upperworld" events such as the contemporaneous Soviet bomb test). What Marvin Lundy—and DeLillo—sees is that we live more and more in a world incapable of such authenticity. All such experience is pithed as it becomes endlessly replicated as mass consumption image or soundbite. In "The Power of History" DeLillo speaks of "the debasing process of frantic repetition that exhausts a contemporary event before it has rounded into coherence." This is the point of the Texas Highway Killer videotape, repeated screening of which encapsulates our experience with all media spectacle and with a host of related simulacra in a "culture" that "continues its drive to imitate itself endlessly—the rerun, the sequel, the theme park, the designer outlet—because this is the means it has devised to disremember the past." The paradox resembles the one Freud identified in repetition compulsion: ostensibly grounded in a desire to take control of a painful reality (the absence of the mother in the famous *"fort/da"* illustration of *Beyond the Pleasure Principle*), repetition presently reveals itself as a drive to recover a prior inorganic state. Some such death wish, DeLillo intimates, lies behind the culture's sick love affair with repetition.

Television news routinely screens and rescreens footage of sensational crime or disaster: Ruby murdering Oswald, assassinations attempted and carried out, the Rodney King beating, the terrible fall of *Challenger*, and the terrorist attacks on the World Trade Center. DeLillo's cautionary remarks about this media phenomenon make clear the way or ways in which his imaginary Texas Highway Killer videotape functions in *Underworld*:

> you're staring at the inside of a convenience store on a humdrum night in July. This is a surveillance video with a digital display that marks off the tenths of seconds. Then you see a shuffling man with a handgun enter the frame. The commonplace homicide that ensues is transformed in the image-act of your own witness. It is bare, it is real, it is live, it is taped. It is compelling, it is numbing, it is digitally microtimed and therefore filled with incessant information. And if you view the tape often enough, it tends to transform you, to make you a passive variation of the armed robber in his warped act of consumption. It is another set of images for you to want and need and get sick of and need nonetheless, and it separates you from the reality that beats ever more softly in the diminishing world outside the tape. ("Power of History")

Diminishing reality—like the home run ball that dwindles to a speck as it sails out of the stadium. With instant replay, however, the diminishment is compounded—not, as one might think, reversed or arrested. The point of the Bobby Thomson baseball is that it embodies a wholly memorable piece of reality—of history, even—precisely because it could not be "replayed." It remains *un*-diminished as an experience of reality because it was never transformed to media simulacrum. Although it can embody bad luck, it remains the story's grail, brimming with the redemptive blood of historical truth. A tiny speck of unique experience and real history, the baseball is in the car with Judson Rauch at the time of his fatal encounter with the Texas Highway Killer. If this detail goes unnoticed at a first reading, all the better for DeLillo's point: the simulacrum elbows aside its counterpart in reality, overwhelms the old model of experience (memorable because unique, and literally, unrepeatable).

The baseball is also a textual nexus, linking virtually all of the novel's themes and motifs—including the theme of connectedness itself. Knocked into the stands on the same day that the Russians tested an atomic device, it is at one point described as the size of a bomb's "radioactive core" (172). In the hand it seems fruitlike, as if one could "juice it or milk it" (131) and thereby produce something like the orange juice that also figures motivically here. The authorities use orange juice to wash the subway trains tagged by Moonman 157 and others. Charlie Wainwright, who owns the baseball at one point, "wanted to pitch the Minute Maid account. He thought about orange juice all the time" (534). Present in the car of a victim of the Texas Highway Killer (indeed the videotaped death may be that of Judson Rauch himself), the ball eventually passes into the hands of the novel's protagonist, for whom, in the watches of the night, it becomes an uncanny intermediary between the different world he once inhabited—a world before the diminution of reality—and the world of guilt in which he still lives. A fan of the defeated Dodgers, Nick knows the answer to his rhetorical question about Ralph Branca, the pitcher with whom he identifies: "What's it like to have to live with one awful moment?" (97). Perhaps also, he half-consciously recognizes, in the vagaries of his own volition, a bond between himself and the Texas Highway Killer. Whether an example of the acte gratuit or of the minimal volition Father Paulus calls velleity (539), the "life-defining act" of Nick Shay's boyhood finds its terrible reflection in the senseless killings carried out by Richard Henry Gilkey, the psychopath. At one point Nick is jocularly taken for the killer (79).

In addition to the textual reticulation (the product merely of an author's forethought or craft), the baseball subsumes as well the idea of a more genuinely metaphysical—even religious— connectedness that remains indeterminate and often debased as superstition or paranoid delusion. Thus the desire to conceptualize cyberspace as heaven's gate, or the traditional fear—chiefly articulated by Nick—of the number 13, or the two Edgars' convictions regarding a universal grid of germs or Communists alike embody the yearning for a rational principle, even if it takes the form of paranoia. In Vietnam Matt Shay notices "black drums"(462) that "resembled cans of frozen Minute Maid" (463): "how can you tell the difference between orange juice and agent orange if the same massive system connects them at levels outside your comprehension?" (465). The "cans of Minute Maid" (820) recur on the billboard in which Sister Edgar sees Esmeralda, and DeLillo suggests that indeed some massive system links advertising, Vietnam, and bogus miracles.

"Everything connects in the end" (465), thinks Matt Shay, and the text enacts this theme relentlessly. In the closing pages Sister Edgar becomes its exemplar, her late passion suggesting the fragility of faith on the eve of the millennium. When she dies she goes not to heaven but to cyberspace, the contemporary secular world's often paranoid model of universal linkage where, again, "[e]verything is connected" (825, 826) amid "intersecting systems" (826) now virtualized. One reads her fate as a kind of poetic justice for a person whose devotional commitment seems to have been corrupted by a faith in the endlessly seen—movie stars—and in nondivine forms of the unseen: germs, radiation, Communists among us. Though she abandons the movie stars, Sister Edgar remains a committed anticommunist with a fervor little short of religious. "The faith of suspicion and unreality. The faith that replaces God with radioactivity, the power of alpha particles and the all-knowing systems that shape them, the endless fitted links" (251). The nun has in fact made of her obsessions a graven image, violated the First and Second Commandments. One way or another she shares more than a name with the paranoid director of the FBI, whose company in the infinitely linkable spaces of the Internet will provide little comfort, for death is not user-friendly and admits no such easy navigation.

Although all around him are ranged the ones and zeroes of embattled belief and hardened despair, Nick Shay continues, curiously enough, a believer, and in the gross tonnage of secular ore this trace element of belief contributes to his survival. In the end Nick's emotional and psychological condition seems to approximate and perhaps surpass the state of achievable psychological equilibrium that Freud called "ordinary everyday unhappiness." Although still given to waking up in the middle of the night and clutching the baseball that may or may not retain a special meaning, he notes a renewed intimacy with his wife, from whom he no longer withholds the secrets of his past, and he finds bearable, at least, the longings that must go unfulfilled. He experiences moods of near tranquility, the muted countercurrent flowing from the vision imparted by the old Jesuit's teachings and nurtured, perhaps, by Nick's lifelong habit of reading. "I . . . feel a quiet kind of power because I've done it and come out okay, done it and won, gone in weak and come out strong" (803). In a passage that follows and qualifies yet another description of the Shay family's conscientious recycling, he even experiences his dead mother as a spiritual presence:

> The long ghosts are walking the halls. When my mother died I felt expanded, slowly, durably, over time. I felt suffused with her truth, spread through, as with water, color or light. I thought she'd entered the deepest place I could provide, the animating entity, the thing, if anything, that will survive my own last breath, and she makes me larger, she amplifies my sense of what it is to be human. She is part of me now, total and consoling. And it is not a sadness to acknowledge that she had to die before I could know her fully. It is only a statement of the power of what comes after. (804)

One detects in this passage no trace of ironic reservation, and one notes, in passing, that DeLillo has dedicated *Underworld* "To the memory of my mother and father."

The ironic reservation, however, does color the interestingly parallel language with which DeLillo evokes Sister Edgar's perception of the miraculous presence in the orange juice billboard: "She sees Esmeralda's face take shape under the rainbow of bounteous juice and . . . there is a sense of someone living in the image, an animating spirit" (822). Although DeLillo affirms that the generally mean-spirited Sister Edgar experiences a moment of exaltation, he simultaneously denies its ultimate validity. The nun has duped herself—as presently even she realizes. Her misguided transports concluded, "[t]here is nothing left to do but die" (824), the author declares, perhaps meaning to echo, with Eliot, the lines from Goldsmith suggesting that only death remains "when lovely woman stoops to folly." Yet, if DeLillo does not represent the billboard manifestation as a genuine miracle, he remains deeply sympathetic to the spiritual yearning it feeds. Thus he allows Lenny Bruce's mock-hagiographic story of the "illiterate sad-eyed virgin" (630) who can blow smoke rings from her vagina gradually to become, with a kind of dwindling satirical malice, that of a girl "hiding in the empty lots" of the South Bronx, where she lives with her junkie mother" (632–33). Unnamed, she anticipates the Esmeralda martyred 30 years later.

Yet regardless of which miraculous story is under review, hagiography remains a narrative imperfectly sanctioned by metanarrative. However moving her story, in other words, one cannot seriously imagine Esmeralda a saint. She is the gauge, merely, of a widespread and poignant yearning for sanctity and its miraculous trappings. One can agree only up to a point then with critics who see DeLillo as a religious writer. According to Vince Passaro, for example, "the subdued religious sentiment that runs through all his work has never been more evident than in *Underworld*" (74). John A. McClure takes a similar view: "DeLillo's work . . . insistently interrogates secular conceptions of the real, both by focusing the reader's attention on events that remain mysterious or even 'miraculous,' and by making all sorts of room for religious or spiritual discourses and styles of seeing" (142–43). But, one must simultaneously recognize DeLillo's tough-minded disinclination to accept moments of spiritualized perception as grounds for a more structured faith. As he told British interviewer, Andrew Billen, "I feel a drive towards some kind of transcendence, perhaps religious but not in traditional ways."

Striving to keep the faith, Sister Edgar fears, late in life, "that all creation is a spurt of blank matter that chances to make an emerald planet here, a dead star there, with random waste between. The serenity of immense design is missing from her life, authorship and moral form" (817). Thus she embraces a false miracle. Perhaps she enjoys a moment of grace when she briefly recognizes in Esmeralda "her virgin twin who is also her daughter" (824), but this identification seems sharply qualified when the narrative shifts to Sister Edgar's continuing consciousness in cyberspace. The momentary nexus of the Internet's many connections, her consciousness finds, as hyperlink, the H-bomb web page corresponding to her obsession in life. Here she "feels the power of false faith, the faith of paranoia" and mistakes "fifty-eight megatons" (825) for the Merkabah.

In the aftermath of her religious credulity the author shifts to second-person address, as at the opening ("He speaks in your

voice, American''), and the language here resonates powerfully
with other meditations on belief in this text:

> And what do you remember, finally, when everyone has gone home
> and the streets are empty of devotion and hope, swept by river wind? Is
> the memory thin and bitter and does it shame you with its fundamental
> untruth—all nuance and wishful silhouette? Or does the power of tran-
> scendence linger, the sense of an event that violates natural forces,
> something holy that throbs on the hot horizon, the vision you crave
> because you need a sign to stand against your doubt? (824)

The images of wind and sign have their complement in the weary
yearning of Nick's mother, Rosemary Shay. "Sometimes faith
needs a sign. There are times when you want to stop working at
faith and just be washed in a blowing wind that tells you everything" (757). Emblem of terrifying vacuity for Sister Edgar, the
wind embodies a Pentecostal hope for Nick's long-suffering
mother. Yet, neither receives the desiderated sign, for its absence
in modern times has become, at least since Eliot's "Gerontion," a
spiritual given. As background to his great poem of spiritual arid-
ity, one recalls, Eliot invokes a Launcelot Andrewes' sermon on the
New Testament text in which the Pharisees demand of Christ:
"Master, we would see a sign." Christ answers in words suited to
what he repeatedly calls a "generation of vipers" (Matt. 12:34—the
phrase also supplies the title of Philip Wylie's midcentury castiga-
tion of American shallowness): "An evil and adulterous generation
seeketh after a sign; and there shall no sign be given unto it" (Matt.
12:39). But, like the early Eliot, DeLillo may well feel that the sign is
withheld not because the countenance divine remains averted but
because it has long since fossilized and cracked.

RECYCLING

In Nick's frequent references to the conscientiousness he and his
family bring to recycling one sees something more than the author's desire to equip his character with traits appropriate to his
professional involvement with waste:

> At home we removed the wax paper from cereal boxes. We had a
> recycling closet with separate bins for newspapers, cans and jars. We
> rinsed out the used cans and empty bottles and put them in their

proper bins. We did tin versus aluminum. On pickup days we placed each form of trash in its separate receptacle . . . We used a paper bag for the paper bags. We took a large paper bag and put all the smaller bags inside and then placed the large bag alongside all the other receptacles on the sidewalk. We ripped the wax paper from our boxes of shredded wheat. There is no language I might formulate that could overstate the diligence we brought to these tasks. We did the yard waste. We bundled the newspapers but did not tie them in twine. (102–3)

This passage is itself recycled, a version of it having appeared earlier (89)—nor does it conclude the recycling, for at least two more variants will appear in the story (803–4, 806–7). Verbal recycling takes place, moreover, even within the brief confines of the present example (the repetition of the point about wax paper and cereal boxes, the repetition of individual words such as "receptacles" and "paper bags"). Freighted with dread, the affirmation of ecological "diligence" here frames and partly masks a half-conscious hunger for the larger recycling of spiritual waste. The speaker, that is, cannot disguise a deep disquiet that his recycling efforts (not to mention his almost obsessive recounting of them) do not keep at bay. Like Jack Gladney poking through the trash in *White Noise* or *End Zone*'s Gary Harkness encountering the excrement in the desert, Nick fears that "[w]hat we excrete comes back to consume us" (791), that human beings must eventually become the garbage they generate in such quantities.

The recycling theme of *Underworld* subsumes a vision of art that lends itself to conclusions about the entire DeLillo oeuvre. Early in the narrative, Nick Shay visits his former lover Klara Sax, an artist whose "career had been marked at times by her methods of transforming and absorbing junk" (102). So given is Klara to using cast-off materials that she has been called "the Bag Lady" (70). Her recycling extends even to some hundreds of decommissioned B-52s. The author intimates that Klara is not unique. Like Simon Rodia, who created Watts Towers out of junk, she is somehow, surprisingly, an archetypal artist. Indeed, as Michiko Kakutani remarked in a review of this novel, DeLillo himself "has taken the effluvia of modern life, all the detritus of our daily and political lives, and turned it into a dazzling, phosphorescent work of art." DeLillo may think of Pound's injunction to "make it new" as an enthymeme, a syllogism with an unstated premise—in this case the dereliction or desuetude of "it." As they transmute suffering into beauty, artists transmute "the great squalor of our lives" (810). Art, like religion, promises the redemption of human waste. It recycles.

Underworld embraces an aesthetic of recycling that complements the obsessions of its protagonist. "Perhaps in keeping with the novel's theme," as Jesse Kavadlo points out, "portions of *Underworld* are themselves recycled, having been published previously in a number of magazines and journals." Moreover, the novel recycles elements of earlier DeLillo fictions, several of which glance at the theme of waste. As DeLillo told Diane Osen at the time of *Underworld*'s publication: "I'd been thinking about garbage for twenty years." This recycling ranges from small details to major themes to that favorite DeLillo device, the grail-like object of universal desire.

Indeed the pursuit of *Underworld*'s baseball represents an especially artful reimagining of the pursuits that structure DeLillo's other fictions, for DeLillo shares with Thomas Pynchon a tendency to structure novels as quests. Pynchon favors the highly factitious grail—V., the Trystero, the Rocket—which becomes the emblem of humanity's need for order and coherence, however spurious. V. confers structure on Herbert Stencil's century; the Trystero offers to Oedipa Maas the promise of an exit from "the absence of surprise to life"; and the Rocket holds the key to humanity's Faustian drive for knowledge and power. A DeLillo novel, on the other hand, though it often revolves around some fixed point of general yearning, favors the grail less than what Hitchcock called the MacGuffin, the simple device that sets the plot in motion: a scientific formula, missing diamonds, a stolen warhead. Possessed, the MacGuffin effects no paradigm shift: it often proves as literally valueless as the Maltese falcon in the familiar Hammett novel. Thus in *Great Jones Street* most of the characters seek either the mountain tapes or the mystery drug developed by the government and stolen by Happy Valley; in *Running Dog* virtually everyone pursues the Hitler film. Only occasionally do DeLillo's characters strive for something more genuinely grail-like or metaphysical, something that, like Dylar in *White Noise*, or the code that will explain the message from Ratner's Star, or the rationale behind the cult in *The Names*, promises to transform our thinking in some radical way. *Underworld*'s baseball, however, is at once MacGuffin and grail, and the author presents it with considerable ambiguity—as an object of yearning, yes, but also as an emblem of bad luck, perhaps even as vitiated relic, something like Chaucer's "shrine from which the seinte is oute."

One sees DeLillo's inspired recycling as a localized or self-bounded illustration of the principle of intertextuality. To speak of recycling then is not to reproach the artist for some creative failure. All discourse, after all, reconfigures prior discourse. Thus, when DeLillo's Lenny Bruce mocks as "linguists" the "cops on special duty" (594) in his audience, he echoes a phrase about the repressive "king's linguists" in *Great Jones Street* (68). Similarly, when Nick Shay visits Frankie's Tropical Bar (617) one may recognize the establishment from *Running Dog*. *Underworld*'s theme of nuclear anxiety, by the same token, reimagines that of *End Zone* at the same time that it recontextualizes the argument in *Libra* for the Kennedy assassination as *fons et origo* of the late-century decades of dread (the dread—of the bomb—was there already, part of the background to the Bay of Pigs, itself widely perceived as somehow linked to the killing of the President).[3] From *The Names* DeLillo recycles reluctant adulterers and the emphasis on onomastics. The lonely passion of Bill Gray, central to *Mao II*, seems to lie behind the sense, projected in the *Unterwelt* set piece, of the artist's oppression by the host of benighted attitudes that swell the wave of societal devolution. The deserts of *Underworld*—literal ones in Arizona and Kazakhstan, figurative ones in agent-oranged Vietnam and the Bronx—are of course a familiar DeLillo motif. Opening in the desert and periodically returning there, the Nick Shay narrative ends in the wastes of Kazakhstan and in the wilderness around Phoenix.

In Nick's story finally one returns to the Oedipal drama that informs both *Americana* and *Running Dog*. Seducing an older woman, an artist, Nick reenacts David Bell's consummated desire for the artist-mother Sullivan. As Glen Selvy defies a father in Earl Mudger, then flees Cao and Van, the murderous agents of Oedipal retribution, so does Nick, shooting George Manza (who tells him, paternally, "Stay in school" [693]), unconsciously take revenge on his absconding father. More Orestes, even, than Glen Selvy, Nick subsequently struggles with Furies that take the form of filial guilt, sexual remorse, and forces that make him live at a distance from those in his own household.

All of these forces do what advertising was said to do in *Americana*: they turn subjects into third-person automatons. In *Underworld* as in his first novel DeLillo explores the unmoored self so familiar to postmodernity. *Americana*'s David Bell, telling his story in first person yet objectifying himself as movie character, destabilizes the boundary between first person and third. In *Ratner's Star*, by the same token, as the world advances into the Mohole, a series of first-person headings complicates the otherwise third-person narration. These shifts may remind one of the effects in certain war fictions. For example, in *Meditations in Green*, Steven Wright's 1983 Vietnam novel, the narrator represents himself in first person in the present when he is a near derelict, suffering from war wounds both physical and mental. But, over half of the novel is set in Vietnam during his service there—and these sections are narrated in third person, as if two wholly different people—notwithstanding their shared name and DNA—have had the experiences reported to the reader. Similarly in Salinger's "For Esmé, with Love and Squalor" the narrator begins in first person but concludes in third. Salinger also reserves third person for his picture of combat fatigue, a state of profound disjunction from the happier, more integrated self of "Sergeant X" just before and long after the Normandy invasion. This example may be the clearest indicator of what DeLillo seeks to represent here—a sense of the divided or alienated self during a war that, however cold, threatens at any moment to become the hottest ever. Thus, in *Underworld* one of the formal elements of which is the shift between first-person, third-person, and (at certain moments) second-person narration for the story of Nick Shay (murderer, thief, sexual predator, waste executive, survivor), DeLillo goes well beyond his previous experiments with point of view. The novel's shifts of viewpoint, like its dislocations of temporality (seen in the scrambling of chronology as well as in the mixing of present-tense and past-tense narration), hint at the self's liability, especially vis-a-vis memory, which ranges forward and backward in time, at once registering and qualifying the individual's alienation.

Underworld may also be said to incorporate and recycle artistic conventions and styles. As Philip Nel has argued, "DeLillo's recent fiction in general and *Underworld* in particular challenges the validity of the modern-postmodern binarism."[4] Part of the greatness of this novel is the way that, at the end of the 1990s, it seems a compendium of literary fashion from turn-of-the-century naturalism, through modernist and postmodernist reaction, to hybridized millennial vision. In other words it offers the insights of naturalism qualified by elements of that movement's successor styles: dislocated chronology; abundant, often conflicting perspectives; intricately motivic construction modeling a near-paranoid dream of universal connectedness; deconstructions of national and religious myth; a self-referring model of history; and a treatment of language that seems to map out contending views on the limits of referentiality.

Seldom formally allusive, DeLillo incorporates elements that have, as it were, pedigrees. This author's work must not be read in a vacuum, for like any other body of writing it follows or coexists with a host of literary currents. As Martin Amis observed in his review of *Underworld*, "DeLillo has always been a literary writer; deeply literary, and also *covertly* literary." *Underworld*, in other words, benefits from judicious contextualization—necessarily judicious, because anything approaching a comprehensive canvassing of its intertexts would require a discussion of some hundreds of pages.

In a novel with waste as central metaphor one expects at least traces of *The Waste Land*, and, sure enough, *Underworld*'s protagonist is a combination of Phlebas ("[r]esidents of Phoenix," Nick notes, "are called Phoenicians" [120]) and the prophet who is asked: "Can these bones live?" (Ezek. 37: 3). Both works feature a Belladonna and both glance in passing at abortion. Both ladle material from the cauldron of unholy loves described by St. Augustine. Both problematize the compulsion to art (the Matisse remark that Klara quotes, "painters must begin by cutting out their tongues" [78], may even remind the reader of Eliot's primal artist, the tongueless Philomela). Both invoke the shored fragments of a moribund Christianity (including the Grail legend) to arrive at a vision of peace.

One's understanding of *Underworld* also benefits from an awareness of—not the influence, exactly, but the looming, fraternal presence of certain of the big novels DeLillo has mentioned reading, notably *Ulysses*. Thus one discerns something of Joyce's cuckolded *homme moyen sensuel*, Leopold Bloom, in DeLillo's similarly cuckolded, similarly curious, similarly sympathetic Albert Bronzini. Similarly peripatetic as well, both men walk the streets perpending odd words and their etymologies. But the assimilated Jew here is Klara Sax, DeLillo's Molly Bloom, and she—not the "consubstantial" son of spiritual kinship—is the artist whose work, which involves the recycling of cast-off or waste materials, reflexively mirrors that of the author. The ephebe in this family romance, though apparently not called to art, struggles like Joyce's Stephen with complexes of paternity, duty to the mother, and the remorse of conscience. Indeed, both Stephen Dedalus and Nick Shay muse on obscure works of the fourteenth century: *Agenbite of Inwit* and *The Cloud of Unknowing*, respectively.

Similarly there are broad resemblances with the early work of James T. Farrell. The Catholic, baseball-loving protagonist of the Studs Lonigan trilogy survives a tough urban boyhood (Chicago, rather than the Bronx), becomes involved with "underworld" figures, and is eventually destroyed, in the classic naturalist manner, by social, economic, and biological forces that make him their hapless puppet. DeLillo also acknowledges the enormous forces ranged against individuals of the underclass—absentee fathers, poverty, biological urges, drugs, crime, racism. These are only the immediate or local forces. Beyond them are the powerful currents of history: the bomb, the Cold War, big business, the media, advertising, and so on. Yet in the end DeLillo presents, in Nick Shay, a protagonist sufficiently self-aware to hold his own against social, biological, and historical determinism. Nick exercises something like free will, and thus does the author himself resist doctrinaire naturalism's final, coercive argument. As John N. Duvall observes, "an awareness of one's alienation is the last best hope to construct an opposition to the forces of consumer culture."[5]

DeLillo's Bronx, finally, resembles the Newark of Philip Roth's *American Pastoral*, published the same year as *Underworld*. Both authors meditate on a once-vital immigrant community and its fate in the late decades of the twentieth century. Roth's central character, the brilliant and gifted Seymour Levov, known as "Swede," passes through—and survives—trials remarkably similar to those of Nick Shay. If Swede's father, unlike Nick's, remains a forceful presence in the protagonist's life, the vexed relationship with a younger brother and the infidelity of a wife are direct parallels. The pivotal taking of a life also figures—Swede's disturbed daughter sets a bomb to protest the war in Vietnam and kills an innocent man. Both authors refuse to soften the toll that survival takes on their protagonists, who are nonetheless spared the fate of Mc-Teague, Clyde Griffiths, Jude Fawley, et al. Nick and the Swede diverge only in the price each pays: where Roth's character cannot finally restore the happiness and integrity of his family, DeLillo's can congratulate himself, late in his story, on having "gone in weak and come out strong" (803).

Yet, in the Epilogue Nick remains subject to feelings of loneliness, loss, and confusion: "I don't know what happened, do I?" (807). Set in the 1990s (but otherwise, as he told Peter Körte, "temporally unspecific" [translation by the author]), the novel's concluding section begins in Moscow, proceeds to Kazakhstan, and ends in Phoenix, where Nick may or may not be a candidate for rebirth from his own ashes. Only here does Nick himself engage in the present-tense narration that has hitherto been reserved for the Texas Highway Killer videotape and accounts of the mythic baseball's early career (that is, all of the sections narrated from the point of view of Cotter Martin or his father Manx). Nick comes to terms with Jimmy Costanza's desertion, concluding that his father simply "went under," without giving much thought to his abandoned family. But "[t]he failure it brought down on us does not diminish" (809). Confronting Brian Glassic, another of DeLillo's reluctant adulterers, Nick momentarily threatens to become Jack Gladney redux, the cuckold who embraces atavistic violence (the reader may recognize in Nick a version, as well, of the Albert Bronzini who loses a mother to death and suffers—with Nick himself in the Brian Glassic role—a spouse's betrayal). On the verge of confrontation, Nick reflects on himself as some kind of impostor: "Brian thought I was the soul of self-completion. Maybe so. But I was also living in a state of quiet separation from all the things he might cite as the solid stuff of home and work and responsible reality. When I found out. . . . I was hereby relieved of my phony role as husband and father, high corporate officer. Because even the job is an artificial limb. Did I feel free for just a moment, myself again, hearing the story of their affair? . . . None of it ever belonged to me except in the sense that I filled out the forms" (796). The last phrase suggests that one might switch roles (or identities) as one switches jobs: just fill out more application forms. It also suggests that one's roles in life merely approximate—fill out—certain ideals or "forms" of the Platonic variety. Nick had once helped the marginally literate George Manza to fill out forms (690), and the figure, repeated, hints at a symbolic role for George as the shadow self that drifts into addiction and untimely death while another, more privileged self fills out other forms. More than the circumstance that shapes a naturalistic literary action, then, Nick's murder of George is a slaying of the double, the self that by rights Nick (a drop-out at 16) was destined to be.

But, in the Jungian system one must integrate—not deny or destroy—the shadow self, and Nick's act takes a psychological toll

throughout his life. His occasional experience of something like serenity at the end must vie with more durable feelings of incom-
pleteness. Nick qualifies his sense of having survived most
revealingly when he thinks: "I'll tell you what I long for, the days
of disarray, when I didn't give a damn or a fuck or a farthing"
(806). DeLillo told Diane Osen that he considers this a "telling" ad-
mission. Nick "ultimately expresses his regret and longing for the
days when he felt physically connected to the earth. The days when
he had freedom to commit transgressive acts. And it's not a nostalgia for innocence, it's a nostalgia for guilt." Nick's expression of
yearning for the gutter encourages the reader to see the true psychological and sociological complexity of this story. It cannot end
with some unqualified affirmation or renewal in the city named for
an archetype of resurrection—for the conflicting perceptions and
the heavy weight of history conspire to allow only the most fitful
visitations of grace, only occasional reversals of the anomie that
has grown unchecked through a century of weapons, waste, and
woe. This tough-minded adherence to a postlapsarian reality principle makes of *Underworld* something greater than a simple ubi
sunt elegy for the passion, the certainty, the simplicity of youth. It
is the companion piece to those great documents of bitter reconciliation to a lost vitality—texts such as Willa Cather's *The Professor's
House*, Frost's "The Oven Bird," and the Immortality Ode. "You
used to have the same dimensions as the observable universe," remarks Marian Shay to Brian Glassic, her feckless lover: "Now
you're a lost speck" (170).

NOTES

1. No one has described the density of this title better than Tom LeClair, who
noted in his review published in *Atlantic* (October 1997) that the novel packs together "Dante, the Mafia, hollowed earth, humankind's sediment, ghetto life, underground politics, the subconscious, and linguistic roots." To LeClair's
enumeration one might add the idea of an artistic underworld as represented in
works such as *Unterwelt* and the literally subterranean graffiti of Moonman 157.
Both homosexual, Eisentein and Munoz dwell also in sexual underworlds.

2. Diane Osen, "A Conversation with Don DeLillo," *Publishers Weekly/National
Book Foundation* (April 2001).

3. As Peter Knight has persuasively argued, "*Underworld* revises the anatomy
of popular American paranoia that DeLillo has conducted in his previous novels,
pushing back the inquiry before the assassination of President John F. Kennedy,
which had previously served as the watershed event in his work, and reaching

ahead into the as yet unconfigured world beyond the end of the Cold War" (812). Knight contrasts what he calls the "secure paranoia" of the Cold War with the more recognizably postmodern "insecure paranoia" (817) that began on the fateful November day in Dallas. He is also an especially able cataloguer of *Underworld*'s many connections, but where I have emphasized the purely textual or modernist element in these connections (with consideration of the way they buttress world views now superstitious, now metaphysical or religious), Knight underscores the picture of world capital's emergent and progressive connectedness. He makes the telling point that this secret history of the Cold War pays virtually no attention to its end: the fall of the Berlin Wall and the New World Order. Rather, the Cold War's secure paranoia gradually gives way to "an underground current of increasing awareness and consternation that slowly everything is becoming connected" as "social and economic relationships within a global economy" (825).

4. Philip Nel, "'A Small Incisive Shock': Modern Forms, Postmodern Politics, and the Role of the Avant-Garde in *Underworld*," 737. This important 1999 article "argues that *Underworld* complicates traditional distinctions between modern and postmodern by drawing on both a high modernist aesthetic and those residual elements of the historical avant-garde that characterize certain postmodernisms" (725–26).

5. John N. Duvall, "Introduction: From Valparaiso to Jerusalem: DeLillo and the Moment of Canonization," 561. For the argument that Nick "has neither historical nor aesthetic self-consciousness," see Timothy L. Parrish, "From Hoover's FBI to Eisenstein's *Unterwelt*: DeLillo Directs the Postmodern Novel," 719. Parrish is especially good on DeLillo's conceptualization of the J. Edgar Hoover character as another of the novel's postmodern artists, but one resists his attempt to read the Dodgers-Giants game as an event that is as "apprehended through the media" as the Texas Highway Killer's "murdering spree" (709). In another article by Duvall (on "Pafko at the Wall" and written before the story's reappearance as part of *Underworld*), one encounters the similar argument that "the mediation of radio, both for Hodges and his listeners, has become as invisible as an FBI wiretap. When a media form comes to seem transparent, when its role in the construction of aura is experienced paradoxically as an unmediated mediation, then we have entered, the novella suggests, the realm of the postmodern, technological sublime" ("'Baseball as Aesthetic Ideology: Cold War History, Race, and DeLillo's 'Pafko at the Wall,'" [303]). Such arguments are intrinsically valuable, but they fail (for obvious reasons, in Duvall's case) to take sufficiently into account DeLillo's patent contrasting, in "The Power of History," of the past and its low-tech media with the present and its Möbius-strip journalism. In one an idea of the historical survives; in the other it is vitiated.

Don DeLillo's Logogenetic *Underworld*

STEVEN G. KELLMAN

PACE SAINT JOHN, THE WORD IS BOTH THE BEGINNING AND THE END OF *Underworld*. "He speaks in your voice, American," are the first, reflexive, words of the novel's Prologue, and for the final paragraph of the Epilogue Don DeLillo provides a solitary word: "Peace." *Underworld* is, among much else, a parable about the creative, and destructive, powers of language. "I was driving a Lexus through a rustling wind" (63) is the way that Nick Shay begins his story, much as his author tells all his stories, by driving a lexis through the windy expanses of preverbal thought. More than angst over the inexorable approach of death or mirth over that angst, language itself is the engine of DeLillo's writing, including *Underworld*.

In a 1993 interview DeLillo addressed the contention that his novels are gloomy and the implicit premise that it is the responsibility of the novelist to provide solace for a troubling world. Insisting on the primacy of language in the shape that writing takes, DeLillo calls attention to the nuances of style and structure that some critics, intent on reading him exclusively for his somber themes, neglect:

> I don't offer comforts except those that lurk in comedy and in structure and in language, and the comedy is probably not all that soothing. But before everything, there's language. Before history and politics, there's language. And it's language, the sheer pleasure of making it and bending it and seeing it form on the page and hearing it whistle in my head—this is the thing that makes my work go. (Begley 306)

DeLillo stands out from other contemporaries who depict a similar landscape by his playful deployment of and anxious attentiveness to the English language—from the depersonalized jargon of bureaucracy in *White Noise* (1985) and of football in *End Zone* (1972) to the Italian-inflected street patois of immigrants and their children in the final section of *Underworld*, a novel that echoes with a variety of voices, registers, and tongues. Echolalia drives the plot of *The Body Artist* (2001), in which an aphasic refugee from a mental hospital shows up in Lauren Hartke's house and offers distorted mimicry of her dead husband's speech. The site of the entire story in *End Zone* is an institution in west Texas called Logos College, and there is a sense in which *logos*—that is, the word—is the inspiration and not just the medium for all of DeLillo's work.

It is very often even the impetus of the plot. *Valparaiso* (1999), the first work that DeLillo published after *Underworld*, is propelled by a *faux mot*. In the two-act absurdist play Michael Majeski's destination is determined by the linguistic accident of geographical homonymy; he ends up in Florida and Chile, and world-famous, because they also happen to hold cities with the same name, Valparaiso, as the one he had intended to visit in Indiana. In *The Names* (1982), whose title testifies as well to the arcane power of words, a homicidal cult (whose password is: "How many languages do you speak?") allows language—a congruence of initial letters in person and place—to determine the location and victim of each of its operations. Because Michaelis Kalliambetsos is killed in Mikro Kamini and Hamir Mazmudar in Hawa Mandir, James Axton is in mortal danger while in Jebel Amman. Such deadly verbal games—like the ball games in *End Zone* and *Underworld* and the mathematical puzzles in *Ratner's Star* (1976)—are a bid to contain and explain chaos. So are the compulsive chess matches into which Albert Bronzini initiates young Matt Shay.

In *End Zone* it is a telling paradox that the late founder of Logos College, Tom Wade, was mute and that a school named for the Word offers a course in the untellable, in which students are required to memorize and recite long poems in a language they do not understand. When he arrives at Logos from upstate New York, narrator Gary Harkness is disturbed by the menacing silence of the bare west Texas terrain:

> It hung over the land and drifted across the long plains. It was out there with the soft black insects beyond the last line of buildings, beyond the prefabs and the Quonset hut and the ROTC barracks. Day after day my eyes scanned in all directions a stunned earth, unchangingly dull, a land silenced by its own beginnings in the roaring heat, born dead, flat stones burying the memory. I felt threatened by the silence. (24–25)

The fact that it can inspire such lyricism in Harkness demonstrates that silence is not only the negation of language but also its necessary context. At the conclusion of *Great Jones Street* (1973) sinister conspirators inject Bucky Wunderlick with a drug that neutralizes the sector of the brain that processes and generates speech. But, the novel's final pages recount how, one by one, words—and the world—begin to return, as Wunderlick is slowly restored to "the mad weather of language" (265) in which the reader lives. Each of DeLillo's verbally ingenious fictions is explicitly a victory over the stubborn hush of the nonhuman. It is revealing that *Unterwelt*, the fictive 1930s film by Sergei Eisenstein that gives *Underworld* its name, is silent. And, what the movie's muteness tells us is that silence is the foundation of all expression. As DeLillo's environmental artist Klara Sax, alluding to the opening sentence of Henri Matisse's 1957 book *Jazz*, notes: "painters must begin by cutting out their tongues" (78).

So also, suggests Klara, must physicists. The desolate site in the New Mexico desert to which Nick Shay is driving his rented Lexus when we first encounter him in *Underworld* is where Klara and her crew are transforming a fleet of 238 abandoned B-52 bombers into an open-air gallery of monumental art objects. They are not far from Los Alamos, where the Manhattan Project created the first atomic bomb, which, as Klara notes, J. Robert Oppenheimer, who directed the research, felt compelled to refer to euphemistically as *merde*: "He meant something that eludes naming is automatically relegated, he is saying, to the status of shit. You can't name it. It's too big or evil or outside your experience" (77).

Haunted by a nameless dread, much of *Underworld* is activated by the futile quest to match language to the scatalogically ineffable, as if to join oral and anal. The *merde* that Oppenheimer could not put into words is refuse, at least of a verbal sort. Klara explains: "It's also shit because it's garbage, it's waste material" (77). So Nick, as an executive at Waste Containment, an international recycling corporation, can define himself as one of the "cosmologists of waste" (88), engaged in a sacred enterprise: "Waste is a religious thing. We entomb contaminated waste with a sense of reverence and dread. It is necessary to respect what we discard" (88). Suffused by secret "shit," like J. Edgar Hoover's stolen garbage, *Underworld* is an attempt to recycle the words of the tribe into fit language for unspeakable dread.

In Kazakhstan, where a company called Tchaika obliterates dangerous waste in underground nuclear explosions, Viktor Maltsev tries to expound on the mystic significance of debris, how "waste is the secret history, the underhistory, the way archaeologists dig out the history of early cultures, every sort of bone heap and broken tool, literally from under the ground" (791). And for Matt Shay, "There may have been an underworld of images known only to tribal priests, mediums between visible reality and the spirit world" (466). Replete with such images, *Underworld* is an attempt to write the secret history, the underhistory, of the second half of the twentieth century, by excavating the littered lots of the Bronx and the housing tracts of Phoenix, a city named for the creature recycled from its own ashes.

Gary Harkness comes to Logos College in order to play football, and much of the sport is conceived of as shaped by language—the vapid motto that their martinet coach, Emmett Creed, uses to motivate players (for example, "It's only a game but it's the only game"[105]), the insults, imprecations, and incantations employed by players (for example, "Nigger kike faggot" [119]), and the names of plays ("Middle-sift-W, alph-set, lemmy-2" [95]) that dictate action on the field. Although he admits to knowing nothing about football, Wally Pippich, Logos College's Sports Information Director, promotes the team by coining catchy nicknames, phrases, and slogans. But, it is Coach Creed who rules absolutely, and he derives his authority from his control of words. "This was his power," observes Harkness, "to deny us the words we needed. He was the maker of plays, the name-giver" (110).

According to Harkness, football "is the one sport guided by language, by the word signal, the snap number, the color code, the play name" (90). Like the novel itself, football is a matter of negotiating a linguistic system. In the author's own interpolation DeLillo explains that in writing about football in *End Zone* he has rendered it as verbal play:

> The author, always somewhat corrupt in his inventions and vanities, has tried to reduce the content to basic units of language and action. ... Much of the appeal of sport derives from its dependence on elegant gibberish. And of course it remains the author's permanent duty to unbox the lexicon for all eyes to see—a cryptic ticking mechanism in search of a revolution. (90)

The same might be said about any of the other subjects— advertising, pop music, science, espionage, academe, and waste

management—that DeLillo has tackled throughout his writing career. And in *Underworld* DeLillo manifestly offers baseball as another sport guided by language. Russ Hodges, the play-by-play
announcer for the New York Giants, recalls his work of simulation,
the years he spent sitting in a radio studio recreating major league
games from information coming off a teletype:

> Somebody hands you a piece of paper filled with letters and numbers
> and you have to make a ball game out of it. You create the weather,
> flesh out the players, you make them sweat and grouse and hitch up
> their pants, and it is remarkable, thinks Russ, how much earthly distur-
> bance, how much summer and dust the mind can manage to order up
> from a single Latin letter lying flat. (25)

DeLillo constructs his universe out of just such bits of language,
even as the deconstruction of the elegant gibberish—for instance,
"white noise"—that defines our lives has been the continuing project of his texts. Much of *Underworld* in particular is an attempt to
gain access to what Marvin Lundy calls the "ESP of baseball, an
underground what, a consciousness" (179).

In *White Noise* Jack Gladney provides a comic example of how
language both facilitates and constrains experience. Though he is a
professor of Hitler Studies, Gladney is embarrassed enough over
his inability to speak the language of the Nazi Führer that he takes
private lessons in German. As host of a conference in his field held
at the College-on-the-Hill, Gladney at first officially welcomes the
other scholars in a very halting, inexpressive version of the language and then retreats to the safety of his office, afraid to attempt
any further communication in German.

Neither does Billy Mast know German, but in *End Zone* the football player relieves his anxieties over the violent game by reciting
German words whose meaning he does not understand. What is
for him gibberish serves the same function as a team prayer. Like
the nonsense syllables "pee-pee-maw-maw" (*Great Jones Street* 118)
to which prolific musician Bucky Wunderlick has reduced his lyr-
ics, it serves the same function as the trade name "Toyota Celica"
does for Jack Gladney's young daughter, Steffie, who repeats it in
her sleep, as "part of a verbal spell or ecstatic chant" (155). In an
underground beneath the conscious level the child has appropriated the catchwords of consumer culture, its white noise, as a
kind of verbal talisman against her fears of airborne toxic events

and other, unnamed terrors. This is language that consoles and protects although and because it ceases to signify.

It is the kind of rapture induced by transcending language that Bucky Wunderlick experiences when listening to that "music of a dead universe" (*Great Jones Street* 166) that is the telephone dial tone: "Source of pleasure and fear never before explored. It was always the same, silence endowed with acoustical properties" (166). It is what the adolescent Gary Harkness experienced when staring at the banal aphorism, "WHEN THE GOING GETS TOUGH THE TOUGH GET GOING" that his father had posted on his bedroom wall:

> The sentiment of course had small appeal but it seemed that beauty flew from the words themselves, the letters, consonants swallowing vowels, aggression and tenderness, a semi-self-re-creation from line to line, word to word, letter to letter. All meaning faded. The words became pictures. It was a sinister thing to discover at such an age, that words can escape their meanings. A strange beauty that sign began to express. (13–14)

Like the cybernetic, monosyllabic conclusion to *Underworld*, it is a signature moment in DeLillo's fiction, when a strange beauty is born through language deployed to transcend the merely linguistic.

As if respecting the reticence of metaphysical mysteries, the rootless international businessmen who wander through *The Names* find elemental reassurance in the fact that they do not understand the babel of ambient tongues, a kind of Levantine white noise, spoken in the Mediterranean and Asian countries through which they travel. The novel concludes with a flashback to archeologist Owen Brademas' childhood in the Midwest. Both disturbed and intrigued by a rapturous church service in which the congregants speak in tongues, Brademas is described as "tongue tied" (335) over the phenomenon of glossolalia. "The gift was not his," we are told, in spelling that simulates the boy's awkwardness, "the whole language of the spirit which was greater than Latin or French was not to be seized in his pityfull mouth" (338). In the final sentence of *The Names* young Brademas runs outside the church into the rain, into "the nightmare of real things, the fallen wonder of the world," (339) forced, like all flawed authors and readers, to make do with words inadequate for the language of the spirit.

Nick Shay draws on his family roots for a word to describe the project of articulating the elusive forces that govern the universe. "There's a word in Italian," he says during an orientation session for Waste Containment. "*Dietrologia*. It means the science of what is behind something. A suspicious event. The science of what is behind an event" (280). *Dietrologia* is the attempt not only to understand whether Waste Containment is really run by the Mafia or some other malignant power or to locate sinister patterns elsewhere throughout the novel. DeLillo's continuing novelistic enterprise itself can be understood dietrologically, as a laboratory for what Nick calls "the science of dark forces" (335).

The first DeLillo novel, *Americana* (1971), concludes with David Bell's drive through downtown Dallas, past the Texas Book Depository, Dealey Plaza, and Parkland Hospital. The three sites have been familiar landmarks of the American popular imagination since 22 November 1963. DeLillo was still working for an advertising agency in New York when John Kennedy was killed in Texas, and in a sense all of his subsequent books are a gloss on the lingering enigma of the national trauma of presidential assassination. *Libra* (1988) was an explicit attempt to make sense of the events, but so, indirectly, are his other works, each a parable of frustration in the quest for coherence. A bootleg copy of the Zapruder film, twenty seconds of lethal images caught on an eight-millimeter movie camera, makes an appearance in *Underworld* (488) and does nothing to dispel the mystery of the Kennedy murder. Jimmy Costanza's cryptic disappearance, how he walked out one day for a pack of Lucky Strike cigarettes and never came back, is, for his sons Nick and Matt, the domestic equivalent of the nation's loss of its vigorous young leader.

In his effort to ascertain which is the authentic baseball that was actually socked into the left-field stands by Bobby Thomson to clinch the pennant for the Giants in 1951, Marvin Lundy pores through a vast array of evidence. It is as if he is trying to determine the grammar for a lost, arcane language. "I looked at a million photographs," he tells Brian Glassic, "because this is the dot theory of reality, that all knowledge is available if you analyze the dots" (175). Like a pointillist painter, DeLillo constructs his elaborate fictions less in terms of straight lines stretching from beginning to middle to end than as isolated dots dependent on an active reader for integration into a complete, coherent design. Yet, his figurative Jamesian "figure in the carpet" remains elusive, if not illusory, a tantalizing possibility that seems to linger just beyond the grasp of characters and readers, as if finding design is an exercise in dietrology.

Underworld is constructed out of several overlapping fields of action. Like an old movie plot tied together by the penny, violin, or pistol that passes through very different hands, *Underworld* finds such unity as it has in the very different people who have touched or been touched by the Thomson home-run baseball that we, along with Jackie Gleason, Frank Sinatra, Toots Shor, and J. Edgar Hoover, witness determining playoff victory in the novel's Prologue. DeLillo mixes separate riffs on Cotter Martin, the Harlem boy who skips school to sneak into the Polo Grounds, where he becomes the first link to the fateful ball; a mysterious drive-by murderer called the Texas Highway Killer; Esmeralda, a twelve-year-old Bronx waif beatified by popular culture after her violent demise; J. Edgar Hoover and his companion, Clyde Tolson, cavorting at Truman Capote's 1966 Black & White Ball; a genius of subway graffiti who signs his creations Moonman 157; and Lenny Bruce rapping about the deadly forces that converge to create the Cuban Missile Crisis.

In *Underworld* DeLillo's characteristic paranoia over patterns takes the specific form of triskaidekaphobia—a tendency to regard the entire universe as organized around the number thirteen. Nick notes that Ralph Branca, the Dodger hurler who served Thomson his home-run pitch and won 13 games that year, wore the number thirteen on the fateful day, 10/3. The winning hit occurred at 3:58, another variation on thirteen if you add the last two digits. Before he disappeared, Jimmy Costanza, whose name consists of thirteen letters, made his living as a numbers runner. Is that profession a paradigm for reading the universe? Does numerology explain the enigmas of Nick Shay's life and times, and ours? Or, does the conjunction of numbers indicate mere happenstance?

"Find the links," insists Hoover to his aide and companion Clyde Tolson. "It's all linked" (577). A quest for links will turn readers into re-readers of *Underworld*, a paradigm of the postmodernist renunciation of master narratives—"a single narrative sweep, not ten thousand wisps of disinformation" (82)—that resolve everything in a single thread. "Longing on a large scale is what makes history," claims the narrator (11), and *Underworld* makes history into an immense, engaging puzzle of unfulfilled desire. "What good's a story without an ending?" (313) asks Marvin

Lundy's wife, Eleanor, but DeLillo's readers learn to live with plots that lack resolution.

"Reality doesn't happen until you analyze the dots," (182) says Marvin Lundy, the merchant of baseball's sacred memorabilia. But, connecting and analyzing the dots is no simple task, and reading DeLillo is often like looking at one of those M. C. Escher visual riddles offering multiple perspectives that are mutually exclusive. A viewer can make sense of Escher's inky lines by processing them as a flock of birds or else as a school of fish, but not as both simultaneously. According to Bucky Wunderlick, the reclusive rock star in *Great Jones Street*: "Life itself is sheer ambiguity. If a person doesn't see that, he's either an asshole or a fascist" (132). Whether sheer ambiguity is a quality of life, it certainly characterizes DeLillo's fiction. The "asshole" is incapable of seeing additional possibilities for connecting the dots, and the "fascist" insists on asserting only one connection. The author of *White Noise* is, like its narrator Jack Gladney, an expert in Hitler Studies. So many of DeLillo's books are parables of fascist reading, works that encourage us to read intricate systems of signs more flexibly than do many of the characters, to recognize more than one valid way to connect the dots.

A DeLillo novel is typically a quest for a unified theory that would make sense of disparate data, a quest that is shared by the reader and the characters. The DeLillo protagonist is a solitary seeker who is set against a vast, inscrutable landscape—the desert Southwest in *Underworld*, the continental United States in *Americana*, the cosmos in *Ratner's Star*. In *Ratner's Star* Billy Twillig attempts to decipher radio messages from space, and, beyond him, Jean Sweet Venable attempts to make sense of his attempts within the novel she is writing. In *The Names* James Axton tries to discover a pattern to ritual murders in the Middle East. In *Libra* Marguerite Oswald and Nicholas Branch separately seek some single explanation that would explain all the sundry facts about the Kennedy assassination. In these and other instances DeLillo suggests caution in how we choose to connect the dots, as well as resistance to the fascism of those who would impose exclusive patterns on us.

Conspiracy is another way of talking about imposed patterns, and the DeLillo universe is rife with intimations of conspiracy. Large, clandestine, coercive organizations such as the CIA, the FBI, and the KGB are prominent players in several of the novels, including *Players* (1977) and *Running Dog* (1978) as well as *Underworld*. Tightly organized groups of spectral terrorists dominate the plots in *The Names* and *Mao II* (1991). Billy Twillig's Field Experiment Number One falls victim to a hostile takeover by a Nazi megacorporation named ACRONYM in *Ratner's Star*. Reflecting on the media conglomerates that seem to control everything in *Great Jones Street*, Bucky Wunderlick, who is unsuccessful in his bid to opt out of the music industry, coins the term "Transparanoia"—"for our spreading inkblot of holding companies, trusts, acquisitions, and cabals" (138). A DeLillo novel is itself just such a spreading inkblot, but the fact that inkblots can be interpreted in myriad ways enabled Hermann Rorschach to devise his famous diagnostic test. The spectacle of unconnected dots could inspire panic, pride, or imaginative agility, depending on whether the spectator is distressed by the lack of structure, insistent on connecting the dots in only one way, or open to several possible patterns. While diagnosing paranoia as a reasonable reaction to the collusion of large, insidious forces, DeLillo liberates us from fascists with designs on us, by imagining alternative ways of seeing patterns.

Of course the touchstone for American speculation about conspiracy is the Kennedy assassination, which has spawned innumerable theories to counter the facile conclusions of the official Warren Commission Report. In *Libra* DeLillo's David Ferrie speaks for all conspiracy theorists when, upset over the possibility of clandestine collusion between Washington and Havana, he posits secret machination as a universal principle: "There's something they aren't telling us. Something we don't know about. There's more to it. There's always more to it. This is what history consists of. It's the sum total of all the things they aren't telling us" (321). The reader of a DeLillo novel, which demands that readers be re-readers, is always left with the feeling that there is more to it. And no omniscient author intercedes to tell us what to make of things. Unfounded suspicion of hostile collusion is paranoia, but the reader can reasonably found such suspicion on patterns that have been planted in the text.

Or are they mere coincidence? According to DeLillo's *Libra*, on 9 September 1963, Oswald, working in New Orleans with both pro- and anti-Castro forces, makes a mental list of all the odd concurrences in his life—among them, the fact that Guy Banister was searching for him when Oswald walked through his door and asked for an undercover job, the fact that the revolver and the carbine that he ordered six weeks apart arrived on the same day, the fact that both he and John Kennedy have brothers named Robert and wives who are pregnant. The experience of reading DeLillo's fictions simulates paranoia, except for the fact that he allows multiple interpretations to compete for our credence—as well as the possibility that, ultimately, the dots cannot be connected at all. Haunting all of the stories is the plausibility of Win Everett's pyrrhonism: "He believed that nothing can be finally known that involves human motive and need. There is always another level, another secret, a way in which the heart breeds a deception so mysterious and complex it can only be taken for a deeper kind of truth" (260).

Yet, according to Sister Alma Edgar: "Everything is connected in the end" (826). In the end of *Underworld* the Bronx nun dies in her sleep, but instead of being transported to Christian heaven finds herself in an electronic one, cyberspace, where everything is linked to everything else: "Everything is connected. All human knowledge gathered and linked, hyperlinked, this site leading to that, this fact referenced to that, a keystroke, a mouse-click, a password—world without end, amen" (825). The DeLillo Underworld begins to resemble Emerson's Oversoul. In her posthumous meditations Sister Edgar, a gentle doppelgänger to J. Edgar Hoover, the FBI Director who is professionally inclined to find connections, concludes *Underworld* by tying together the disparate threads of that book. Her musings from and about the Internet also recapitulate themes from throughout DeLillo's work—the quest for connection, the replacement of reality by electronic simulation, the generative power of language, the specter of violence. In the book's final line one word in particular—Peace—is sent coursing through the circuits of the World Wide Web, to make its way out—over and under the world. Simulating, supplanting, and sustaining, the world is word without end. Amen.

Pynchon and DeLillo

Timothy L. Parrish

Don DeLillo's remarkable body of work emerges out of his engagement with the interconnected systems of meaning-making that define the postmodern era. As a novelist DeLillo is a genius of multimedia mimicry; everything he writes exhibits his uncanny ability to absorb within his fiction competing technologies (video, film, radio, television, photography, music, tape recorders). Pointing to the ways in which people might be seen as the effects of a particular technology, DeLillo has also been centrally interested in the possibilities and limitations of authorship. *Mao II*, for instance, imagines an author, Bill Gray, who has gone underground in order to preserve the doomed hope that he might write "what the culture needed in order to see itself" (163). No longer confident of his ability to create worlds that can withstand the media machinery that transforms everything—person, idea, thing—into images, Gray chooses to surrender the idea of himself as an author and maker by drifting into an anonymous, futile death. Gray's embrace of oblivion is less a consequence of the familiar observation that neither author nor reader can transcend the language one uses to communicate than the fact that Gray cannot come to terms with how his language is inscribed within various systems that also encode how that language is used and received. Gray makes this point obliquely when he observes that "Beckett is the last writer to shape the way we think and see" (157). DeLillo speaking through Gray does not mean that writing ends with Beckett but that Beckett was the last writer who created narratives that could be imagined to be separate from the systems they described. His suicide at the end of the novel finalizes the death he initiated earlier when he allowed his picture to be taken by a professional photographer. In Gray's mind the writer becomes not his work—his words—but his picture. Gray martyrs himself to the idea of himself as image, one whose reproduction will now be at the mercy of the technological systems of communication and information that his art could not control.

Although Bill Gray may point to Beckett as the last writer to construct narratives untainted by anything except what might be loosely called literature, DeLillo's work points to the central author of the postmodern era, Thomas Pynchon, the one author who might be said to have written the one book—*Gravity's Rainbow* (1973)—that defines the way we see the postmodern era. DeLillo's career might be productively understood as an attempt to make sense of the implications of Pynchon's seminal work. Both DeLillo and Pynchon portray technology as a type of narrative and narrative as a type of technology. Both suspect that whatever the brilliance of one's language, it can only be at the mercy of the systems that it describes. Roughly, where Pynchon's work narrates the shift from a human-centered world to a technology-driven one, DeLillo's work imagines more concretely what happens once that shift has occurred. In order to comprehend how DeLillo responds to Pynchon, a brief analysis of the main themes of *Gravity's Rainbow* is in order.

The opening words of Pynchon's masterpiece strive to convey something outside of language: the shattering sound of a V-2 rocket. The narrator says that this technological marvel of destruction accompanies "the fall of a crystal palace" (3), by which is meant the structures that to that point had defined the Euro-American world order but that have come crashing down with the end of the war. Throughout, *Gravity's Rainbow* relentlessly refuses the comforts afforded by a belief in cause-and-effect reasoning. Suspicious of narrative coherence altogether, *Gravity's Rainbow* never suggests that life has changed as a result of warring nations and armies. Rather, the war is but an incidental effect of a cultural transformation already taking place as a consequence of the technologies that have created the V-2 rocket. The war interests Pynchon not as a consequence of geopolitical conflicts but as a structure that organizes the seemingly random energies that are coming to define a world that actually has little to do with the war as it is conventionally portrayed. "So the populations move," Pynchon writes in a well-known passage, "across open meadows, limping, marching, shuffling, carried, hauling along the detritus of an order, a European and bourgeois order they don't yet know is destroyed forever" (560).

In *Gravity's Rainbow* characters are shaped less by ideological interests or psychic needs (unless one wants to say that the book dramatizes a massive death wish) than by the demands of whatever technology they have pledged their selves to. The war is technology's playground:

> this War was never political at all, the politics was all theatre, all just to keep the people distracted . . . secretly, it was being dictated instead by the needs of technology . . . by a conspiracy between human beings and techniques, by something that needed the energy-burst of the war. . . . The real crises were crises of allocation and priority, not among firms—it was only staged to look that way—but among different Technologies, Plastics, electronic, Aircraft, and their needs which are understood only the ruling elite . . . (530)

This passage implies a teleology and an agency that Pynchon's narrative throughout works to subvert. The "ruling elite" may benefit from new technologies but they cannot predict how the technologies will be used or how people will be used by them. The narrative of the novel, if not the events the novel depicts, coheres around the building and firing of the German supersonic V-2 rocket. A bewildering number of technologies deriving from apparently all disciplines of math and science seem to come together through the narrative's pursuit of the Rocket 00000. At one point the narrator observes that during certain paranoid experiences one is inclined to "the discovery that *everything is connected*" (717 italics Pynchon's). The implication of the diverse and many-layered narratives of *Gravity's Rainbow* is neither that the rocket connects these technologies nor that it is the necessary endpoint. Rather, whether you know it or not, these technologies create and define you, the reader.

As the endpoint that connects the multiple technologies and characters in *Gravity's Rainbow*, the rocket is a narrative necessity that paradoxically we are not to take too seriously as an organizing force. Its primary function is to serve as a metaphor for the impossibility of separating one technology or system of meaning from another. Unlike DeLillo, Pynchon holds out the faint hope that this understanding might be a single individual's necessarily paranoid insight and hence fallible because the logic of universal interconnectedness encourages the reader to posit connections where none may actually exist. The question one must ask but cannot answer is whether this insight is a self-fulfilling one. In *Underworld* DeLillo borrows the line "everything is connected" from Pynchon but now the line's meaning can no longer be ascribed quixotically to a single individual's paranoid delusion. When waste conspiracy theorist Jesse Detwiler remarks that "everything's connected" (289), De-Lillo suggests that Pynchon's line has become the ruling logic that explains how in the second half of the twentieth century humans have become the inventions of their various technological systems.

Since *Gravity's Rainbow* it has become impossible to see contemporary society except through the lens of ever-expanding, ever-shifting technological innovation. Don DeLillo was born a year before Pynchon and his earliest stories precede Pynchon's first novel, *V.* (1963), but he developed as a writer later than Pynchon and his work clearly responds to Pynchon's through *Gravity's Rainbow*. As if responding directly to the implications of the Pynchon passage cited above, DeLillo's narratives consistently involve characters caught up in systems that obligate them toward certain inescapable choices. DeLillo has aptly described his novels as "games" (LeClair and McCaffery 81). Once the game's premise is established, his characters become the narrative solution for whatever the novel's governing technology demands. The death of Selvy in *Running Dog* (1978) or Oswald's murder of Kennedy in *Libra* (1988) result from human choices made inevitable by the technologies of information control in which the characters' desires and choices are defined. Lauren Hartke's evacuation of her self in *The Body Artist* (2001) is implied by the dispersal of her voice into the tape recorder, just as the "retarded" man's ability to mimic her voice and that of her dead husband, Rey, seems to make the retarded man a consequence of the tape recorder's mimetic capacity. It would not be an exaggeration to say that for DeLillo, as for Pynchon, technology rather than character is fate.

DeLillo's characters either consciously or unconsciously work to perpetuate the systems in which they find themselves; Pynchon's characters futilely try either to create or imagine an alternative. They seek a "Counterforce" to the technological logic that controls them. Thus Tyrone Slothrop, the antihero of *Gravity's Rainbow*, is the unwitting "subject" of a variety of technological experiments designed to shape and control his identity. An extraordinarily ineffectual actor in his own life, Slothrop comes to realize dimly how virtually every character who touches him has had a role in controlling him—a plot that in its permutations goes back to his birth. Slothrop suspects that his fate is connected with that of the rocket but neither he nor the reader may discover what the nature of that connection is. Slothrop and the rocket exist in narrative relation as protagonist and antagonist. One orbits the other, but which force is centrifugal remains uncertain. Rather than finding the meaning of the rocket Slothrop meets the bizarre fate of being broken down and scattered across the Zone. He disintegrates. Open to many interpretations, Slothrop's scattering might be seen as the almost certainly failed attempt to avoid the fate of becoming merely the implication of a particular technology. In this reading Slothrop would become the representative figure of the Counterforce, the "We" who try to counteract the seemingly all-powerful "They" who manipulate figures such as Slothrop in order to keep Their Systems operating. His scattering would be a rebellion, a kind of Thoreau-like gesture of stopping the machine by grinding its gears. Such a reading discounts, however, the fact that Slothrop's final incarnation involves a loss of self distinctive in the history of Western literature. That is, because Slothrop disappears as a recognizable human figure but does not die, one could argue that Slothrop's disintegration represents the crumbling of human nature as it has been traditionally understood. From this perspective, the narrative lines of the rocket and Slothrop do not orbit each other but meet in a collision out of which the fragments of Slothrop's humanity take form again as various permutations of technological invention.

As a plot device Slothrop is what makes possible Pynchon's opposition of They vs. We. Pynchon never holds out the hope that They can be toppled, though, because doing so would require the destruction of the System within which this opposition takes meaning. As one character observes, "To believe that each of Them *will* personally die is also to believe that Their system will die—that some chance of renewal, some dialectic, is still operating in History" (549 italics Pynchon's). As I have suggested, Their seemingly all-powerful force derives from the fact Their will seems to be both agentless and organized. In this respect the story of Slothrop is pure plot device, a gigantic red herring, because what matters in *Gravity's Rainbow* is not that a single individual is victimized by technology but that humans actually desire to meld their identities with the technologies available for use. Despite Pynchon's encyclopedic eagerness to venture into intellectual realms (math and science) unplumbed by few other contemporary writers, there is no question that the narrator of *Gravity's Rainbow* experiences the melding of humanity with technology as a violation. In a quest to find transcendence, a way out of the systems it describes, the narrator displays a stunning fearlessness willing to convey all aspects of experience from the level of molecular particles to intimations of life after death. Yet, all indications suggest that even these other realms are but outposts/developments of the same systems of control that dominate the events of "ordinary" life.

If *Gravity's Rainbow* can be said to reveal the culture to itself, then it avoids claiming for itself the kind of mastery associated with representative modernist figures such as James Joyce, Samuel Beckett, and, arguably, even Don DeLillo. One character who works on the rocket at the behest of the book's most obviously evil character, Weissmann/Blicero, realizes that "Weissmann's cruelty was no less resourceful than [his] own engineering skill, the gift of Daedalus that allowed him to put his labyrinth as required between himself and the inconveniences of uncaring" (435). Pynchon here in all likelihood refers to the ingenious technical skill of Joyce (Daedalus) to suggest that the aesthetic mastery that the modernists championed provides no security against the systems that Weissmann perpetrates; in fact, these systems require the gifts of Daedalus to function well. Making no pretense that this book is a self-contained world, a perfect aesthetic universe unto itself, *Gravity's Rainbow* highlights how the techniques described within it are in part responsible for the narrative we are reading, just as the book's open-ended conclusion invites the reader to recognize that the rocket, in all of its technological and metaphorical implications, hovers above us and we are either already on board or about to be hit. Pynchon knows that even if his book is conceived as a rebellious act, it is committed within the same System by which They are authorized. Indeed, we are to understand that the voice of the novel is in a sense Their poet. "Once the technical means of control have reached a certain size," the narrator remarks ominously, "a certain degree of *being connected* one to another, the chances for freedom are over for good" (548 italics Pynchon's).

One does not experience this same sense of loss in DeLillo's fiction because his characters never escape the technological premises on which their lives are structured. In *Players* the identities of stockbroker and terrorist are interchangeable precisely because the two identities are governed by the same systemic and technological assumptions. In *Great Jones Street*, a book heavily indebted to Pynchon's *The Crying of Lot 49*, a rock star tries to disappear from the star-making system—the ubiquity of the media, the power of the marketplace, his role as a counterculture hero—only to find himself further implicated in the various systems he tries to escape. At the conclusion of *White Noise* Jack Gladney may experience intimations of immortality emanating from the supermarket cash register scanners, but this likely reflects Gladney's desire to cling to his bourgeois values in the face of technological forces that are rapidly reproducing "reality" as its own simulacrum. Slothrop's life is controlled by the same forces that make the rocket, but the hope is held out that perhaps he can transcend his technological conditioning. Pynchon's work can seem almost unbearably tender in a way that DeLillo's cannot precisely because DeLillo's narratives take for granted the technological conditioning that Pynchon's characters futilely resist. Thus DeLillo's novels seem to bear no relation to the old orders to which *Gravity's Rainbow* says farewell and lack nostalgia for a time when lives might be perceived to exist outside the realm of technological innovation. *Underworld* concludes with an eerie fusion of technology and transcendence when DeLillo invites us to imagine that we might be joined, author and audience, via an Internet site that reveals authentic miracles. At times in DeLillo's fiction it seems that technology is not the medium for the divine but the divine itself.

Whether or not DeLillo truly understands technology to be an instrument of transcendence, he plays with the possibility in order to convey how all-encompassing technology has become. In pointed contrast to Pynchon, DeLillo betrays little interest in nature—not even as an alternative to the technology-driven world that consumes his characters. DeLillo's characters would be untroubled were one of them to suffer, as one does in *Gravity's Rainbow*, a dream in which a scientist declares that the combinations of molecules found in nature "can be changed, and new molecules assembled from the debris of the given" (420). Frequently, DeLillo implies that there is no nature that can be apprehended and thus transgressed against. In *White Noise* a communication from the local cable television company reads "CABLE HEALTH, CABLE WEATHER, CABLE NEWS, CABLE NATURE" (231), as if to say that "nature" is made possible by television: an invention of the media that is also a product for consumption. Within DeLillo's world, the destruction of nature by the Slothrop family paper mill firm is only a relatively harmless prelude to the colonization of the natural world by television. With his finely ingrained historical consciousness—his uncanny ability to recreate the feeling of places and times that he has not experienced—Pynchon asks his readers to experience the loss of nature as a moral outrage. Though one may reasonably object that DeLillo's stance toward nature in *White Noise* is largely satiric, it is nonetheless true that with the possible exception of the last half of *Ratner's Star*, DeLillo has portrayed nature only as a wasteland of death and destruction (*End Zone, Running Dog, Underworld*).

For the most part DeLillo has not followed Pynchon in attempting to develop a historical perspective that can account for the omnipotence of technology. That his fiction is mostly unmarked by a sense of history that precedes the dawn of the Cold War era is a logical consequence of DeLillo's interest in the material and narrative effects of technology.[1] Pynchon makes technology the culmination of the master narratives of European and American history. DeLillo, by contrast, identifies technology not as the end of a historical sequence but as something that verges on making history irrelevant, if not altogether absent. Works such as *Libra* and *Underworld* are about technology without being about history in any kind of Pynchonesque sense. True, *Libra* portrays "History" as the interconnection of contingent and often conflicting narratives that characters presume to control but ultimately cannot. As many critics have noted, one can derive from the novel a theory of history compatible with the work of major postmodern theorists such as Baudrillard, Lyotard, and Rorty. As historical fiction, however, *Libra* is less suggestive or far-ranging than Pynchon's first three novels with their intricate, unlikely plots that combine astonishing coincidence and extraordinary learnedness on the part of Pynchon. A significant difference between *Libra* and *Gravity's Rainbow* then is that the former novel is made up of events and theories fairly well-known to its audience, most of which are contained in the Warren Commission Report, whereas the latter is a gathering of knowledge that could only be accumulated and pieced together by one extraordinary mind. Such an observation is not meant to diminish the achievement of DeLillo but to suggest how prevalent a Pynchonesque way of seeing is in his work. By focusing on an event that has made paranoia a comfortable and familiar subject, DeLillo has in effect domesticated—made matter-of-fact—the quests that consume Herbert Stencil, Oedipa Maas, and Tyrone Slothrop. Although one might say that DeLillo constructs a plot mainly as a means of questioning plots, *Libra* demonstrates that questioning any one plot is the means by which another plot is inevitably created.

Such an orientation toward narrative implies that whoever tells the most persuasive plot ultimately has the most control over determining what the consequences of that plot will be. From this perspective DeLillo might be understood as a late modernist writing about the consequences of postmodernism. Although DeLillo recognizes the threat that our many postmodern systems of technological representation pose to the autonomy of the novelist, he never doubts his own authorial ability to reproduce those systems within the universe of his novels. If DeLillo's characters cannot resist the systems that contain them, DeLillo-the-novelist is not subject to the same control. DeLillo thus draws a sharp distinction, one that is traditionally modernist, between the artist and the work of art. Even though the plots of novels such as *Libra* and *Underworld* rely on "real" events, their authenticity as fiction is sanctioned by DeLillo alone. In this sense DeLillo creates the "real" events he narrates. Thus, whereas Pynchon dramatizes the impossibility of drawing a distinction between his narrative about technology and the technological narratives he depicts, DeLillo seems to stand outside the worlds he invents. In *Libra* the narrator suggests that the Warren Commission is "the megaton novel James Joyce would have written if he'd moved to Iowa City and lived to be a hundred" (181). In direct contrast to Pynchon's reference to Joyce in *Gravity's Rainbow*, DeLillo invokes Joyce to claim his own aesthetic mastery over the events that led to 22 November 1963. A truth unavailable to the Warren Commission, countless television shows, and untold independent investigators can be expressed in the form of a novel precisely because of its ambiguous character. If literal-minded readers of *Libra* are made paranoid by its convincing deconstruction of the lone gunman theory, then to DeLillo that is a tribute to his art but not a consequence of it.

In *Gravity's Rainbow* the narrator suggests that "Names by themselves may be empty, but the act of *naming*" is a version of the sacred. For Pynchon to give any object or process a name is to turn it into a tool for use. Names include not only words but mathematical equations that can be used to transform the way that the world is perceived, experienced, and ultimately made. Naming is the process by which technological systems usurp nature and come to define what is human. DeLillo, by contrast, with his modernist conception of the artist, reclaims the mystery of naming for the author. Gary Harkness, the narrator of *End Zone*, is fascinated by how in football "each play must have a name." The fact that "all teams run the same plays" matters less than the fact that "no play begins until its name is called" (118). Bucky Wunderlick's power as a rock star in *Great Jones Street* results from his ability to fuse unlikely words, even nonsense syllables, with powerful modes of electronic sound. Bucky thus becomes an avatar of what might be a new kind of language "where all sound is silken and nothing erodes in the weather of language" (265). In *The Names* human lives are sacrificed for the sake of language when lives literally become letters. The narrator suggests that language is what we bring to the temple instead of "prayer or chant or slaughtered rams" (331).

DeLillo's characters are created through specific technologies but those technologies are always the function of a particular language. To DeLillo language is a force before which we may humble ourselves but with which we invent ourselves. *The Names* concludes with pages ostensibly written by a child that are filled with misspellings and typographical errors. Neither mastering nor mastered by the language that passes from his brain through his fingers to the pages being typed, the child is a medium for language's mysterious power. In *White Noise* a plane seems to be on the verge of crashing, and the passengers are of course panic-struck at the prospect. However, when the passengers begin thinking of their flight as resulting in a "crash landing" rather than a "crash," a calmness takes control and soon the plane has indeed safely landed. DeLillo presents the scene as if the plane could be saved by the sudden addition of a word (92). On the other hand characters unable to master language become the victims of that failure. The best example of this is *Libra*'s Lee Harvey Oswald, a precursor to *Mao II*'s Bill Gray. DeLillo portrays Oswald as a failed writer who becomes a misplaced assassin because he cannot implement his vision of the world effectively through language. He goes from being a writer of a plot he cannot complete to being an actor in a plot he does not write. The presumed author of the events of 22 November 1963 becomes instead one of the victims of those events.

In a stunning passage that contrasts markedly with the concluding pages of *The Names* DeLillo imagines Oswald writing at the typewriter, unable to find the language commensurate with his vision. Like Tap, Oswald's sentences are pocked with mistakes.

> Always the pain, the pain of composition. He could not find order in the little field of symbols. They were in the hazy distance. He could not

see clearly the picture that is called a word. A word is also a picture of a word. He saw spaces, incomplete features, and tried to guess at the rest. . . . He watched sentences deteriorate, powerless to make them right. The nature of things was to be elusive. Things slipped through his perceptions. He could not get a grip on the runaway world. (211)

Pynchon's characters cannot get a grip on the runaway world either, but they are portrayed as readers rather than writers. Except for Stencil, there are no writers or surrogate-writers in Pynchon's world because the mysterious power of naming something belongs to the scientist and the mathematician. However, the force that the naming unleashes is never exactly a human power, and thus the great scientists such as Kekulé, the inventer of organic chemistry, do not become god-like figures. Rather the rest of us become bureaucratic functionaries working out the implications of the equation that has been named. DeLillo's Oswald recalls Tyrone Slothrop because he is made to be both subject of and accomplice to plots designed to accomplish his undoing. By framing Oswald as a failed writer, DeLillo seems to suggest that if only Oswald had the mastery of the imaginary Joyce who writes the Warren Report he might have been able to script a better fate for himself.

From the perspective of the author, a better fate would be that of making one's plot work according to one's intention. In *Libra* there are surrogate-author figures: Oswald, CIA operative Win Everett, and CIA historian Nicholas Branch. Each of these characters employs different narrative strategies to script the events of 22 November 1963, but none of them is able to write a plot that defines the event. It is not enough to say, though, that DeLillo becomes the one author who masters these plots because DeLillo does so only by adopting the narrative techniques associated with organizations such as the CIA. Through CIA operative Lawrence Parmenter DeLillo implies his own narrative strategy. Parmenter recognizes that the Agency sees individuals in terms of their capacity to be used for the creation of new fictions, and thus has the primary objective of breeding "deception so mysterious and complex it can only be taken for a deeper kind of truth" (260). DeLillo and the Agency both prize narratives of intricacy and contingency for their capacity to convey a deeper truth. For the CIA the tendency of a narrative to deconstruct or be deconstructed only means that stories can always be rewritten so that the Agency achieves its purpose. For DeLillo this narrative tendency not only reveals the capacity of the

United States government to transform postmodern narrative principles into insidious cultural and political games but becomes an aesthetic goal in its own right.

Whereas Pynchon identifies a seemingly random discovery in order to pursue an impossibly complex chain of related events that eventually render any kind of originating moment superfluous, DeLillo identifies skeins of conflicting plots and technologies that might be attributed to a single author. Although Oswald represents a failed version of this process, *Underworld*'s J. Edgar Hoover is truly DeLillo's postmodern techno-Joyce. Like DeLillo Hoover seems to stand apart from the cultural processes he invents and dominates. DeLillo's Hoover reflects on his

> enemies-for-life and the way to deal with such people was to compile massive dossiers. Photographs, surveillance reports, detailed allegations, linked names, transcribed tapes—wiretaps, bugs, break-ins. The dossier was a deeper form of truth, transcending facts and actuality. The second you placed an item in the file, a fuzzy photograph, an unfounded rumor, it became promiscuously true. It was a truth without authority and therefore incontestable. Factoids seeped out of the file and crept across the horizon, consuming bodies and minds. The file was everything, the life nothing. (559)

DeLillo frames Hoover's dossier as a novel-in-progress—a counterpart to the Warren Report. As a new form of media, Hoover's dossier is more powerful than the Warren Report not simply because it is never released and thus never readable. Rather it acquires power because it does not attempt to formulate a cohesive narrative or reveal an organizing authorial agency. The mere fact of its existence—its unlimited capacity for rumor and innuendo—implies omnipotence. DeLillo describes Hoover's dossier in terms traditionally associated with the novel—a deeper form of truth, transcending facts and actuality. By showing how Hoover coopts novelistic strategies, DeLillo imagines Hoover inventing the kind of postmodern novel that DeLillo writes. Hoover is to *Underworld* as Weissmann is to *Gravity's Rainbow* except that Hoover's technical mastery prevents him from becoming only a moral monster.

In *Underworld* DeLillo's general confidence in the power of the author includes the power to manipulate all technologies not just those rendered in language. For DeLillo everything is connected not through paranoia but through the novelist's art. Here he portrays baseball broadcaster Russ Hodges, junk artist Klara Sax, co-median Lenny Bruce, and the graffiti tagger Moonman 157 as artists who, like DeLillo, employ available technologies in order to write narratives that express their particular sensibilities. Of all these characters, the graffiti artist seems closest to DeLillo's public conception of himself as a novelist writing in opposition to society. Moonman's creative works are complicitous with the cultures he writes over while nonetheless being acts of transgression. His work is also a dangerous act of defiance: "The trains come roaring down the rat alleys all alike and then you hit a train and it is yours, seen everywhere in the system, and you get inside people's heads and vandalize their eyeballs" (435). Moonman's art is created within and even defined by its relation to a particular "system," but unlike in Pynchon, it marks for others (the train riders) his defiance of the system. Even if Moonman's work will eventually be erased he nonetheless succeeds in leaving his mark on their eyeballs and gets inside the heads of his audience as effectively as Hoover.

No author of the past half-century has surpassed Pynchon or De-Lillo in portraying how technology has transformed the way we perceive reality in the postmodern era. In this context, it is not surprising that each author has been obsessed with the kinds of narrative that the technology of filmmaking allows. *Gravity's Rainbow* ends at a movie theater to imply that the novel we have been reading is actually a film we have been watching. *Underworld* takes its title from an apocryphal film, *Unterwelt*, made by Sergei Eisenstein but invented by DeLillo. However, the narrative uses to which they put their film adaptations point up their different orientations toward authorship. The end of *Gravity's Rainbow* occurs as either the film we have been watching or the projector showing that film breaks and we are left instead with "a film we have not learned to see" (775). For Pynchon, the novel gives way to film in a surrender to the forces of technology that have rendered the author helpless before or complicitous with those forces that he would oppose. In the theater of Thomas Pynchon we are left in the dark the moment before the rocket lands. In the theater of Don DeLillo we are treated to many possible films, spliced together by DeLillo, whose projector never breaks. Presenting his novel *Underworld as* the double to the film *Unterwelt*, DeLillo invokes the possibility of mimicking something that does not exist to assert through the form of the novel his status as creator. DeLillo would attribute to the novel the power that moviemaker Gerhardt von Göll of *Gravity Rainbow* claims for his artistry: the power to make reality out of images. In pointed opposition to Gray or Pynchon, DeLillo has embraced the opportunity to meld his imagination with the very technological forces his novels depict—*Underworld* concludes as a site on the Internet. For DeLillo, the author, if not his characters, can still achieve transcendence. Whether DeLillo has successfully bypassed Pynchon's version of connectedness or merely reinscribed it, is a matter for the reader to determine.

Notes

1. Possible exceptions to this claim are *The Names* and *Ratner's Star*. Whereas the former explores language as the ground to all being, the latter portrays the history of mathematics from the ancient Egyptians through the twentieth century. In these novels, though, DeLillo is less interested in depicting a historical sequence of events or the relation between "the past" and "the present" than in exploring the possibilities implied in and created by the logic of certain symbol systems. If DeLillo's work extends *Gravity's Rainbow*'s exploration of the relationship between technology and narrative, it does so to suggest how technology in effect effaces conventional understandings of history.

Conspiratorial Jesuits in the Postmodern Novel: *Mason & Dixon* and *Underworld*

Carl Ostrowski

READERS OF CONTEMPORARY AMERICAN FICTION HAVE LONG BEEN aware that the complementary themes of conspiracy and paranoia inform the novels of Thomas Pynchon and Don DeLillo. In this essay I will assess these themes in the novels *Mason & Dixon* and *Underworld* through attention to an unusual and revealing coincidence that may arise from similar literary-historical sources, sources that have gone unrecognized in their contribution to our postwar literature of paranoia. Pynchon's *Mason & Dixon* and De-Lillo's *Underworld*, published in the same year, both include as important minor characters Jesuit priests who possess knowledge and power beyond everyday experience. The primary Jesuit figure in *Mason & Dixon* is Father Zarpazo, who is single-mindedly dedicated to the conversion, destruction, or enslavement of non-Catholics. In *Underworld* protagonist Nick Shay bonds with Father Andrew Paulus, S. J., who initiates Nick into an underworld of secret knowledge. Two postmodern novels awash in paranoia, two Jesuits who significantly contribute to the plot: this apparent coincidence can be explained in part, I think, by looking at the history of Catholicism as represented in Anglo-American literature and culture. Though indebted to some extent to the cultural connotations that Catholicism in general and Jesuits in particular carry with them, Pynchon and DeLillo transform these shopworn stereotypes to their own artistic ends.

In four centuries of contact with English and American culture Jesuits have acquired some unflattering associations. If, as Arthur Marotti says, "English nationalism rests on a foundation of anti-Catholicism" (37), this intolerance has from an early date tended to focus on Jesuits. The arrival of Jesuit missionaries in England in the 1580s prompted Elizabeth's royal proclamation "Declaring Jesuits and Non-Returning Seminarians Traitors." Jesuit Robert Campion was martyred in England in 1581, and, as Garry Wills has argued, the discovery of Jesuits involved in the Gunpowder Plot to blow up the English Parliament in 1605 intensified anti-Jesuit feelings and contributed to an aura of fear surrounding the order. The influence they gained in European courts as confessors to Catholic monarchs compounded the belief that the Jesuits were the foremost plotters in a worldwide conspiracy to overthrow Protestantism. Also adding to their mystique was a reputation Jesuits earned throughout Europe for cultivating linguistic and logical subtlety into an art of disingenuousness. Two notorious techniques attributed to Jesuits are "mental reservation," by which Jesuit priests contrived to qualify verbal lies with unspoken, mental qualifications (thereby avoiding the sin of lying), and "equivocation," by which the individual turns "a double meaning or ambiguity to [his] own advantage" (Barthel 88). Though these techniques evolved in part as a defensive response to persecution, this reputation for linguistic and ethical double-dealing nonetheless led to the coinage of the word "Jesuitical" as an adjective describing casuistry.

Migrating to the New World, many English colonists naturally brought with them this antipathy toward Catholicism. Seventeenth-century New England Puritanism's legacy of describing the Catholic Church as the Whore of Babylon prefigured in the Book of Revelation continued to influence American ideas about Catholicism in subsequent centuries. Conflicts between the English colonists and their neighbors in New France persisted throughout the eighteenth century, leading one historian to conclude that "Anti-Catholicism, or anti-popery . . . was one of the most prevalent characteristics of New England culture before the American Revolution" (Cogliano 2). Thomas Jefferson and John Adams disapproved heartily of the Society. Its reemergence from papal suppression was characterized in 1816 by Jefferson as "a step backward from light into darkness" while Adams feared "regular swarms of them . . . in as many disguises as a King of the gipsies can assume, dressed as printers, publishers, writers and schoolmen" (quoted in Letson and Higgins 49). Distrust of Catholics in America was also manifested in the Illuminati scare of the 1790s (because the Bavarian Illuminati were believed to be heavily infiltrated by Jesuits) and in the nativist or Know-Nothing movement of the mid-nineteenth century. Richard Hofstadter, who famously identified a "paranoid style" of political thought in American history characterized by grandiose conspiracy theories, noted the confluence of anti-Catholic thought with these instances of political paranoia.[1]

All of these anti-Catholic and anti-Jesuit sentiments naturally find expression in English and American literary history. Although a comprehensive treatment is beyond the scope of this essay, I want to put forward a few representative examples from several centuries of Anglo-American literature in order to establish the history of Catholic representation that precedes Pynchon and DeLillo. An American tradition of anti-Catholicism is initiated in the New World's earliest distinctive literary genre, the Indian captivity narrative. Jesuit missionaries among the Native Americans were held responsible by the authors of some of these narratives for inciting raids and encouraging Native Americans to take captives who could then be converted to Catholicism; Gayle K. Brown writes that "the anti-Catholic theme is strongest in the captivity narratives written by civilians before the French and Indian War" (10), citing several examples that span the period from 1695 to 1756. Later, the English Gothic novel of the late eighteenth century included obvious elements of anti-Catholicism in its use of depraved monks and priests as villains, introducing an element of lurid sexuality into the mix that nineteenth-century American gothicists were quick to elaborate. Maria Monk's 1836 bestseller *Awful Disclosures*—the purported exposé of a nunnery in Montreal by a former inhabitant—sold 300,000 copies and described priests as "inexhaustible lechers who had murdered so many illegitimate children they had to dispose of babies' corpses in a lime pit in the basement" (quoted in Reynolds 261). Other examples of the American "convent tale" or "Catholic captivity tale," which derive in part from a riot against an Ursuline convent in Massachusetts in 1834, play upon this American Protestant "obsess[ion] with the theme of Catholic bondage, particularly in nunneries" (Lewis 154). Images associated with the literature of anti-Catholicism appear in the work of Herman Melville, as in his exposés of corrupt Catholic missionaries in *Omoo* and *Typee* and in *The Confidence-Man* where the herb doctor is suspected of being "one of those Jesuit missionaries prowling all over our country" (938). To continue this lineage into the late nineteenth and early twentieth centuries, the portrayal of certain, usually Catholic European countries as environments rife with corruption, sensuality, and sinister machinations beyond the conception of the straightforward American Protestant mind, as in some of the novels of Henry James, might also be said to derive in part from this association of Catholicism with depravity and duplicity.

In drawing this brief and impressionistic sketch of Catholicism in American political and literary history, I intend to argue that contemporary American novelists come out of a centuries-long cultural tradition that blends a paranoid style of thought with a long and vividly rendered history of Catholic, particularly Jesuit, conspirators. With this background in mind, I turn to the Jesuit characters in recent novels by two acknowledged deans of American paranoia to determine the extent to which Pynchon and DeLillo inherit (and transform) the imagery of this tradition.

Set in the eighteenth century, Thomas Pynchon's *Mason & Dixon* capitalizes on the long-standing importance of the Catholic as "Other" in Anglo-American culture, exaggerating to parodic levels every perfidy of which the Jesuits were presumed capable. Pynchon exploits the lingering anti-French sentiment in America in the 1760s in the wake of the French and Indian War, when some Americans feared a French design to impose Catholicism on the rest of the continent. The Jesuit strand of the plot emerges primarily through the experience of Eliza Fields of Conestoga, Pennsylvania, who is abducted from her home by Native Americans and brought to a Jesuit college in Quebec, where she encounters Father Zarpazo, representative of all of the supposed crimes of the order, whose Spanish ancestry calls to mind Jesuit founder Ignatius Loyola. A Jesuit with a vengeance, Father Zarpazo, also known as the Wolf of Jesus, is too exaggerated to be credible, and Pynchon's comic treatment of his Jesuit subplot, as we shall see, leaves readers with the distinct impression that Zarpazo is a far less tangible threat to the tranquility of the British American colonies than the line that Mason and Dixon inscribe on the surface of the earth.

As James J. Walsh has argued, in the eighteenth century Jesuits were among the foremost physical scientists and astronomers of the day (10), and Pynchon delves profitably into their vaunted scientific and technical ingenuity. Characters throughout the novel, including Benjamin Franklin, proclaim their belief in a so-called "Jesuit telegraph," a means of communicating information across vast distances with the use of balloons, wires, and "Pyro-Elecktrical Fluid" (517). Pynchon shows us the device in action at the Jesuit college, but the only message we see transmitted is the word "IDIOTS" spelled out by a frustrated instructor in front of his slowwitted pupils (516). The telegraph is manned by Chinese converts,

CONSPIRATORIAL JESUITS IN THE POSTMODERN NOVEL

affirming Franklin's suspicions of a "Sino-Jesuit conjunction" that merges "the two most powerful sources of Brain-Power on Earth, the one as closely harness'd to its Disciplin'd Rage for Jesus, as the other to that Escape into the Void, which is the very Asian mystery" (288). In fabricating an alliance that strikes the modern reader as nothing less than bizarre (though Jesuits did serve as missionaries in China in the eighteenth century), Pynchon comically robs the Jesuits of seriously sinister connotations, satirizing the eighteenth-century Anglo-American penchant to find conspirators everywhere, Catholic or otherwise, plotting world domination and the downfall of Protestantism.

The concupiscence attributed to priests and nuns in the literature of anti-Catholicism quickly emerges in Pynchon's novel, though again with a twist, as Eliza is reserved by Zarpazo to become a novitiate in the Widows of Christ, an order of nuns educated in the arts of sexuality for the advancement of Jesuit interests. Trained by experienced nuns for whom she develops sexual feelings, Eliza is fitted with "a device suggested by Jesuit practice" (520), a cilice fastened by a hothouse rose whose thorns pierce her in ways best left to the imagination, and she is made to wear a "Uniform of most shamefully carnal intent, which framed, but did not veil, [her] intimate openings" (525) as she learns that she will eventually be expected to service the Chinese converts. At this point Pynchon's novel blends seamlessly into the novel-within-the-novel called *The Ghastly Fop*, a pornographic Gothic serial being read by one of the characters from Pynchon's framing device, reminding us of how Protestant "reform" writers sometimes cloaked titillating pornography in the guise of anti-Catholic literature. Ironically, though, her experience among the Jesuits does not horrify or demoralize the innocent Eliza, as the eighteenth-century Anglo-American Protestant imagination would certainly have scripted the scene. In fact Eliza seems to enjoy her training. She escapes from a routine, constricting life on a farm to experience an apparently healthy and at times lyrically rendered sexual awakening, experiencing desire for herself, for her companion nuns, and for the mysterious Captain Zhang. In flight from the Jesuits into the Mason and Dixon party, Eliza forges a happy lesbian relationship with Zsusza, a gypsy adventurer who has also attached herself to the surveying party.

Although Pynchon enjoys parodying stereotypes associated with the Society of Jesus, the most thematically important element of the Jesuit subplot involves the conflict between arch-enemies Father Zarpazo and Captain Zhang. Zarpazo, who champions walls, right lines, "Routes of Approach, Lines of Sight, Flows of Power" (522)," defends, as David Cowart notes, "every proposed atrocity in the language of reason," making him "the extreme embodiment of what Mason and Dixon undertake" (347–48). Zarpazo commits his faculty of reason not to religion but to power, as he reveals when instructing his students that "the Christless must understand that their lives are to be spent in Servitude" (524). Pynchon might have in mind here Adorno's critique of the Enlightenment as a will to power, rendering the Mason-Dixon Line as the symbol of this rationalizing will, an idea expressed through Captain Zhang. As the defender of the mystical art of Feng Shui, Zhang clearly represents the authorial voice when he says that the line drawn by Mason and Dixon is a conduit for "Bad Energy," an "ill wind, bringing failure, poverty, disgrace, betrayal. . . . To mark a right Line upon the Earth is to inflict upon the Dragon's very Flesh, a sword-slash, a long, perfect scar, impossible for any who live out here the year 'round to see as other than hateful Assault" (542). If Zhang is right, then Zarpazo is, at least briefly, allied with the worst excesses of the age of reason and the conspiratorial Jesuit as villain is revived. Yet, Pynchon undermines this stereotype with his final reference to Zarpazo, who is reported to have left Quebec to pursue "an irresistible offer to travel to Florida and be one of the founders of a sort of Jesuit Pleasure-Garden, of Dimensions unlimited by neighboring Parcels, tho' the Topick of Alligators has so far adroitly remain'd unaddress'd" (636). Pynchon comically exploits and then himself adroitly sidesteps the more sinister implications associated with the Society of Jesus, or, as Cowart puts it, "Pynchon's Jesuits no doubt owe something to Monty Python" (354).

As is well known, Don DeLillo was educated at the Jesuit-run Fordham University; he has said that he attributes the sense of mystery in his novels in part to his Catholic upbringing.[2] It is not surprising then that he does not buy into the most unappealing stereotypes of the Jesuits, though he is aware of them and could be said to transform them in *Underworld* through the character of Father Andrew Paulus, S. J. Paulus' importance to the novel lies in his relationship to Nick Shay, the waste management engineer whom we meet in the 1990s and whose past gradually comes to light in the more or less reverse chronology of the work. Discussing his career and his worldview, Nick claims that "the Jesuits taught

me to examine things for second meanings and deeper connections" (88). In a novel that hovers obsessively around such meanings and connections, the figure who imparts such an attitude—the
figure who teaches Nick to look at the world the way DeLillo
does—merits close attention. That the reader must wait some 450
pages for Paulus' appearance does not diminish but rather magni-
fies the importance of this Jesuit priest because the span of pages
indicates that Nick has continued to think in the priest's terms
some forty years after his first exposure to the order.

Father Paulus is one of the founders of the Minnesota college to
which Nick is sent after the ambiguously accidental killing that
forms the novel's chief mystery. In the scene where we meet him,
Paulus asks Nick to name the parts of a shoe. Nick makes little
headway, coming up with the sole, heel, tongue, and lace. Paulus
then, with the pedagogical rigor and thoroughness that contribute
to the mystique associated with the order, names and compels
Nick to repeat the names of the cuff, the counter, the quarter, the
welt, the vamp, the aglet, the grommet, and the last. In explaining
the lesson Paulus offers the following: "Everyday things represent
the most overlooked knowledge. These names are vital to your
progress. Quotidian things" (542). Paulus' lesson alerts Nick that a
world of knowledge exists that can be revealed only by an understanding of its language, or as Nick puts it after the lesson, "I
wanted to look up words. I wanted to look up velleity and quotidian and memorize the fuckers for all time. . . . This is the only way
in the world you can escape the things that made you" (543). In
this section the notorious linguistic subtlety of the Jesuits is turned
to benign ends, guiding Nick toward a deeper understanding of
the world. Nick retains this epistemological insight throughout his
life, often meditating thoughtfully about the deeper meanings of
his unusual occupation.

Father Paulus' role in the narrative could be read as having conspiratorial overtones. His linguistic resources give him access to the
kind of secret knowledge that conspiracy theorists project onto
their enemies; he seems to put Nick into possession of a secret
code. More ambiguous, perhaps, is Paulus' role as Nick's confessor
(though he does not literally hear Nick's confession, he is aware of
Nick's past and mentors Nick). This element of their relationship
puts Paulus in the tradition of Jesuit confessors of earlier centuries
who were charged with helping their princes to justify and absolve
themselves of political assassinations and other malevolent in-

trigues. Jesuits in the seventeenth century "enjoyed a virtual mo-
nopoly as confessors to the Catholic monarchs of Europe" in part
because of a perception that they were "not overly scrupulous or
rigorous in their examination of the consciences of others" (Barthel
87). Emerging from reform school, Nick is able in part due to the
agency of the Jesuits to suppress the knowledge of his crime and
return to society. Nick fails to tell his wife about the killing until
the Epilogue of the book, decades into their marriage.

Ultimately, though, DeLillo does not intend readers to see Paulus in a negative light. Whereas Pynchon somewhat playfully made
use of eighteenth-century ideas about Jesuits torturing heretics—
Captain Zhang decided it was time to part company with Zarpazo
when the latter dropped hints about torture (530)—for DeLillo the
Jesuit is a figure not of persecution but of victimization. Nick explains that the founders chose not to name the college buildings
after theologians because

> the Jesuits, according to Paulus, had been treated so brusquely in so
> many places for their attempts to convert and transform, decapitated
> in Japan, disemboweled in the Horn of Africa, eaten alive in North
> America, crucified in Siam, drawn and quartered in England, thrown
> into the ocean off Madagascar, that the founders of our little experi-
> mental college thought they'd spare the landscape some of the bloodier
> emblems of the order's history. (543)

Here, Nick learns to read the landscape for what it does not say, a
kind of inverted application of the principle of mental reservation
and a sign of Nick's increasing linguistic sophistication. And significantly in this novel that traces the history of the Cold War, Paulus' parting words to Nick in this exchange are a sharp critique of
Nick's having followed other students in signing a petition supporting Senator Joseph McCarthy: "So you signed. The others were
shitting, Father. So I shat" (543). As a representative of an order on
which Americans and Europeans have for centuries pinned their
conspiracy theories, Paulus recognizes a witch-hunt when he sees
one. DeLillo alters the conventional relationship between Jesuits
and paranoia, making Paulus defender of the underdog and oppo-
nent of a paranoid habit of mind.

The character of Father Paulus could be important in resolving a
persistent issue in the criticism on *Underworld*, the question of
where DeLillo finally stands in regard to paranoia. Michael Wood

describes *Underworld* as a "post-paranoid" novel that "explores conspiracy's legacy or, more precisely, a world bereft of conspiracy, in mourning for the scary, constricting sense the old secrets used to make." James Wood, on the other hand, harshly criticizes DeLillo's obsession with the theme of paranoia, lamenting that "the novel comes to seem complicit with the paranoia it describes" and that "the form of *Underworld* is paranoid." Peter Knight, who has provided the most convincing treatment of paranoia in *Underworld*, claims that although DeLillo's novel traces unexpected connections—for example, the Father Paulus who instructs Nick in Minnesota in 1955 was approached in the Bronx in 1951 by a friend of the family to tutor Nick's brother Matt in chess and to talk to Nick about college—it does so without pinning a conspiracy theory on any particular agent. In Knight's words the story of recent history as told in *Underworld* is to be found not in "a coherent story of shadowy conspirators," but rather in "the daily ephemera and vast entanglement of multinational consumer capitalism, both more obvious because it is omnipresent, and less detectable because it is so much taken for granted" (820). Father Paulus is the character in the novel who instructs Nick in the technique of looking for connections without imagining Communists lurking around every corner, advocating close attention to the world of the quotidian. To look for connections in the quotidian rather than in an imagined web of conspirators, DeLillo implies, is not paranoia; it is the most constructive, meaningful response to an increasingly complex, fragmented world.[3] Nick looks with a skeptical eye on the many conspiracy theorists of the novel, countering them with his credo, "I believed we could know what was happening to us. We were not excluded from our own lives. . . . I didn't believe that nations play-act on a grand scale. I lived in the real" (82). And, in *Underworld*, this is DeLillo's creed as well.

Both Pynchon and DeLillo use the figure of the Jesuit as conspirator, but, as we expect of writers of their stature, neither does so thoughtlessly or uncritically. Pynchon puts the Jesuit into an eighteenth-century context of conspiracy so far-reaching and unlikely that it collapses under its own weight. Though in his earlier works Pynchon's novels have confronted readers with "every degree of paranoia from the private to the cosmic" (Sanders 140), the degree to which Pynchon has endorsed the paranoid mindset has never been entirely clear. And here I agree with Michael Wood's reading of *Mason & Dixon* as Pynchon's "long, looping farewell to the idea of conspiracy." Mason and Dixon are right to believe that at times they are the pawns of larger institutional entities, but the novel allows them a critical eye toward overzealous conspiracy theorists such as Captain Zhang and permits a considerable degree of individual agency in shaping their own lives. In *Underworld* DeLillo's Father Paulus gives Nick a healthily analytical understanding of the world and warns Nick about the dangers of undisciplined paranoia. In other words, though both authors make use of the connotations that Jesuits bring with them, neither author gives us conspiratorial Jesuits in the stereotypical mode. The prevalence of paranoia as a theme in postwar American fiction can be traced to causes such as the Kennedy assassination, Watergate, the Cold War, globalization, and the increasing sophistication of electronic surveillance devices. And Timothy Melley in *Empire of Conspiracy: The Culture of Paranoia in Postwar America* (2000) has linked American obsession with conspiracy and paranoia to the loss of agency implicit in postmodern theories of subjectivity. My purpose here has been to suggest that American literary paranoia has a pedigree that extends much further into the past than World War Two. Several centuries of literature portraying Catholics as subversives intent on destroying the American way of life might also contribute to the ubiquity and resonance of the paranoid theme. Surely, as *Mason & Dixon* and *Underworld* suggest, Pynchon and DeLillo are sufficiently aware of this tradition to recognize in the Jesuit a potent locus of conspiratorial fears within the American psyche, a figure that provides them with a multivalent symbol for exploring the mechanisms and implications of American paranoia.

NOTES

1. Hofstadter treats the Illluminati scare in "The Paranoid Style in American Politics" from *The Paranoid Style in American Politics and Other Essays*, 21.

2. Anthony DeCurtis, "'An Outsider in This Society': An Interview with Don DeLillo." *Introducing Don DeLillo*, edited by Frank Lentricchia (Durham: Duke University Press, 1991): 55.

3. In his chapter on the novel, "'Everything is Connected': Containment and Counterhistory in *Underworld*," Mark Osteen agrees that DeLillo does not endorse a paranoid worldview: "The narrator [of *Underworld*] invites us to join this community, to make everything connect, not in cyberspace or in the fevered minds of paranoids and bombheads, but in works of imagination that we collaborate in making" (260).

Don DeLillo, John Updike, and the Sustaining Power of Myth

Donald J. Greiner

Baseball is a game of the long season, of relentless and gradual averaging-out.
—John Updike, "Hub Fans Bid Kid Adieu"

Longing on a large scale is what makes history.
—Don DeLillo, *Underworld*

Midway through the twentieth century, the United States created a decade known today as the Fifties. Emerging first from the debacle of the Great Depression and then from the terror of World War Two, America stood preeminent with its economy flourishing and its cities intact. An implacable enemy may have lurked across the ocean as a Cold War took shape, but a victorious nation exhausted by twenty years of economic depression and violent death required renewal rather than confrontation. It is not that Korea, McCarthyism, and racial tensions were ignored but that a generation born into debt and weaned on warfare sought rejuvenation.

From the perspective of today the 1950s look eerily innocent despite the unsettling tremors of cultural imperfection. This is because the decade offered a moment for the society to recharge its myths, to reaffirm the stories that point to its sense of its own identity. Don DeLillo and John Updike acknowledge this imperative, and they do so through two now legendary baseball games that began and ended the 1950s and that, in the succeeding years, have achieved the power of myth. DeLillo's recreation in *Underworld* of the third playoff game between the New York Giants and the Brooklyn Dodgers on 3 October 1951, the game in which Bobby Thomson hit a home run in the bottom of the ninth inning to lift

103

the all-but-beaten Giants to the pennant, brilliantly captures a moment at the beginning of the decade when a nation elevated an apparently insignificant sporting event to the heroic in its need to counter the startling news that the Soviets had on the very same day exploded a nuclear device. Updike's report in "Hub Fans Bid Kid Adieu" of Ted Williams' last game on 28 September 1960, the game in which Williams hit a home run in the final plate appearance of his long career, freezes a moment when the hero encounters the twilight and the Fifties stumble to a close. Both writers recognize the creative use of language as an arbiter of history.

I

There are two important textual states of DeLillo's account of Bobby Thomson's home run: the story "Pafko at the Wall" (1992, Andy Pafko played left field for the Dodgers) and *Underworld* (1997). After revising the magazine version to prepare it as the Prologue to the novel, DeLillo published an account of the genesis of the tale titled "The Power of History" in which he argues the authority of language to counter the triumph of death. Just as Updike will note the ephemeral quality of *Saturday Evening Post* cover drawings in his essay on Ted Williams' final game, so DeLillo begins his article by commenting on the transitory nature of newspaper reports. What he calls "the power of history" can be refigured by the permanence of myth: "The newspaper with its crowded pages and unfolding global reach permits us to be ruthless in our forgetting. But a few weeks later it (the Thomson home run) all came back. I found myself thinking about the event in a different way, broadly, in history, as an example of some unrepeatable social phenomenon, and I couldn't shake the impact of the game's great finish."

The front page of *The New York Times* for 4 October 1951, published the day after Thomson's feat, carried juxtaposed headlines in identical typeface and typesize: "Giants Capture Pennant" and "Soviets Explode Bomb." DeLillo felt the power of history in the pairing of the home run—known as the Shot Heard 'Round the World—and the Soviet mushroom cloud. Yet, the point here is not the startling, parallel headlines but DeLillo's decision to "be objective in the face of something revealed, an unexpected connection, a symmetry." The key word "connection" and variations on it turn out to be the operative thematics in the Prologue to *Underworld*. Rather than stress the potential for the bomb (politics) to dwarf the magic of the home run (myth), he acknowledges the juxtaposition and then celebrates the social connection that the Giants-Dodgers game affirmed. Updike would agree with DeLillo that "a fiction writer feels the nearly palpable lure of large events and it can make him want to enter the narrative." Both novelists understand that through myth and history artists "connect" with humanity even if they "don't feel like team members."

DeLillo locates "a precious integrity in the documents of an earlier decade" that counters today's frenzied craving for time to move faster, a craving fed by the very technological devices—the redial button, the microwave—initially thought to save time. Yet DeLillo and Updike slow down the craving by freezing a moment of unexpected heroics and connecting it to history. Describing, for example, the archival newsreel footage of Thomson's home run, DeLillo in "The Power of History" notes the union between an isolated moment at the beginning of the 1950s and the changelessness of art: "But the shakier and fuzzier the picture, the more it lays claim to permanence. And the voice of the announcer, Russ Hodges, who did the rapturous radio account of the game's final moments, is beautifully isolated in time. . . . Thomson and Hodges are unconsumed." They are unconsumed because they enter the realm of myth, because they answer humanity's need for assurance, continuity, heroism, life.

DeLillo may imagine J. Edgar Hoover as counterpoint to Thomson's exploit, but his larger concern is that the language of fiction carries the power of "counterhistory." Both history and fiction are narratives, but the latter connects humanity to sustaining myth: "It is fiction's role to imagine deeply, to follow obscure urges into unreliable regions of experience—child-memoried, existential and outside time. . . . Such qualities will sooner or later state an adversarial relationship with history. . . . Language lives in everything it touches and can be an agent of redemption" ("The Power of History"). This is where DeLillo (and Updike) soars, where he challenges history's (and Hoover's) "triumph of death," where he sustains us with a fixed moment of myth located in the artistic use of language.

In this deeply felt essay DeLillo pointedly announces his understanding of *Underworld*. History is always infiltrated by the novelist's art, by what DeLillo defines as "the tendency of the language to work in opposition to the enormous technology of war that dominated the era (the 1950s) and shaped the book's themes. The writer sets his pleasure, his eros, his creative delight in language and his sense of self-preservation against the vast and uniform Death that history tends to fashion as its most enduring work." Language can be artistic, sustaining, necessary. It can connect rather than separate, affirm rather than deny. Fiction, concludes DeLillo, is "our second chance."

II

A major analysis of DeLillo's take on Bobby Thomson's heroics, published in 1995, would have it otherwise. In a thoughtful Marxist discussion John N. Duvall reads the magazine version of the Prologue to *Underworld* as a political document in which DeLillo exposes the Cold War fears and racial divisions of the 1950s. For Duvall's DeLillo (but not mine), the memorable Giants-Dodgers game is not the catalyst for a life-sustaining myth but the destructive transcendence of what Walter Benjamin famously calls "aura"—the cloaking of a work of art in its ritual function. Thus for Duvall, "Pafko at the Wall" is an "examination of baseball as an aesthetic ideology that masks troubling political realities. . . . to show how baseball serves in popular culture a function equivalent to T. S. Eliot's high-culture tradition. . . . in short, like Eliot's tradition, baseball's tradition is ahistorical" (286, 291).

Duvall is interested in Marxist notions such as "the American mythos of capital" (289) and "cultural imperialism" (290), and he argues that DeLillo wrote "Pafko" to reveal "the dangerous tendency of baseball to aestheticize and erase international politics" (295). As part of his evidence he cites what for him are two telling passages. The first is the scene in which the white adult, Bill, chases the black teenager, Cotter, who has retrieved Thomson's home run ball. Bill calls the fleet young man "nigger" (68). The second passage is the final line of the magazine version of the tale—"It is all falling indelibly into the now" (70)—which, says Duvall, demonstrates that America's longing to be ahistorical remains a cultural failing even today.

The problem with Duvall's readings of these two scenes is that, although they may or may not apply to "Pafko," they do not apply to *Underworld*. Duvall published his essay in 1995, three years after the story but two years before the novel. These two years are critical because during them DeLillo revised the two passages Duvall cites. The revisions are seemingly slight but finally telling. Exchanging, for example, "nigger" for "goofus" (56), DeLillo downplays the racial tension of the 1950s that Duvall stresses and features instead the absurd comedy of a grown man pursuing a kid to grab a scuffed baseball. More important, DeLillo changes one crucial word in the final sentence of the Prologue so that in the novel it reads, "It is all falling indelibly into the past" (60). With this single emendation—from "now" to "past"—he emphasizes not the ahistorical but the mythic. DeLillo's J. Edgar Hoover may prefer the dance of death located in Bruegel's articulation of history, but DeLillo and Updike offer the language of fiction as counterpoint, as a celebratory affirmation of life.

III

Rather than name the Prologue to *Underworld* "Pafko at the Wall," DeLillo uses the title of Bruegel's famous sixteenth-century painting *The Triumph of Death*, a magazine reproduction of which Hoover examines while ostensibly watching the game. For DeLillo the green spaciousness of the stadium at the Polo Grounds suggests an immediate counter to the blackness of World War Two, and the baseball teams themselves are the social glue of a culture. Although there are thousands of empty seats (thus uncannily presaging the thousands of no-shows at Ted Williams' last game at the end of the Fifties), Russ Hodges understands that the game connects the present to the past in a historical continuity of heroic achievement: "Polo Grounds—a name he loves, a precious echo of things and times before the century went to war. . . . When you see a thing like that, a thing that becomes a newsreel, you begin to feel you are a carrier of some solemn scrap of history" (15, 16).

Sitting together in the stands, Frank Sinatra, Jackie Gleason, Toots Shor, and Hoover personify the opposite perspective. They are Bruegel's skeletons dancing on the backs of the living. Yet, even Shor, a vulgar saloonkeeper, intuitively understands that both history and fiction are narrative constructs and that the artist is the person who has the words to tell the tale: "This is a miracle year. Nobody has a vocabulary for what happened this year" (18). He is wrong, of course. Hodges and DeLillo have the words. Hoover focuses on the blast of the Soviet bomb because he yearns to link the 1950s to the deaths in World War Two and to the specter of Communism, but despite also being unified by the threat of atomic annihilation, DeLillo and the fans focus on the blast from Thomson's bat because they sense the connecting authority of myth. Stories that join a culture give it the will to resist death. The point is not that myth fosters forgetfulness but that myth offers renewal.

DeLillo makes the contrast explicit. Here is Hoover, brooding in the stands, longing but failing to join with the anonymous fans: "He wants to feel a compatriot's nearness and affinity. All these people formed by language and climate and popular songs. . . . But there is that side of him, that part of him that depends on the strength of the enemy" (28). Now, here is Hodges, musing in the broadcast booth: "a souvenir baseball, a priceless thing somehow, a thing that seems to recapitulate the whole history of the game every time it is thrown or hit or touched" (26). Cotter and Bill, the two regular fans whom DeLillo particularizes, agree that baseball in the 1950s means connection and that connection means life: "'That's the thing about baseball, Cotter. You do what they did before you. That's the connection you make. There's a whole long line'. . . . Cotter likes this man's singleness of purpose, his insistence on faith and trust. It's the only force available against the power of doubt" (31). Bill's "trust" becomes ironic later when he challenges Cotter's right to the home run ball, but for the moment Cotter and Bill speak for the millions of people who, in Hodges's words, are "connected by the pulsing voice on the radio, joined to the word-of-mouth that passes the score along the street" (32).

DeLillo and Updike affirm a society's need for faith, for what the former calls "magic" and the latter calls "miracle." To believe is to hope and to hope is to live. It is not that they are ahistorical, or that the bomb did not explode, or that Korea, McCarthyism, and racial tension did not exist but that a nation turning toward Bruegel and Hoover rather than toward the myths created by Thomson and Williams is a nation depleting itself. Late in the game, for example, with the Giants on the edge of defeat, the crowd unifies in rhythmic applause, and "the repeated three-beat has the force of some abject faith, a desperate kind of will toward magic and accident" (36).

DeLillo's irony, on the other hand, reduces Hoover to a merchant of death. As the magazine pages with the reproduction of Bruegel's painting flutter onto his shoulders, "It is clear to Edgar that the page is from Life. . . . and what is the connection between Us and Them? . . . It's not enough to hate your enemy. You have to understand how the two of you bring each other to deep completion" (41, 51). To parry Hoover's commitment to death-in-life, DeLillo posits Thomson's home run as a feat of strength and skill that both mythologizes a moment in history and forges a unity among the living. Not only do "people make it a point to register the time"; they "wish to be connected to the event. . . . This is the nature of Thomson's homer. It makes people want to be in the streets, joined with others" (44, 45, 47).

DeLillo's point is that the joining becomes a sustaining legend. As a friend says to Hodges, whom DeLillo casts as an artist because of his command of the appropriate vocabulary, "I'll tell you one thing's for certain, old pal. We'll never forget today" (54). Neither will America. Bill's ridiculous pursuit of Cotter following the game surely indicates that serious cultural tensions are *always* present, that heroic stories do *not* eradicate grievous flaws, but for a nation just recovering from global conflict to ignore its need for myths is to propel that nation toward loss. DeLillo takes his cue from E. M. Forster: "only connect."

The conclusion of the Prologue to *Underworld* is cautiously affirmative, a celebration of the power of language—both DeLillo's and Hodges's—to construct the narratives that embrace life:

> Russ thinks this is another kind of history. He thinks they will carry something out of here that joins them all in a rare way, that binds them to a memory with protective power. . . . Isn't it possible that this mid-century moment enters the skin more lastingly than the vast shaping strategies of eminent leaders, generals steely in their sunglasses—the mapped visions that pierce our dreams? Russ wants to believe a thing like this keeps us safe in some undetermined way. (59–60)

DeLillo would like to believe with Hodges, though he knows, of course, that the bomb is always there. The final line of the Prologue, so slightly yet significantly emended from "Pafko at the Wall," memorializes the magic by which the mundane game of the day slides into the eternity of myth: "It is all falling indelibly into the past" (60).

IV

The Fifties ended with a similar moment of magic. On 28 September 1960, John Updike bought a ticket to Fenway Park to watch

Ted Williams play what would turn out to be his final game. Updike's account of that legendary contest, titled "Hub Fans Bid Kid Adieu," has been praised as consistently as any of his much-anthologized short stories. Like DeLillo's recreation of the Thomson home run, "Hub Fans" has multiple important textual states. The essay was first published in *New Yorker* (22 October 1960) without explanatory footnotes. Updike later added the notes to the second state when he collected "Hub Fans" in *Assorted Prose* (1965). Interestingly, the British edition of *Assorted Prose* (London: Deutsch, 1965) omits "Hub Fans Bid Kid Adieu" entirely, presumably because baseball is as foreign to the British as cricket is to the Americans. Then, in 1977, Updike published the third state of the essay in a limited edition of 326 signed copies (Northridge, CA: Lord John Press) for which he wrote a four-page Preface.

The context in which Updike created his meditation on heroism is set not by the contemporaneous *Rabbit, Run* (1960) but by "Packed Dirt, Churchgoing, A Dying Cat, A Traded Car," a little-known story that he published in *New Yorker* (16 December 1961) before collecting it in *Pigeon Feathers* (1962). In the tale the narrator responds to a sailor's question about why he bothers to write: "We in America need ceremonies, is I suppose, sailor, the point of what I have written" (279). "Packed Dirt" and "Hub Fans Bid Kid Adieu" appeared little more than a year apart, at a time just before the disasters of the 1960s sullied the American glow first emanating from the victory in World War Two and then sustaining the nation through the undercurrent of death fed by the twin demons of McCarthyism and the Cold War.

Like DeLillo researching the specifics of the Giants-Dodgers game in back issues of *The New York Times* and in Hodges's recorded play-by-play account, Updike resorted to an "outdated" record book and the Boston newspapers (128). His goal was not an expository reconstruction of the event but a meditative exploration of the moment. Played on a dreary, chilly New England afternoon, the game turned into an unanticipated ceremony of mythic proportions that, when looked at retrospectively, seemed to bring the 1950s to a close.

Updike's description of Fenway Park cleverly presages the paradoxes of the man he will laud in the essay. Fenway offers "a compromise between Man's Euclidean determinations and Nature's beguiling irregularities" (127). Like Ted Williams, not to mention American society itself, Fenway Park is far from perfect in its oddities and twists. And yet it is also the locale of heroic action, "a lyric little bandbox of a ballpark" that before the game features a uniformed groundkeeper on top of the famous left field wall, "picking batting-practice home runs out of the screen, like a mushroom gatherer seen in Wordsworthian perspective on the verge of a cliff" (127). Updike plays on the contrast between the irregular and the precise throughout the essay, as when he juxtaposes the gray day, the thousands of empty seats, and the meaningless game against the Baltimore Orioles ("It was not a very interesting game" [144]) on the one hand to the life-affirming green of the stadium, the presence of Ted Williams, and the fans's longing for a miracle from the aging hero on the other hand.

By the third paragraph, however, it is clear that the fans linked together on this cold afternoon represent Americans needing rejuvenation at the end of a spent decade. They have come to see the greatest hitter of the era, and they recognize the potential for myth in the event:

> The affair between Boston and Ted Williams was no summer romance; it was a marriage composed of spats, mutual disappointments, and, toward the end, a mellowing hoard of shared memories. It fell into three stages, which may be termed Youth, Maturity, and Age; or Thesis, Antithesis, and Synthesis; or Jason, Achilles, and Nestor. (128)

Just as DeLillo counters J. Edgar Hoover in order to acknowledge the authority of myth, so Updike resists perennial nay-sayers in order to honor the affirmation of heroism: "Greatness necessarily attracts debunkers." Williams' "basic offense against the fans has been to wish that they weren't there" (130).

On this particular day in Fenway, Updike's Ted Williams becomes god, hero, and artist for reasons beyond his career-long prowess with the bat. First he cares about his "art." Then he personifies "the intensity of competence" (134). Finally he represents the consistency of greatness. Playing in a game that means nothing because the Red Sox are mired in next-to-last place and thereby illustrate the inevitability of defeat, Williams is the 1950s' last best hope for heroism. What was "magic" for DeLillo turns into Updike's "miracle": "All baseball fans believe in miracles; the question is, how *many* do you believe in? . . . It was for our last look that ten thousand of us had come" (137, 139 italics Updike's).

Lest debunkers agree with Hoover and smile cynically at America's need for mythic heroes and miraculous feats, Updike gently mocks the fans, himself included ("We applauded ourselves lustily" [142]), before he challenges the saccharine portrayal of the national essence dispensed in the 1950s mass media via Norman Rockwell's magazine covers: "Whenever Williams appeared at the plate. . . . it was like having a familiar Leonardo appear in a shuffle of *Saturday Evening Post* covers" (144). The reader of DeLillo and Updike can hardly fail to notice the parallel dismissal of *Life* and the *Post* as shapers of American culture.

Fittingly for those who enter myth, Williams rallies the populace as he walks to the plate for his final at-bat in his final game. The dreary day, the boring contest, the washed-out decade—all point to the triumph of death. Yet, Updike and DeLillo celebrate the creativity of language and the power of art: "Understand that we were a crowd of rational people. . . . Nevertheless, there will always lurk, around the corner in a pocket of our knowledge of the odds, an indefensible hope, and this was one of those times . . . when a density of expectation hangs in the air and plucks an event out of the future" (145). Williams swings, and the ball, "less an object in flight than the tip of a towering, motionless construct. . . . was in the books while it was still in the sky" (146). Never vainglorious, never playing to the crowd, always committed to his art, he circles the bases, refuses to lift his cap to the imploring fans crying "to be saved," and steps into the permanence of myth: "Immortality is nontransferable. The papers said that the other players, and even the umpires on the field, begged him to come out and acknowledge us in some way, but he refused. Gods do not answer letters" (146). DeLillo and Updike know this truth. But, they also know they can shape the language of fiction to memorialize the exploits of the gods that connect a society in the face of diminishment and loss. Myth counters death.

V

In the years since its original publication "Hub Fans Bid Kid Adieu" has achieved a special status. For example David Halberstam included the essay in *The Best American Sports Writing of the Century* (Boston: Houghton Mifflin, 1999). Even more significant was Williams' response to Updike's account of his heroics. In the Preface to the 1977 limited edition of "Hub Fans," Updike reports that Williams, through an agent, invited Updike to write his biography. The invitation was declined. Yet, Updike uses the Preface to confirm the longevity of myth. Gods may not answer letters, but, 16 years after the miracle, Updike is pleased that true gods remain aloof. Unlike "some former superstars" Williams "does not appear on Brut television commercials or in Marilyn Monroe biographies" (ix). The allusions to Willie Mays and Joe DiMaggio are barely hidden.

Like DeLillo, Updike does not doubt that art shores up a culture or that a culture needs ceremonies. Thus, at the close of the Preface, he shifts from the message to the means; from the heroics described to the description of heroics; in other words, to language: "Love shows. Readers sense, an inch or so under the words, love or its absence . . . so these paragraphs must be, or they would not have so long survived their occasion" (xii). The point is clear. Mythic feats and artistic language outlive the political turmoil of their times. Don DeLillo and John Updike confirm that a society is finally sustained by the stories it remembers to tell.

In the Nick of Time: DeLillo's Nick Shay, Fitzgerald's Nick Carraway, and the Myth of the American Adam

JOANNE GASS

IN THE OPENING CHAPTER OF *UNDERWORLD* DON DELILLO RECREATES the 3 October 1951 afternoon when Bobby Thomson hit a three-run home run that gave the New York Giants the National League pennant and broke the hearts of Brooklyn Dodger fans everywhere. The event has come to be known in baseball mythology as the Shot Heard 'Round the World. It confirmed for many Americans their belief in heroes. But, even as the public bathed in the glow of unabated optimism, a second, more sinister, event occurred on the same day that would eclipse that sunny explosion of optimism—the Soviet Union's successful underground detonation of an atomic bomb. DeLillo says of those two events:

> The ball game was a unifying and largely joyous event, a kind of event in which people come out of their houses in order to share their feelings. . . . With the onset of the cold war, the communal sense started to become associated not with celebration but with danger and loss. The catastrophic events since then, events framed and defined by television, seem to have become predominant, events such as assassination, terrorist acts, even natural disasters. In my private record of events, this ball game represents a sort of transitional moment between the second world war and the beginning of the nuclear age. (quoted in Jones)

DeLillo marks this moment as one in which the traditional celebratory function of communal events shifts, and fear, paranoia, and death displace community, joy, and life. J. Edgar Hoover's sinister presence at the Giants-Dodgers game evokes that shadow of paranoia as he admires the reproduction of Bruegel's *The Triumph of*

Death that drifts down along with the clouds of confetti and receives the news of the Soviet Union's successful test.

Underworld traces the fortunes of the United States, of its anguished paranoia, and of Bobby Thomson's home run baseball from that eventful day in 1951 to the eve of the new millennium. It looks back and asks, "How have we come to be as we are?" "Where have we been, and where are we going?" Nick Shay, the novel's sometimes narrator and hero—if there is such a thing in the late twentieth century—seems to stand for America itself—cynical, tired, lost, and nostalgic for a time when baseball was the national game and its heroes represented action, impetuosity, and purpose. DeLillo asks what has happened to the American hero at the end of this century. As such, his Nick Shay evokes another Nick: Nick Carraway, the narrator of F. Scott Fitzgerald's *The Great Gatsby.* That Nick is disillusioned as well, disillusioned by events that transpired shortly after the beginning of the twentieth century. Both Nicks, it seems to me, represent America at crucial times in its history, and both are descendants and heirs of the American Adam— that mythic figure that came to symbolize the young, expanding, frontier America of the nineteenth century.

In 1955, at the fulcrum of our twentieth century, R. W. B. Lewis published *The American Adam: Innocence, Tragedy, and Tradition in the Nineteenth Century* in which he traces the myth of the American Adam as it developed in nineteenth-century America into the mid-twentieth century where Adam and the American Dream seem to have lost their way. For Lewis, the nineteenth-century American Adam was a radical innocent of the New World, divorced from the corruption of the Old World. The "American myth," he says, "saw life and history as just beginning. It described the world as starting up again under fresh initiative"—a new chance after the disastrous fall of the Old World. And, to carry out this second chance:

> the hero of the new adventure; an individual emancipated from history, happily bereft of ancestry, untouched and undefiled by the unusual inheritances of family and race; an individual standing alone; self-reliant and self-propelling, ready to confront whatever awaited him with the aid of his own unique and inherent resources. (5)

The American Adam faces the world alone, having dispensed with the trappings of history, family, tradition, friends, and community. Lewis quotes Emerson to argue that the American Adam is the "simple genuine self against the whole world" (6), a self-fashioning, independent being. Our image of this Adam is of a young man striding forth toward some frontier. He is, as Lewis described it, "the hero in *space*" uniquely identified with landscape and space "surrounded, detached, in *measureless oceans* of space" (91 italics Lewis'). In other words, the landscape is his to conquer, not to understand. It is the great unknown, which he will challenge.

Adam's innocence and impetuosity, combined with his willful rejection and forgetting of history, lead to disillusionment, for he has learned nothing from the past. And, the price of rejecting the past out of hand is high. As Lewis reminds us, "we are conscious, no longer of tradition, but simply and coldly of the burden of history. And without the vision, we are left, not with a mature tragic spirit, but merely with a sterile awareness of evil uninvigorated by a sense of loss" (9). Lewis attributes this willfulness and its subsequent sense of loss to "the American habit of resistance to maturity" (129).

Lewis wrote at a moment in American history when it appeared that the nineteenth century's "party of Hope," as he called it, had been defeated by the forces of evil. The coincidence of Bobby Thomson's home run, which struck a blow for optimism and joy, with the Soviet Union's successful testing of an atomic device—an event whose shadow would eventually eclipse the sun of Thomson's heroic act—went virtually unnoticed by the then-cheering public, despite the fact that *The New York Times* featured both events on the front page in parallel stories the next day. But by 1955, Thomson's heroism and the explosion of joy and optimism that had followed the Allied victories over the evil empire—Germany—in World War Two had been replaced by cynicism, skepticism, and paranoia fostered by McCarthyism at home and by the dawning realization that one evil empire had possibly been replaced by another—the Soviet Union—and that evil itself might be a game of infinite substitution. Lewis felt this growing cynicism keenly. In his Epilogue he deplores the "mordant skepticism" of his time (196), which has replaced the "fertile and alive" irony of the nineteenth century, which represents, for him, "one of the modes of death" (196). Thus, for Lewis, fiction in the mid-twentieth century lacked irony—that trope of innocence betrayed by the truth that life is inherently tragic and will break even the most impetuous and stalwart Adam.

In 1955 Lewis mourned the loss of that impetuosity, that tragic innocence, and he cited two causes for it: "antagonism to nature" and "distrust of experience" (198). What happened to the American Adam? Does Lewis perceive his extinction? No. Fitzgerald's *The Great Gatsby*, he says, "demonstrates once more the dramatic appeal of the hero as a self-created innocent" (197).

Lewis asserts that Jay Gatsby is the tragic American Adam of the early twentieth century, and I would not disagree with him. But, Gatsby's narrator, Nick Carraway, may provide us with a more fruitful look at the fate of the American Adam in the twentieth century, especially if he can be compared to Nick Shay who, it seems to me, represents the last half of the twentieth century and the consequences of the perpetuation of the myth of the American Adam. I will make the comparison based upon Lewis' own criteria: the American Adam's attempts at self-creation require that he turn his back on history, home, and community, and that he venture into the American landscape from which he is alienated in a quest to find himself.

Nick Carraway, ostensibly not the hero of *The Great Gatsby*, is nevertheless its main character (because we see everything through his eyes) and its narrator. Nick's narration of Gatsby's life and death reveals more about Nick than it does of Gatsby himself. Gatsby acts as a screen upon which Nick projects his own ambivalence and shifting attitudes. The self-created Gatsby, who mesmerizes Nick, is a sham, a petty grifter whose grail is to possess the shallow Daisy Buchanan. The single act that redeems Gatsby for Nick and for us, I suppose, is his self-sacrifice—he dies for Daisy after first assuming responsibility for Myrtle's death and thus allowing Daisy to continue her irresponsible existence. Gatsby makes a single heroic gesture that, in Nick's eyes, redeems him. But there is no "Gatsby" at the center of Gatsby; his one true act may be heroic but only if we accept that Daisy is worth dying for. Everything else about him is a glittering, enamel facade of lies. When Daisy will not redeem him by swearing that she never loved Tom Buchanan, Gatsby loses his reason to live and his sacrifice loses some of its luster. Although Lewis of course famously disagrees, there is nothing at the core of Jay Gatsby save a quixotic love for an undeserving woman.

But, Nick Carraway is a man of substance, our representative of America in the first quarter of the twentieth century, aware in the end of his ironic situation. Gatsby cannot be awarded this appellation; he is neither self-aware nor ironic. Our attention must be

drawn to him because he stands for the millions of young men who
returned from World War One having had their innocence and ideals stripped from them. They did not reject out of hand their history, traditions, and values; their history, traditions, and values
were forcibly and irreparably stripped from them. They sacrificed
themselves, as did Gatsby, for an ideal that turned out to be a hol-
low illusion. Of his service in the war, Nick says sarcastically, "I
participated in that delayed Teutonic migration known as the Great
War. I enjoyed the counter-raid so thoroughly that I came back
restless" (7). Nick's restlessness leads him to turn his back on his
"well-to-do" "prominent" family whose roots reach back three
generations in "a middle-western city" (7) that no longer was "the
warm center of the world" but instead "now seemed like the rag-
ged edge of the universe" (7), and to go east to make his way in the
bond business, to seek his fortune. He believes he has left the Midwest behind for good, that he is "a pathfinder and an original set-
tler" in West Egg and that "life was beginning over again with the
summer (of 1922)" (8). Nick presents himself to us as an expatriate
from the burden of his Midwest culture that he indicts for its
"bored, sprawling, swollen towns beyond the Ohio, with their in-
terminable inquisitions which spared only the children and the
very old" (185). Nick's goal is to remake himself in exile; he will
conquer the bond business and in the pastoral setting of "the great
wet barnyard of Long Island Sound" (9) remake himself into the
"'well-rounded man'" (9). In other words, feeling fragmented by
his experiences, he imagines that he can through an act of will invent a unified self. He says of his plans, "This isn't just an epi-
gram—life is much more successfully looked at from a single
window, after all" (9). Like Gatsby, Nick is in search of his ideal,
unified self. Unlike Gatsby, however, Nick has the power of self-
reflection and self-irony; disillusionment, for him, leads to retreat
not collapse and death.

What Nick finds in the East is not a new beginning. What he
finds is a wasteland—the "valley of the ashes," a "fantastic farm
where ashes grow like wheat into ridges and hills and grotesque
gardens" (27). Nick, Gatsby, Tom, Daisy, and Jordan must pass by
this bleak landscape on their trips to the city. It is a part (and I emphasize "part") of the pastoral setting in which these characters
find themselves. It symbolizes, as many have pointed out, the
waste land at the heart of the Lost Generation. It is, however,
merely a stop on the trip from West Egg to New York (they pick

up Myrtle, Tom's mistress near there). Nick, our modern American Adam, moves through the space of landscape; he does not, to borrow from Ian Johnston, have a "mystical sense" of the landscape; "it is essential to him, of course, as a place to move through and as a source of events which define him. . . . [But] no gods whisper from the mountains or the bushes"; he is indifferent to it. Nick's reportorial tone and matter-of-fact approach to the valley, to West Egg and East Egg, demonstrate his detachment from them. He is not a part of nature; he is apart from it.

Even at the end of the novel, when Nick decides to return to the Midwest, his memories of it have a proprietary and transient quality about them. He remembers nostalgically returning by train from prep school and college at Christmas time: he refers to the snow as "our snow"; he calls it "my middle-west" (184). Although he insists that his identity is tied up with the wintry landscape of his returns home from other places, he points out that he and his friends who were returning with him were "unutterably aware of our identity with this country for *one strange hour,* before we melted indistinguishably into it again" (184 italics mine).

Nick returns to the Midwest because he has found that the myth of the American Adam, in the person of Gatsby, is bankrupt, and yet he cannot "find another faith to live by" (Noble 152). He tells us at the novel's beginning that when he returned, he "felt that [he] wanted the world to be in uniform and at a sort of moral attention forever" (6). He wants order to be restored. He looks back on Gatsby's dream and the lost Eden that lit the way for the first settlers in America, "Gatsby believed in the green light, the orgastic future that year by year recedes before us. It eluded us then, but that's no matter—tomorrow we will run faster, stretch out our arms farther. . . . And one fine morning—So we beat on, boats against the current, borne back ceaselessly into the past" (189).

Gatsby believed it, he says, but Nick does not believe it anymore; he has already told us, just pages before: "I was thirty. Before me stretched the portentous, menacing road of a new decade" (143). We are reminded here of "the American habit of resistance to maturity" (Lewis 129). Nick's bleak assessment of his own future makes a fine, ironic counterpoint to Gatsby's "orgastic future that year by year recedes before us." That youthful hope has been lost, and growing up holds no charm. Gatsby's chivalric sacrifice, the individual act in the face of a corrupt and corrupting society, may be the one redeeming spot in Nick's vision of the coming decade:

> Nick knew that this dream had not found fulfillment and never could. But like Fitzgerald, he cannot imagine an alternative to this "greatest of all human dreams." Stoically, he accepts the burden of innocence which dooms him to the hypocrisy and sterility of the Lost Generation. He can see no other future but that which "year by year recedes before us. . . . So we beat on, boats against the current, borne back ceaselessly into the past." (Noble 160)

Nick Carraway, the American Adam of the first part of the twentieth century, faces the future by retreating to his home in the Midwest disillusioned, burdened by the irony of his realization that "the Europeans' arrival in the New World signaled the end of something, not the beginning" (Bizzell 782). Nevertheless, he is still willing, I think, to "run faster" and "stretch [his] arms out farther" to that receding future, if only because Fitzgerald cannot himself envision an alternative route for Nick to take.

Nick Shay, the American Adam of the last half of the twentieth century, is virtually everything that Nick Carraway is not in terms of privilege and education, and yet the two share one crucial trait: disillusionment. Fitzgerald's Nick, on that fateful thirtieth birthday, reflects, "Thirty—the promise of a decade of loneliness, a thinning list of single men to know, a thinning briefcase of enthusiasm, thinning hair" (143).

Nick Shay, when we meet him, is also disillusioned. In his late fifties, his future is behind him, and, with an irony equal to Nick Carraway's vision of the lost green world, he observes, "Most of our longings go unfulfilled. This is the word's wistful implication—a desire for something lost or fled or otherwise out of reach" (803). That "mid-century moment" (60) when Bobby Thomson hit the home run is forty years behind him, and the ball Thomson hit, which Nick owns, lies mostly unnoticed on his library shelf. Nick says, "I tend to forget why I bought it" (809). Nick has reached comfortable late middle age, comfortable in the sense of material comfort—the amenities that a successful career can bring. He is a grandfather; his marriage, having overcome infidelities on both sides and a brush with heroin addiction on Marian's part, is stable; he is a success in every sense of the word. He and Marian are collectors; they fill their house with objects, but now those objects fail to satisfy:

> There is something somber about the things we've collected and own, the household effects, there is something about the word itself, *effects,*

the lacquered chest in the alcove, that breathes a kind of sadness—the wall hangings and artifacts and valuables—and I feel a loneliness, a loss, all the greater and stranger when the object is relatively rare and it's the hour after sunset in a stillness that feels unceasing. (808 italics DeLillo's)

Nick's reflections reveal a dusty preoccupation with death. The objects he has collected are the "effects" of other lives, rootless history that has no significance other than the monetary value placed upon old and rare items acquired because their owners have died. Seen in another light, they are rubbish; they are the cast-offs of another generation. They do not bring Nick any satisfaction or solace; having does not fill the great pit of his loss. Despite his assertion that he "tends to forget" why he bought it, at other times, Nick makes his reasoning clear: "It's all about losing. . . . It's about the mystery of bad luck, the mystery of loss" (97).

Nick Shay, unlike Nick Carraway, had no comfortable, middle class, Midwest upbringing, no privileged prep school and Ivy League education to turn his back on, and no father whose sage advice he can recall, as Nick Carraway does when he is about to embark upon his journey east. As with Nick Carraway's, Nick Shay's quest for a unified and coherent self begins with betrayal, loss, anger, and expulsion. Nick's loss began early when his father Jimmy Costanza, a small-time bookie and charmer of women, left for cigarettes and never returned. He left his wife and two small sons to fend for themselves in a poor, tough Italian neighborhood in the Bronx. Jimmy's disappearance lies at the center of Nick's loss and of his anger. Whereas Nick Carraway feels betrayed by civilization and the war and seeks a new self by selling bonds and settling in pastoral Long Island, Nick Shay's betrayal pierces more deeply into his psyche. He will never forget his father's desertion; even at 57, Nick thinks about that long ago betrayal. Time and again, in the midst of other thoughts, Nick's memories return to this fundamental loss, this terrible betrayal:

We built pyramids of waste above and below the earth. The more hazardous the waste, the deeper we tried to sink it. The word plutonium comes from Pluto, god of the dead and ruler of the underworld. They took him out to the marshes and wasted him as we say today, or used to say until it got changed to something else. (106)

All associations inexorably lead back to Jimmy Costanza's disappearance, the "final family mystery. All mysteries of the family

reach their culmination in the final passion of abandonment," Nick
says (87). Jimmy's disappearance, the original sin, precipitates
Nick's Fall.

Before the Fall, Nick, like any small boy, idealized his father.
Nick remembers his father shaving:

> He used to shave with a towel draped over his shoulder, wearing his
> undershirt, his singlet, and the blade made a noise I liked to listen to,
> a sandpaper scrape on his heavy beard, and the brush in the shaving
> cup, the Gem blade and the draped towel and the hot water from the
> tap—heat and skill and cutting edge. (106–7)

There is a certain romance implied in Nick's description—the romance of the knight in his singlet heroically applying his blade—
especially because the memory is wrapped in another memory of
loss, the loss of the Latin mass and the beauty of the Latin language. (The juxtaposition of *Dominus vobiscum* to Jimmy's ablu-
tions suggests that he resembles as well a priest intoning mass.)

Jimmy's abandonment changes an adoring boy into an angry
teenager, a bully, and a thief who suffers another series of losses
that eventually leads to murder. Bronzini's description of sixteen-
year-old Nick to Father Paulus and Klara's memory (related to Acie
years after her affair with Nick) delineate the contradictions in
Nick's character. Bronzini appeals to Father Paulus on behalf of
Nick's mother to try to save him. He describes Nick as "[b]right, I
think, but lazy and unmotivated. He's sixteen and can quit school
any time he likes. . . . But what a waste if a youngster like this were
to end up in a stockroom or garage" (671). Klara remembers him
differently. Although she describes him at seventeen as a man and
a "juvenile delinquent," Nick, to Klara, "didn't seem to make too
much of [their affair] himself. He was, [she] thought, remarkably
unconfused and even-keeled" (484). Klara drastically misconstrues
Nick's response to her ending of their affair, I think, just as she fails
to plumb the depths of Nick's feelings about the affair. She does
not know Nick's first name, much less his full name, until the day
she ends the affair (752). She did not then (nor does she later) sense
Nick's explosive anger until it is too late. Klara's rejection exacer-
bates the wound Jimmy's disappearance opened. Klara has not
cared enough to find out his name; Nick has attempted to know
her in a most intimate way:

> Never mind the body. He's never looked at a woman's face so closely.
> How he thinks he knows who she is from her face, what she eats and

how she sleeps, from the lookaway smile and the uncombed hair, the hair over the right eye, how her face becomes everything she is that he can't put into words. (752)

Nick never tells Klara these things. His pride not only prevents him from using his feelings to plead with her but it makes him try to hurt her as he leaves. But Klara's loss looms large in Nick's psyche no matter how hard he tries to contain the waste from his past; how else explain his trip to the airplane graveyard forty years later? Klara rejects Nick again: "This is a long way, Nick. We're a long way from home" (73). Nick's response evokes his own careful study forty years before: "I wanted her to see me. I wanted her to know I was out there, whatever crazy mistakes I'd made—I'd come out okay" (73).

Nick loses Klara just one year after the Dodgers lost to the Giants and six years after Jimmy "loses" his family. One month later Nick kills the hapless heroin addict, George—it is October, 1952. Clearly in killing George, Nick tries to "kill" his father, but George has also betrayed Nick. Thinking himself streetwise, Nick learns "a lesson in serious things" when George reveals his heroin addiction (727): "It took Nick a minute to understand all this. This was new to him. Drugs. Who used drugs around here? He felt dumb and confused and very young suddenly. . . . Nick felt dumb all right. He felt like someone had just sandbagged him in an alley. Wham. He almost put a hand to the back of his neck" (726).

Nick feels "he'd lost some standing" with George (760). This loss of face puts Nick at a disadvantage with George, he feels. The final loss comes when Mario tells Nick that "Jimmy was not in a position to be threatened by serious people" (765). Nick's father was not important enough to warrant the attention of the local mob; therefore, Jimmy has also lost face. Nick's version of Jimmy's disappearance depends on his importance in the community as a numbers runner. It depends on the myth that Jimmy was a somebody. Mario's misplaced reassurance that "Jimmy was not in a position where he could offend somebody so bad that they would go out of their way to do something" (765) reduces him to a nobody. Although Nick "didn't think he had to accept the logic of the argument," he surely has lost face once again. Matt, Nick's brother, thinks he knows why Nick must believe that his father's death was the result of a plot:

He'd told Janet the story, how Nick believed their father was taken out to the marshes and shot, and how this became the one plot, the only conspiracy that big brother could believe in. Nick could not afford to succumb to a general distrust. He had to protect his conviction about what happened to Jimmy. Jimmy's murder was isolated and pure, uncorrupted by other secret alliances and criminal acts, other suspicions. (454)

The adult Nick clings to this complete plot just as tenaciously as did the seventeen-year old Nick, who could not afford to lose the logic of it. George then becomes the scapegoat for all of Nick's losses.

The primal sin—murder of the "father"—leads to expulsion from society. Nick is sent first to upstate New York and then to Minnesota, far from the corruption of the city and into pastoral America where he constructs a new self. Like Nick Carraway, Nick Shay wants to look at life "through a single window" (9). The angry teenager sent upstate embraced the concept of correction: "When I entered correction" he says, "I wanted things to make sense. . . . I was a convert to the system. . . . I believed in the stern logic of correction. . . . I didn't want sweetheart treatment. . . . this was how I began to build an individual" (502–3). Building an individual requires that our Adam, after having left behind home, family, and community, actively reject his history and begin anew in a setting wholly unlike the Old World from whence he came. Upstate New York and Minnesota prove to be New Worlds far removed from the Bronx. But they are not isolated and without connections. McCarthyism reaches its tentacles into the Jesuit school, and Nick signs his name to a supporting petition. In upstate New York Nick's counselor, Dr. Lindblad, tries to get him to connect to his past, but he "didn't know if [he] accepted the idea that [he] had a history" (511). To Nick, history, like the narrative of his father's death, must have "some sort of form and coherence" (511). Nick rejects Dr. Lindblad's assertion that he has a history that he is "responsible to." She tells him, "You're answerable. You're required to try to make sense of it. You owe it your complete attention" (512). Nick chooses not to devote his "complete attention" to his history; he chooses instead to "escape the things that made [him]" by learning words (543). Language, and Nick's mastery of it, creates the coherent, orderly "I" who moves west, until he finally ends up in Phoenix, where "history does not run loose. . . .

They segregated visible history. They caged it, funded and bronzed it, they enshrined it carefully in museums and plazas and memorial parks" (86).

In the end Nick does succeed; he acquires the material signs of success: nice house, nice wife, nice kids, nice belongings. He describes himself as "a country of one. . . . a measured separation like my old man's" (275). He has perfected the concept of *lontananza*:

> Distance or remoteness, sure. But as I use the word, as I interpret it, hard-edged and fine-grained, it's the perfected distance of the gangster, the syndicate mobster—the made man. Once you're a made man, you don't need the constant living influence of sources outside yourself. You're all there. You're made. You're handmade. You're a sturdy Roman wall. (275)

Both his brother Matt and his wife Marian see these qualities in him. Matt describes his older brother as "shaped and made. First unmade and then reimagined and strongly shaped and made again" (416). Marian also feels Nick's command of distance and control:

> She had a demon husband if demon means a force of some kind, an attendant spirit of discipline and self-command, the little flick of distance he'd perfected, like turning off a radio. She knew about his father's disappearance but there was something else, hard and apart. This is what had drawn her in the first place, the risky and erotic proposition. (261)

Marian feels the magnetic and equally repellant force of the self-made man. And yet, that surface detachment and outward control and calm conceal an existential void. Nick cannot contain and control the waste buried in his heart. "Waste," he thinks, "is an interesting word that you can trace through Old English and Old Norse back to the Latin, finding such derivatives as empty, void, vanish and devastate" (120). Controlling that devastating void has become Nick's obsession. At 57, he finds himself explaining to himself and to us. He wants us to know that he "turned out okay." But, the irony of his success is not lost on him; this self-made man who has become everything that his father was not, responsible, successful, careful, looks back nostalgically:

> I long for the days of disorder. I want them back, the days when I was alive on the earth, rippling in the quick of my skin, heedless and real. I

was dumb-muscled and angry and real. This is what I long for, the
breach of peace, the days of disarray when I walked real streets and
did things slap-bang and felt angry and ready all the time, a danger to
others and a distant mystery to myself. (810)

Ironically, he longs for that Adamic time when anything was possible and the future was a series of obstacles to be conquered, when
disorder was his way of life. Nor is the irony lost on us, especially
when we learn that Nick Shay's success is in garbage. The American Eden has become a true wasteland, Nick is a waste manager,
and America's future lies in managing its waste.

The America that Nick confronts resembles Nick Carraway's
America only in its geographical contours. Whereas Nick Carraway passed *through* a valley of ashes; Nick Shay's America has *become* a valley of ashes. The landscape itself has turned into a refuse
heap, as has society and even culture. DeLillo's novel catalogues
the sweep of our irresponsibility. From the cascading paper trash
that follows the Thomson home run; to the monumental effort to
conceal our everyday garbage in vast, efficient pits; to the most
dangerous of all our garbage, nuclear waste, and our willful pretense that it can be harmlessly dealt with; to our shameful treatment of the homeless and the poor as though they were no more
valuable than the trash that periodically chokes New York City
during garbage strikes. In his pursuit of more efficient methods of
waste management Nick travels to the former Soviet Union to witness a demonstration of the disposal of waste via a nuclear blast.
Trash has even become aesthetic; Klara Sax, Nick's first lover, has
become a trash artist. Nick finds her painting cast-off B-52s in the
Arizona desert, where, in fact, there is an enormous aircraft graveyard. Nick and Klara have become connoisseurs of garbage. They
are collectors in the sense that Walter Benjamin defined them as he
looked at nineteenth-century Europe:

> Perhaps the most deeply hidden motive of the person who collects
> can be described this way: he takes up the struggle against dispersion.
> Right from the start, the great collector is struck by the confusion, by
> the scatter, in which the things of the world are found. . . . The collector
> . . . brings together what belongs together; by keeping in mind their
> affinities and their succession in time, he can eventually furnish infor-
> mation about his objects. Nevertheless—and this is more important
> than all the differences that may exist between them—in every collector
> hides an allegorist, and in every allegorist a collector. As far as the col-

lector is concerned, his collection is never complete; for let him discover just a single piece missing, and everything he's collected remains a patchwork, which is what things are for allegory from the beginning. On the other hand, the allegorist—for whom objects represent only keywords in a secret dictionary, which will make known their meanings to the initiated—precisely the allegorist can never have enough of things. With him, one thing is so little capable of taking the place of another that no possible reflection suffices to foresee what meaning his profundity might lay claim to for each one of them. (211)

The collector struggles in the collecting activities to create order out of impending chaos, whereas the allegorist discerns significance in particularity; to the allegorist a world of meaning lurks behind every individual incident and object, and each particularity, when read properly, has the potential of unlocking the secrets of the universe. For the allegorist, as is frequently asserted in *Underworld*, "everything is connected." The tension in the collector/allegorist personifies the paranoia inherent in the American character in the late twentieth century. The collector/allegorist suspects hidden plots everywhere, clawing a way through history's detritus and trying to save something from the wreckage and waste. Paradoxically, the collector/allegorist also longs for the good old days of the Cold War when there was a plot, when the Soviet Union provided a clear and present danger, when the enemy was clearly identifiable, when we faced the danger together. In the face of chaos, of a world filled with information but little meaning, the American Adam collects to resist dispersion, to forestall entropy.

The consequences of ignoring the past have caught up with us, and yet we continue to go on, as though America were a frontier to be conquered. We bury the evidence of our irresponsibility; we render it invisible and pretend that the yuccas and the hawks are somehow unaffected. We, and Nick, remain as disconnected from nature and the landscape as our nineteenth-century American Adam.

Underworld, like *The Great Gatsby*, ends in a vision of the future. Fitzgerald's ending mourns the tragic loss of innocence and of the American dream; DeLillo's vision embraces, in a way, "connectedness" at the same time as it evokes the specter of formlessness, in a vision of cyberspace as the new frontier, a frontier in which everything is reduced to "a single fluctuating impulse now, a piece of coded information. Everything is connected in the end" (826).

Just as Sister Edgar and J. Edgar Hoover are joined together in cyberspace "all conflict programmed out," so are the exploding bombs that materialize on the screen replaced in a click by "a seraphic word"—a word that promises much but is merely another piece of coded information:

> and you try to imagine the word on the screen becoming a thing in the world, taking all its meanings, its sense of serenities and contentments out into the streets somehow, its whisper of reconciliation, a word extending itself ever outward, the tone of agreement or treaty, the tone of repose, the sense of mollifying silence, the tone of hail and farewell, a word that carried the sunlit ardor of an object deep in drenching noon, the argument of binding touch, but it's only a sequence of pulses on a dullish screen and all it can do is make you pensive—a word that spreads a longing through the raw sprawl of the city and out across the dreaming bourns and orchards to the solitary hills.
> Peace. (827)

The word can do no more than cause longing, not unlike the longing Gatsby feels as he gazes at that green light or the longing Nick Shay feels as he rearranges his books, builds new shelves, enumerates his collections and "[stands] helpless in [his] desert place looking at the books" (810).

Fitzgerald ends with the natural landscape, that lost Eden of the New World, receding into the past even as we race toward it. DeLillo, in spite of his evocation of "the raw sprawl of the city and . . . the dreaming bourns and orchards to the solitary hills," removes us even further from the natural landscape we have despoiled, and from the garbage we have buried that nonetheless "has not ceased to exist merely because it has disappeared; it continues in another place, festering and radiating" (Helyer 1002).

What has happened to the myth of the American Adam at the dawn of the twenty-first century? Well, nothing, really; we persist in clinging to its promise. Like Nick Carraway, we still believe in the promise of the American frontier where we can remake ourselves in whatever image we choose. We still admire in our movies and novels the self-made individual who challenges the status quo and sets out on a quest for fame and fortune. We still believe in the power of the individual. We also practice a blissful ignorance of the consequences of our frontier brinksmanship. DeLillo's cautionary tale reminds us that the cost of our progress is high indeed. We still look out across our American landscape and see opportunities; we do not see ourselves as a part of the landscape; we see it as a commodity. And, if we have ruined the landscape, we move into cyberspace—our isolation from nature is complete. We continue to plow forward recklessly, gobbling up the natural resources, leaving behind a wasteland of refuse, a wasteland to which we turn a blind eye even as we pick through that garbage, collecting the memorabilia, trying to make sense of our past. Forging ahead into a new century, we, like Nick Shay, manage our garbage.

Don DeLillo, T. S. Eliot, and the Redemption of America's Atomic Waste Land

Paul Gleason

T. S. ELIOT'S *THE WASTE LAND* AND DON DELILLO'S *UNDERWORLD* MEDI-
tate the meaning of waste in different periods of twentieth-century
history. For Eliot, the waste of World War One persists in the nihilistic actions of modern humanity. For DeLillo, the waste created in
the atomic bomb factories of the Cold War remains after the imminent threat of nuclear war dissipates with the fall of the Berlin Wall
and the dissolution of the Soviet empire. Both Eliot and DeLillo
recognize that, as Jesse Detwiler points out to Big Sims and Nick
Shay, one can learn a lot about a civilization by examining its garbage.

The Waste Land and *Underworld* uphold Detwiler's point about
the semiotics of waste. But they reach quite different conclusions
about the relation of waste to literature and history. Eliot and
DeLillo agree that waste and literature function as cultural productions that illuminate the civilizations from which they derive.
But by similarly creating literary works in which waste defines
specific historical epochs, Eliot and DeLillo offer different com-
mentaries about the role of literature in history. Because *Underworld* echoes many of *The Waste Land*'s concerns—particularly
sexual morality, asceticism, prophecy, and the meaning of the
word "peace"—it exposes the nihilistic impulse that motivates
Eliot's vision of history and literature.[1] In contrast to Eliot, who
suggests that the writer respond to an essentially meaningless
twentieth-century history with a mythic aestheticism that ideal-
izes and privileges the past, DeLillo proposes art and language
as means by which the individual can reinvent and redeem the
waste that defines America in the second half of the twentieth
century.

The Metaphysics of Waste

The different historical situations in which Eliot wrote *The Waste Land* and DeLillo wrote *Underworld* inform their different understandings of the metaphysics of waste. For Eliot, who wrote *The Waste Land* before the advent of nuclear power, waste is not eternal but a psychological and moral state that can be eliminated if humanity rediscovers the religious consciousness with which it lived in past eras. In *"Ulysses*, Order, and Myth" (1923), an impassioned defense of *Ulysses* published one year after *The Waste Land*, Eliot comments on the bleak status of contemporary history, proclaiming it an "immense panorama of futility and anarchy." He posits the "mythical method"—specifically, Joyce's manipulation of "a continuous parallel between contemporaneity and antiquity"—as "a way of controlling, of ordering, of giving a shape and a significance" to contemporary history (177).

This analysis of Joyce's use of the mythical method in *Ulysses* illuminates the way in which Eliot defines history as waste in *The Waste Land*. He employs *From Ritual to Romance*, Jessie L. Weston's anthropological study of the grail myth, and other mythic and literary sources to impose nihilism on modern humanity.[2] According to Eliot modern humanity no longer possesses the religious consciousness that made human existence meaningful in the past. He begins "The Burial of the Dead" with these famous lines:

> April is the cruellest month, breeding
> Lilacs out of the dead land, mixing
> Memory and desire, stirring
> Dull roots with spring rain.

$$(\text{ll.}1–4)$$

Eliot inverts the opening lines of Chaucer's Prologue to *The Canterbury Tales*, which in Nevill Coghill's modern translation are as follows:

> When in April the sweet showers fall
> And pierce the drought of March to the root, and all
> The veins are bathed in liquor of such power
> As brings about the engendering of the flower . . .

Eliot refers to Chaucer's Prologue to contrast the religious certainties of the Middle Ages to the nihilism of modernity. The Prologue
posits April as a month of seasonal renewal, in which Christians
band together to make pilgrimages. Eliot's speaker, however, does
not recognize April as the month of renewal. He misconceives of
April as cruel, opposing himself to the "breeding" and "desire"
that affect the rebirth of nature in the spring. Eliot's later reference
in "The Burial of the Dead" to the "Son of man" (l. 20) suggests
a Christian interpretation of the speaker's comments. In aligning
himself against the spring, the speaker also aligns himself against
Christ, whose crucifixion, death, and resurrection parallel the seasonal cycle of fall, winter, and spring. By not understanding the
seasonal cycle through religious consciousness, the speaker expresses his desire to remain a corpse, a piece of human waste buried beneath "the dead land."

Eliot then suggests that individuals become waste when they do
not act with religious conviction. In his early "Portrait of a Lady"
he writes of a "conversation" that "slips / Among velleities and
carefully caught regrets" (ll. 14, 15). The word "velleities" indicates
human volition at its lowest level. In *The Waste Land* Eliot posits
that velleity plagues his speaker and modern humanity, transforming them into waste. In "The Burial of the Dead" the speaker remains waste because he does not want to participate in the cycle of
death and rebirth. Later in "The Burial of the Dead" the speaker
has the opportunity to revitalize himself and the waste land
through a sexual encounter with the Hyacinth Girl. In *The Golden
Bough*, another of Eliot's sources for the poem, James George Frazer
says that the hyacinth "heralded the advent of another spring and
gladdened the hearts of men with the promise of a joyful resurrection" (320). Eliot's speaker, however, fails to initiate a sexual encounter with the Hyacinth Girl: "Yet when we came back, late,
from the hyacinth garden, / Your arms full, and your hair wet, I
could not / Speak" (ll. 37–39). He does not overcome his velleity
by performing the linguistic act that would lead to the sexual revi-
talization of the modern world.[3]

By associating waste with velleity, Eliot suggests that it is not
eternal but a phenomenon that can be eliminated if modern humanity acts with conviction and recognizes its position in the cycle
of birth, death, and resurrection. In so doing he expresses the possibility that humanity can respond to modern history's "immense
panorama of futility and anarchy" by performing linguistic and

sexual acts that will inaugurate an era of religious consciousness ordered by the seasonal cycles. As I hope to show, however, *The Waste Land* ultimately suggests that this is impossible.

In contrast to Eliot, DeLillo does not hold that waste can be eliminated in language or sex, nor does he idealize the past. Rather, he attempts to locate redemption in humanity's existential experience of a culture whose phenomenology is rooted in waste. For DeLillo two forms of waste define culture in the second half of the twentieth century: nuclear waste and the waste produced by mass-media capitalism. DeLillo contemplates the persistence of nuclear waste in "Das Kapital," the Epilogue to *Underworld*, in which the American waste managers Nick Shay and Brian Glassic visit Polygon, a former Soviet nuclear test site in Kazakhstan. Their host Viktor Maltsev runs a company that "destroy[s] contaminated nuclear waste by means of nuclear explosions" (791). Nick describes the landscape through which they drive on their way to the test site, noting "the remnant span of a railroad trestle, a sculptured length of charred brown metal resting on concrete piers" and "the weathered posts and I-beams left to the wind, things made and shaped by men, old schemes gone wrong" (792). Nick's description of the deserted site and allusion to the wind directly recall the landscape of *The Waste Land*, which Eliot's speaker characterizes as sterile, void of human habitation, and home only to the wind.[4]

After alluding to Eliot's poem to establish Polygon as a nuclear waste land, DeLillo considers the horrific deformities of the inhabitants of Kazakhstan who came into contact with nuclear waste. Viktor takes Nick and Brian to the region's Medical Institute, where Nick sees a "boy with skin where his eyes ought to be, a bolus of spongy flesh, oddly like a mushroom cap, springing from each brow" (800). Despite Viktor Maltsev's venture to destroy it in underground nuclear explosions, nuclear waste indelibly marks the people with whom it comes into contact. Indeed the boy's "mushroom cap" is an eternal reminder of the mushroom clouds that led to his deformity.

In the essay "The Power of History" DeLillo targets the media as another cause of waste, criticizing its "fame-making apparatus [that] confers celebrity on an individual in a conflagration so intense that he or she can't possibly survive." He goes on to argue that America's celebrity culture is indicative of "the larger cultural drama of white-hot consumption and instant waste." According to DeLillo, the media advances this culture of "instant waste" by promulgating a "debasing process of frantic repetition that exhausts a contemporary event before it has rounded into coherence." In Baudrillardian terms the media imprison people and historical events in a capitalist simulacrum, creating them as commodities to be consumed as products and discarded as waste. Because the media ultimately transform people and historical events into waste, they oppose humanity's quest to discover existential "coherence" in historical experience.

The first section of "Elegy for Left Hand Alone," the second part of *Underworld*, dramatizes DeLillo's critique of the media in "The Power of History." Matt Shay watches on television a young girl's videotape of "the tenth or eleventh homicide committed by the Texas Highway Killer" (159). DeLillo describes the way in which "Taping-and-playing intensifies and compresses the event" so that it becomes "an act of shadow technology, of compressed time and repeated images, stark and gray and unremarkable" (159). The media's repeated playing of the videotape destroys the homicide's historicity, depriving it of its significance as the senseless death of a man. By the end of the novel Nick notes that the Texas Highway Killer has become the detritus of the pop-cultural conversation: "No one talks about the Texas Highway Killer anymore" (807).

Unlike Eliot's waste land, whose nihilistic inhabitants insure its sterility, DeLillo's nuclear waste land is a place of belief. DeLillo told interviewer Diane Osen that "the time is coming when we will begin to feel a nostalgia for the Cold War. For its certainties and its biblical sense of awesome confrontation." In *Underworld* the Cold War resembles Eliot's Middle Ages: it is a period when not God but the atomic bomb functions as a stabilizing, metaphysical presence in which the characters *believe*. Sister Edgar, DeLillo's "cold war nun" (245), most overtly establishes the connection between atomic and religious belief. Just as she lines "the walls of her room with Reynolds Wrap as a safeguard against nuclear fallout" (245), she maintains a rigorous regimen of prayer. DeLillo's other Edgar, J. Edgar Hoover, sees the Soviet atomic threat as a communal force: "All these people formed by language and climate and popular songs and breakfast foods and the jokes they tell and the cars they drive have never had anything in common so much as this, that they are sitting in the furrow of destruction" (28). As Klara Sax walks through New York during the "rooftop summer" (371), she contemplates the city's "late medieval texture" (391), experiencing an era similar to Eliot's age of religious consciousness. Moreover,

Louis T. Bakey, a crewmember of the B-52 Long Tall Sally, recounts a mystical experience he had while flying through a mushroom cloud during an atomic simulation in the Nevada desert: "A glow enters the body that's like the touch of God. . . . I swear to Jesus I thought this was heaven. . . . I thought I was flying right through Judgment Day" (613). In Viktor Maltsev's words to Nick and Brian, the Cold War makes it advisable to "Believe everything" (801).

Because the second half of the twentieth century is a time of belief for DeLillo, it is also a time of prophecy. His prophets affect humanity's political and metaphysical perceptions, whereas Eliot's simply observe and lament humanity's nihilistic sexual actions. Eliot writes in his commentary that Tiresias, the ancient Greek prophet who appears in "The Fire Sermon," is "the most important personage in the poem, uniting all the rest. . . . What Tiresias *sees*, in fact, is the substance of the poem" (70 italics Eliot's). Tiresias sees the young man carbuncular and the typist engaged in a mechanistic and nihilistic sexual encounter that does not result in the redemption of the waste land.[5] As the witness of this encounter Tiresias functions as the poem's religious consciousness, his presence clearly articulating Eliot's central theme of sexual immorality. But, he is simply a witness, an impotent prophet who neither prevents the young man carbuncular and the typist from engaging in sex nor tells them how to approach sex with religious consciousness.

DeLillo's Eisenstein, like Eliot's Tiresias, is a prophet-figure whose vision—his film *Unterwelt*—unifies the main themes of the work in which he appears. Gerald Howard comments on how "the Eisenstein film unites so many strands of meaning and imagery in *Underworld*," and during his interview with Howard, DeLillo himself talks about the importance of the "film suppl[ying] a Russian presence right in the middle of the book." DeLillo's "Russian presence" is associated with bisexuality: "You try to imagine Eisenstein in the underground of bisexual Berlin . . . and he's dishing Hollywood gossip with men in drag" (444). [6] But in contrast to Tiresias, whose transsexuality allows him to understand sex from both the male and female perspectives,[7] Eisenstein signifies sexual repression, and his film expands the meaning of the word "underworld" so that it encompasses sexual repression, nuclear war, and Cold War politics. Just as Eisenstein conceals his sexuality in the "underworld" of repressed sexual desire, *Unterwelt* allegorizes the suffering of the inhabitants of an atomic waste land: "There was no plot.

Just loneliness, barrenness, men hunted and ray-gunned, all happening in some nether-land crevice" (430). As the film culminates with the authorities returning the escaped men to their underground prison, DeLillo notes how "it is all vigilance and suppression, the FBI in peace and war and day and night, your own white-collar cohort of the law" (444). DeLillo's reference to the FBI universalizes the film so that it transcends political ideology and reflects the Cold War experience of both the Soviets and the Americans.

Like Eisenstein, Lenny Bruce, DeLillo's other prophet, is a historical and artistic figure not a mythic seer who symbolizes an eternal standard of morality. By including him in the novel DeLillo indicates that artists cannot use eternal standards to judge history but must create their art from their participation in history.[8] Of course, Bruce's repeated prophecy during the Cuban Missile Crisis that *"We're all gonna die"* responds to the imminent threat of Soviet nuclear attack; and DeLillo imagines "Lenny in his primitive Christian mode, doing offbeat sermons to desert rabble" (586) and has him reiterate his own theory of the biblical significance of the atomic bomb: "the atomic bomb is Old Testament. It's the Jewish bible in spades. We feel at home with this judgment, this punishment hanging over us" (592). Bruce's cry *"We're all gonna die"* bonds his audience into a community, inspiring in them a primitive fear:

> And his voice sent a weird thrill shooting through the audience. They felt the cry physically. It leaped in their blood and bonded them. This was the revolt of the psyche, an idlike wail from their own souls, the desperate buried place where you demand recognition of primitive rights and needs. (547)

Bruce's cry releases the Cold War fears that reside in the "buried" underworld of the psyche and becomes a ritualistic chant that he uses to emphasize the political insights of his sermons. He asserts that one should "Never underestimate the power of language" (582), and during his act in Miami he repeats the cry after he hilariously analyzes the uncommon first names of some of the most powerful authorities in the American government of the early 1960s. For Bruce, the first names of the "men . . . deciding our fate" (591)—he cites Adlai Stevenson, Dean Rusk, McGeorge Bundy, Roswell Gilpatric, and Llewellyn Thompson, among others—

signify the power that their exclusive "family" wields over human-ity. In articulating their names and reconfiguring them in the context of his act, Bruce points out the reality of the exclusivity of nuclear power: it is a divisive political force not a communal force like the primitive fear released by his cry.[9]

Similar to Bruce, Nick Shay realizes the power of language, but he is a negative theologian not an apocalyptic prophet in the Old Testament tradition. Talking with Donna about his reading of *The Cloud of Unknowing*, he speculates on the connection between lan-guage and God: "Instead we cherish [God's] negation. . . . And we try to develop a naked intent that fixes us to the idea of God. *The Cloud* recommends that we develop this intent around a single word" (295). For Nick, God is a secret that we cannot know posi-tively. He says to Donna that he uses *"Todo y nada,"* a phrase from John of the Cross, to focus his intent on God and argues that "sex is the one secret we have that approximates an exalted state . . . that we share" (297). Nick's ritualizing of sex reflects Eliot's mythic vision in *The Waste Land*, but DeLillo denounces his hero's mystical theory. Indeed Nick is about to have an affair with a married woman who is attending a sexuality seminar for swingers, and Donna herself tells him before they make love that "Sex is not so secret anymore. The secret is out" (297). This is spring 1978, after all, and the scene's true power comes when Nick lets his own se-cret out for the first time in the novel, telling Donna that when he was seventeen he shot and killed George the Waiter. Here, DeLillo indicates that language can focus attention on God and bring out the past from the buried and secret "underworld" of history and human memory.

DeLillo then conceives of burial differently from Eliot. Whereas Eliot considers burial as a metaphor for a nihilistic humanity that is neither willing nor able to act with religious conviction, DeLillo thinks of it in terms of concealment. For DeLillo, in the manner of Martin Heidegger, truth remains concealed until the work of art reveals it.[10] This is why the novel's "backward" structure is so im-portant to DeLillo's theory of language and art. As the novel's nar-rative moves into the past, the characters offer their own narratives of the secret events that the reader encounters "first-hand" later in the novel. For example, as we have just seen, Nick reveals to Donna in 1978 a secret that the reader eventually experiences in its forma-tion later in the novel when DeLillo narrates it as a story in his sec-tion on the Bronx in the 1950s. DeLillo's narrative method in

Underworld ultimately demonstrates how language and art irreducibly participate in history. It also speaks of the redemptive power of aesthetic experience, showing how the past becomes meaningful and true when the individual uses language and art to interpret personal and historical experience.

WASTE, ASCETICISM, AND THE MEANING OF PEACE

Eliot concludes *The Waste Land* with the redemptive rain not having reached the parched land and his speaker "Fishing, with the arid plain behind [him]" (l. 425). In *From Ritual to Romance* Weston cites war, the Fisher King's sexual impotency, and the grail knight's failure to inquire into the Fisher King's ailment as the three causes of the waste land (21). Eliot's waste land remains unredeemed at the conclusion of his poem because his speaker neither asks the grail knight's question when he reaches the chapel nor initiates a religious sexual relationship. The speaker then becomes an ascetic, fishing for meaning among the chaotic fragments of modern history. In so doing he propounds a moral vision taken from Hindu mythology. Near the conclusion of the poem the divine thunder pronounces the syllable "DA," which the speaker interprets as three words: "Datta, Dayadhvam, and Damyata" (l. 433). These words translate as three moral commandments: give, sympathize, and control. Earlier in the poem the young man carbuncular does not heed these commandments when he and the typist have sex. But, by presenting them after his depiction of humanity's nihilistic sexual practices, Eliot enunciates their aesthetic origin in mythology. Indeed they have no inherent foundation in humanity's consciousness; rather they are constructs that make existence possible. Commenting on "Datta," or give, Eliot's speaker stresses the pragmatic nature of this mythic construct: "By this, and this only, we have existed" (l. 406).

At the conclusion of the poem the moral commandments combine with Eliot's other mythic references to reaffirm the chaotic nature of modern historical experience. Eliot ironically uses the word "Shantih"—which means "The Peace which passeth understanding"—to conclude the poem, as well as to confirm the fragmentary nature of modern history. He leaves his reader stumbling for meaning among the fragments of mythic texts from which he constructs his poem, just as humanity strives for coherency in the chaos of contemporary history. For Eliot then peace does not exist in modernity. According to him the modern individual is an ascetic like the Fisher King, struggling for meaning in a desert of nihilism. Ultimately, in contrasting the religious eras studied by Weston and Frazer to the modern world, Eliot exposes modern nihilism and proposes mythology as an aesthetic and moral construct that upholds Nietzsche's famous dictum from *The Will to Power* that "We possess art lest we perish of the truth."

DeLillo also concludes his work with the word "Peace," but he does not share Eliot's nihilism. This is because he posits language and art as ways in which humanity can redeem historical experience. Like Eliot's speaker at the end of *The Waste Land* DeLillo's heroes Nick Shay and Klara Sax are desert ascetics. In contrast to Eliot's speaker, however, they linguistically and artistically strive to redeem the waste land they inhabit. DeLillo fashions Nick as an ascetic who contemplates America's culture of waste from atop a bronze office tower in the desert city of Phoenix, Arizona. Nick's contemplation centers on words. Like Stephen Dedalus in Joyce's *A Portrait of the Artist as a Young Man*, Nick is trained by the Jesuits to appreciate the power of language.[11] Nick's mentor Father Paulus discusses "intense actions" and "a persevering will" as means of combating "velleity" (539), the modern sickness that plagues Eliot's *Waste Land*. Later in the conversation he dismisses his discussion for its abstract nature and says that Nick would "be better served looking at [his] shoe and naming the parts" (542). Nick learns from Father Paulus that knowing words allows one to investigate "[q]uotidian things" (542)—that is, commonplace things that one tends to overlook. As one of DeLillo's "Church Fathers of waste" (102), Nick practices what he learns from Father Paulus, revealing in narrative language the universality of waste, a "quotidian thing" (88) that most people overlook. Of course Nick cannot use language to account for all the "second meanings and deeper connections" (88) that contribute to waste's universality, and, like the author of *The Cloud of Unknowing*, his devotion to the object of his contemplation ultimately cannot be expressed in words. Indeed, discussing the ritualistic care with which he and his family handle their trash, he says: "There is no language I might formulate that could overstate the diligence we brought to these tasks" (103).

As Klara Sax, DeLillo's other great desert ascetic, tells a French reporter, the atomic bomb is another piece of waste that humanity cannot name: "You can't name it. It's too big or evil or outside your experience. It's also shit because it's garbage, it's waste material" (77). Klara goes to the Arizona desert to lead an artistic project that aspires to reinvent the bombers that carried these unnamable waste materials during the Cold War. She says that in repainting the bombers and configuring them in the Arizona desert, she and her staff express a "survival instinct . . . a graffiti instinct—to trespass and declare ourselves, show who we are" (77). For Klara and DeLillo, art is an assertion of freedom, a way in which humanity can reject and survive an American culture whose mass-market capitalism and weapons of mass destruction threaten individualism and human life.

Considering the extent to which DeLillo focuses on language in Nick's narrative, it is not surprising that he points out the relationship between art and language in his section on Klara's project. One of the bombers on which Klara works is the same Long Tall Sally in which Louis T. Bakey served in Vietnam. Klara refuses to paint over the name as it appears on the nose because it signifies "somebody's hometown girl. . . . somebody's first love. . . . an individual life" and functions as a "sign against death" (78). Klara's refusal indicates DeLillo's understanding of the sacred role of art and language in preserving and revealing individual human lives. Art and language, according to DeLillo, rescue individual lives from the waste of history.

Just as DeLillo believes in the redemptive power of art and language, he also upholds the redemptive power of aesthetic experience. From a hot-air balloon Nick and Marian Shay observe Klara's 230 airplanes lined up on the desert floor. After seeing Klara's piece, Marian asserts that she "can never look at a painting the same way again," and Nick responds that he "can never look at an airplane" (126). Through this conversation, DeLillo proposes that the work of art can forever transform one's perception of art and the commodities of America's waste culture. But, more important, Klara's art affects the way in which Nick and Marian perceive phenomenological reality. Nick says that after their aesthetic experience, "Everything [they] saw was ominous and shining, tense with the beauty of things that are normally unseen, even the cars gone to canker and rust" (126). Klara's art, like Father Paulus' language, reveals the hidden beauty of quotidian phenomena, among which Nick includes the cars that are decaying into waste. By later describing Klara's aesthetic response to the Watts Towers—another work of art constructed out of refuse—DeLillo offers a possible explanation of the inspiration for her desert project, noting how for her the Towers signify freedom: "She looked up through the struts of the tallest tower. Such a splendid independence [the artist, Sabato Rodia] was gifted with, or likely fought for" (492). In providing garbage with a new aesthetic form, DeLillo suggests that the artist works in a continuum with other artists who also represent the persistence of humanity's struggle for freedom.

DeLillo equates this struggle for freedom with peace. Like Eliot in *The Waste Land*, he concludes *Underworld* with the word "Peace." His conception of peace, however, is not ironic but hopeful. His preceding discussion of Sister Edgar's resurrection in cyberspace considers the universality of the World Wide Web. For DeLillo, the Web is similar to the garbage dump because it is a place where everything is connected and where eternal life is possible. But, according to DeLillo, peace ultimately does not exist in the Web's universality; rather, the Web imprisons the individual in a system in which "[t]here's the perennial threat of virus" (825), just as during the Cold War the threat of nuclear annihilation plagued the individual. In opposition to the paranoia and imprisonment wrought by the Web's universality, DeLillo proposes language. He describes the word "Peace" as it appears on a computer screen, noting how it becomes "a thing in the world, taking all its meanings, its sense of serenities and contentments out into the streets somehow, its whisper of reconciliation" (827). Words, according to DeLillo, have both the power to reconcile and to reveal: just as they universalize phenomena in the peace of reconciliation, they reveal their individual aspects. For example, DeLillo describes the phenomenology of some of the quotidian things on the writer's desk, including "the curl of the braided wick . . . and the yellow of the yellow of the pencils" (827). For DeLillo then peace resides in language and in the power of works or art to bond individual lives and distinct phenomena in the universality of their individualities.

CONCLUDING SPECULATIONS

In many ways Eliot's modernist *Waste Land* anticipates much postmodernist thought. His notion that morality is an aesthetic or linguistic construct resembles Nietzsche's theories in *On the Genealogy of Morals* and *The Will to Power*, two texts that influence the

142					PAUL GLEASON

thinking of key postmodernist figures such as Michel Foucault. Like Foucault, whose philosophy risks simplifying art and other cultural productions so that they only function as expressions of power, Eliot's *Waste Land* posits art as a futile practice. Indeed art becomes pointless when it merely indicates nihilism without seeking to overcome it.

In *Underworld* DeLillo attempts to redeem art from nihilism. Like Baudrillard and Jameson, he holds that postmodernism is a cultural condition determined by mass-market capitalism. Moreover, he understands the phenomenology of this condition in terms of waste. The artists of *Underworld*—particularly Lenny Bruce, Eisenstein, Klara Sax—and DeLillo himself combat this cultural condition. In the manner of Shelley and Camus, they rebel against the society in which they live. They reject twentieth-century waste culture, redeeming history by alluding to the individuals who struggle against its tyranny. As Martin Amis remarked in his review of *Mao II*, DeLillo "is an exemplary postmodernist" who "is also pointing somewhere beyond" by writing "about the new reality—realistically." This suggests the extent to which DeLillo remains rooted in postmodern reality while simultaneously attempting to differentiate himself from postmodern writers. DeLillo's new realism in *Underworld* considers the ways in which the artist responds to an America whose waste culture undermines human freedom. It is a realism of redemption and hope.

Notes

1. Tom LeClair, David Wiegand, and Philip Nel have all briefly noted the presence of *The Waste Land* in *Underworld*, but none of them has commented extensively on the implications of DeLillo's references to Eliot's poem. See Tom LeClair, "An Underhistory of Mid-Century America"; David Wiegand, "We Are What We Waste," *San Francisco Chronicle*; and Philip Nel, "'A Small Incisive Shock': Modern Forms, Postmodern Politics, and the Role of the Avant-Garde in *Underworld*," 739.

2. In "Notes on *The Waste Land*" Eliot expresses his debt to *From Ritual to Romance*, stating that "the plan and a good deal of the incidental symbolism of [*The Waste Land*] were suggested by [it]" (68).

3. John B. Vickery, *The Literary Impact of "The Golden Bough*," 251.

4. See the opening lines of "The Fire Sermon," the third section of *The Waste Land*, 58.

5. Eliot clearly expresses the mechanistic nature of the sex. As the young man carbuncular departs, having "Bestow[ed] one final patronising kiss" (l. 247), the

typist is "Hardly aware of her departed lover" (l. 250) and "smooths her hair with automatic hand / And puts a record on the gramophone" (ll. 255–56).

6. Eisenstein's bisexuality parallels the bisexuality of another artist, the graffitist Moonman 157, a narrative of whom appears in the same chapter of *Underworld*.

7. See Ovid's *Metamorphoses*, Eliot's source for his presentation of Tiresias in *The Waste Land*, particularly 94–95.

8. Here I agree with Philip Nel, who argues that "DeLillo's work hits the pause, freezes the frame, not to efface the material world but to challenge us to reconnect to it, to remind us of what came before and what will come after— especially if this reminder makes us uneasy" (744).

9. For DeLillo the divisive force of the atomic bomb is emblematic of America's political turmoil in the 1950s and 1960s. In the same part of *Underworld* in which Bruce's sermons appear, DeLillo also writes about the national division caused by the civil rights movement and by the Vietnam conflict.

10. I do not have the space to provide a lengthy explication of Heidegger's theory of art as the revelation of concealed truth. See "The Origin of the Work of Art," in *Basic Writings*, 143–212. Simply put, Heidegger argues that art does not indicate truth as a monolithic and eternal standard but grants insight into the existential reality of a historical people.

11. The scene in *Underworld* in which Father Paulus questions Nick about the names of the different parts of a shoe (536–43) recalls the scene in *A Portrait* in which Stephen and the dean discuss the meaning of the words "tundish" and "funnel" (185–90).

The Unmaking of History: Baseball, Cold War, and *Underworld*

Kathleen Fitzpatrick

> It is true that once the substitute Brooklyn pitcher, Ralph
> Branca, whose mere presence in the game seems not amenable
> to narrative explanation . . . released the ball, and once the fifth
> New York batter, Bobby Thomson, began his swing of the bat,
> a combination of a few special cases (mainly ballistic) of the
> general laws of motion with the National League ground rules
> on home runs suffices strictly to entail that Thomson hit a home
> run. It is hard, however, to envision the combination of condi-
> tions and laws that would strictly entail a decisive precondition
> of that home run: to wit, that Thomson decided to swing at
> Branca's pitch in the first place.
>
> —J. H. Hexter

> It takes a great deal of history to produce a little literature.
>
> —Henry James

IN 1968 J. H. HEXTER APPROPRIATED THE NEW YORK GIANTS' MIRACULOUS
1951 National League pennant victory as a historical event through
which he could explore several basic principles of historiography.
The resulting article, "The Rhetoric of History," has since achieved
classic status among postmodern historians whose work draws
upon Hexter's conclusion that history is built not simply of facts
but of narratives.[1] By arguing that the full communication of one's
knowledge about history requires use of a nonscientific, and even
metaphoric, language, as well as a rhetoric that owes much to
storytelling, Hexter anticipated the reconsideration of the practice
of historiography by poststructuralist theorists from Jacques Der-
rida to Linda Hutcheon. Far from positing the writing of history
as a pseudoscientific, objective communication of facts and figures,
Hexter instead uses the example of the Giants' win over the Brook-

lyn Dodgers to unearth the inevitably subjective impulses behind all historical study:

> The original question, "How did it come about that . . . ?", has become the more amorphous "Tell me (or let me find out) more about. . . ." The demand is no longer for further *explanation*. A reasonably full explanation is presumably already in hand. That explanation itself has led reader and writer of history alike to shift the ground of their interest. Because of it they have become aware that they have stumbled onto one of the great events in baseball history, the event that culminated in Bobby Thomson's home run—the equivalent (in its sphere) of the defeat of the Armada, the battle of Stalingrad, the Normandy landings. What they want under these circumstances is not more or fuller explanation; what they want is confrontation with the riches of the event itself, a sense of vicarious participation in a great happening, the satisfaction of understanding what those great moments were like for the ordinarily cool Russ Hodges, Giant radio announcer, who, as the ball arched from Thomson's bat into the stands, went berserk and screamed into the microphone, "The Giants win the pennant! *The Giants win the pennant!* THE GIANTS WIN THE PENNANT!" And what those moments were like for those who saw what he saw and for those who heard him. (42–43 italics Hexter's)

The best means by which one can evoke this "sense of vicarious participation" is, Hexter argues, narrative; only in telling stories about the past can the historiographer move beyond the facts and figures of the game's statistics to the announcer's hoarse screams, the maddening roar of the crowd, and the shower of paper raining down over the left-field wall.

Hexter's choice of the Shot Heard 'Round the World as the moment from which to build his inquiry into the historical effectivity of narrative should come as little surprise to readers of Don De-Lillo. The 1992 publication of "Pafko at the Wall" produced much excited discussion among DeLillo's readers about the interrelationships of baseball and history. This novella brings its readers inside the Giants' 1951 pennant win by presenting the game from a number of different perspectives: that of Russ Hodges, of course, calling the game from the chaotic press box; but also that of Frank Sinatra, Jackie Gleason, Toots Shor, and J. Edgar Hoover, watching the game from Leo Durocher's box seats; and that of Cotter Martin, an African-American teenager watching illicitly (he has both skipped school and jumped the turnstile[2]) from the bleachers. From these various perspectives we are able to piece together an understanding of the cultural value of this moment, of what DeLillo describes as "another kind of history," a memory with "protective power" (70). And thus, on first reading, it would appear that DeLillo's project in "Pafko" ·is precisely that which Hexter describes, a move from explanation to vicarious participation. But as John N. Duvall points out (292–95), the effect of the baseball game as DeLillo writes it is to steal focus from that much more looming event that takes place in the background, outside the consciousness of everyone present except Hoover: the second Soviet atomic test blast. And, in fact, the rest of the novel *Underworld*, of which "Pafko at the Wall" was mere prologue, provoked disappointment in a number of sport-literature critics when it turned out that the narrative in its entirety was not about baseball after all, but instead about the Cold War that the game had hidden.[3] Hexter's comparison then of Thomson's home run with "the defeat of the Armada, the battle of Stalingrad, the Normandy landings" highlights not simply the power that narratives of history might reveal, but also what their peculiar focus might leave out.

In this essay I will explore *Underworld*'s interplay between baseball and history, suggesting that the novel's relationships to both the game and the Cold War reveal a move beyond the self-reflexive logic of postmodernity—in which history is its writing—and into a new logic of unmaking. In this new logic history's textuality is called into question, as traces of the past are seen to conceal as much as they reveal about the workings of history; these traces must be dismantled in order for history to be understood. This logic of unmaking, I will further argue, produces a dramatically altered relationship between the individual and the mythic, a concept that once indicated the sacred, a higher truth, but now instead connotes an untruth—a shift that bears profound consequences for the conception of the self.

HISTORY, MYTHOLOGY, NARRATIVE

The interconnections of baseball and history have long surfaced in sports fiction, ranging from imaginative reconsiderations of historic incidents (as in W. P. Kinsella's *Shoeless Joe*), to narratives that explore the interconnections of past and present (Kinsella's *Iowa Baseball Confederacy*; William Kennedy's *Ironweed*), to explorations of the mythic underpinnings of accounts of both games and times past (Bernard Malamud's *The Natural*). Robert Coover's *The Universal Baseball Association, Inc., J. Henry Waugh, Prop.* most explicitly takes on the relationship between baseball's overwhelming production of text—in the form of scorecards, statistics, game reports, league analyses, newspaper articles and columns, and so on—and the production of history itself. In this novel history does not merely exist or reside in textual form but is rather *brought into being* by text itself. Henry's role as "auditor" (26) for the UBA, as he quite cannily describes it to the B-girl he has brought home, extends from statistical record-keeping to the more explicitly historical work of keeping "a running journalization of the activity, posting of it all into permanent record books, and I help them with basic problems of burden distribution, remarshaling of assets, graphing fluctuations. Politics, too. Elections. Team captains. Club presidents. And every four years, the Association elects a Chancellor, and I have to keep an eye on that" (27). This work that Henry describes, maintaining the "official archives" (55) of the UBA—otherwise known as the Book[4]—reveals the way that written records create history, sliding as he does from numbers to texts to politics, with each seeming to lead automatically to the next. Henry takes obvious pleasure in pondering the interconnections of his records and the history that they create, teasing his friend Lou with his veiled insights:

> At 4:34 on a wet November afternoon, Lou Engel boarded a city bus and spilled water from his hat brim on a man's newspaper. Is that history?
> "I . . . I dunno," stammered Lou, reddening before the sudden distrustful scowl of the man with the newspaper. "I (wheeze) guess so."
> "Who's writing it down?" Henry demanded. (50)

Henry's causality here is clear—present actions become history by being written down. The writer alters worlds. Henry's texts ultimately produce political factions, religious rituals, infighting, death. Hexter's concern then with the "rhetoric of history" becomes crucial as the form that history takes will largely be determined by the manner in which it is recorded.

This concern resurfaces in very different form in *Underworld*; the differences between Coover's treatment of the production of history and DeLillo's reveal something of a paradigm shift in the post-

Cold War period. Echoing Hexter's title and coincident with the fall, 1997, release of *Underworld*, DeLillo produced a brief article entitled "The Power of History." This article works most plainly to illuminate the relationship, for DeLillo, between his novel's uses of history and its forays into the imagination. In the article DeLillo describes two contradictory senses of history's power with regard to narrative. The first is the power of history to draw the novelist in, to give him access to material larger than himself: "A fiction writer feels the nearly palpable lure of large events and it can make him want to enter the narrative." History can thus "reinvigorate the senses," giving the novelist a "subject of strong and absorbing proportions." On the other hand, history's power over narrative comes to be perceived as a trap, and one from which only the novelist's use of imaginative language can help the reader escape: "Language lives in everything it touches and can be an agent of redemption, the thing that delivers us, paradoxically, from history's flat, thin, tight and relentless designs, its arrangement of stark pages, and that allows us to find an unconstraining otherness, a free veer from time and place and fate." The novelist's rhetoric, far from *creating* history, instead helps the reader escape history.

A fundamental contradiction lingers then in DeLillo's dual conception of history as something that should be sought out and as something that must be escaped; history as inspiration and history as trap. In his essay DeLillo distinguishes two distinct kinds of history, kinds that may perhaps be understood as differences in historical medium:

> Newsreel footage of Bobby Thomson's home run resembles something of World War I vintage. But the shakier and fuzzier the picture, the more it lays a claim to permanence. And the voice of the announcer, Russ Hodges, who did the rapturous radio account of the game's final moments, is beautifully isolated in time—not subject to the debasing process of frantic repetition that exhausts a contemporary event before it has rounded into coherence.

History, here again created by the records baseball leaves behind, is for DeLillo at its purest, its most "permanent," when those records are least complete; historical significance here seems to vary inversely with picture quality. The problematic nature of history, history as trap, arises when the picture becomes too clear, when the historical event and its recorded traces become most identical.

These recorded traces are the "flat, thin, tight and relentless designs" from which the novelist hopes to deliver us—from history reified into photographic, or filmic, or otherwise concrete form.

DeLillo's concern with the damage that reification works upon history echoes Baudrillard in "History, a Retro Scenario": "Photography and cinema contributed in large part to the secularization of history, to fixing it in its visible, 'objective' form at the expense of the myths that once traversed it" (48). The previously mythical stature of history has been transformed by these technologies of ostensible preservation into something fixed, into DeLillo's "flat, thin, tight and relentless designs." But, in order to read this "secularization" as a genuine "expense," one must have a very specific understanding of the nature of the mythic. Myth functions here not as Barthes's ideological structure nor as Benjamin's potentially fascistic aura but rather as a narrative repository for the sacred, for the transhistorical. The secularizing force of visual media, in other words, by defusing history's myths, demotes it from the teleological to the momentary, from the universal to the quotidian. This transformation, according to Baudrillard (a judgment with which DeLillo seems to concur) bears great consequences for the novel: "The age of history, if one can call it that, is also the age of the novel. It is this *fabulous* character, the mythical energy of an event or of a narrative, that today seems to be increasingly lost" (47 italics Baudrillard's). That mythical energy is still clearly at work in Coover's *Universal Baseball Association*, and thus its loss cannot be easily read as a symptom of the fragmentation of the experimental postmodern novel. In fact the subterranean connections between mythology and Coover's metafictional strategies bear this out; as Deeanne Westbrook points out, "mythology" derives from two related roots, *mythos*, "word," and *logos*, "word" (5). Mythology may thus be thought of as words about words and so is always operating at the same metadiscursive level as metafiction. The loss of "mythical energy" in narrative then cannot be casually attributed to postmodernist experimentation or disaffection; at issue is a much deeper, later reassessment of myth, of history, and of narrative itself, a reassessment that lies at the heart of *Underworld*.

Returning then to my earlier suggestion that *Underworld* is, on the whole, not about baseball but rather about the history of the Cold War that begins in the background of the Giants' victory: this argument, although perhaps generally accurate, overlooks two important facts about the book. First, that the Cold War's history is told not forward in time but backward, retracing a path from the post-Soviet 1990s to the Russian H-bomb tests in 1951. And second, that although this may not be a story about baseball, it is in fact a story about *a baseball*, the ball with which Bobby Thomson hit the Shot Heard 'Round the World. The novel's structural inversions reveal a need to free the narrative from the "objective" forms of a demythologized history. Similarly, a breakdown in baseball's own mythic nature—a mythicity that, as Deeanne Westbrook points out, is inherent in the game itself[5]—has similarly secularized it, fixing the game's meaning in its physical objects. These objects, from the piles of memorabilia in a New York basement collector's shop, to Marvin Lundy's replica of the Polo Grounds scoreboard, to the baseball itself, condense and reify the game's lore into something with exchange value rather than mythical value. Russ Hodges thinks of such a souvenir baseball as "a priceless thing somehow, a thing that seems to recapitulate the whole history of the game every time it is thrown or hit or touched" (26). This particular baseball does indeed retain some sentimental or emotional value for its owners, but that value degrades over its lifespan until it reaches Nick Shay, who claims that he "didn't buy the object for the glory and drama attached to it. It's not about Thomson hitting the homer. It's about Branca making the pitch. It's all about losing" (97). What history of the game still inheres in "the object" is a history of loss; its sentimental value has become inextricably entangled with—and, one might argue, degraded by—exchange value. This baseball is no longer priceless, as Russ Hodges would have thought, as it is repeatedly bought and sold; it is *not* thrown or hit, but rather removed from the game altogether.

If myth has been replaced by commerce, a profound loss that demonstrates a fundamental change in American culture, the change is irrevocably tied to the Cold War itself. The connection of the sport's commodification and postwar politics is made most evident in the photographic remnants of the Prologue's mythical showdown between Branca and Thomson; the pair appear in every era the novel encounters, photographed with each successive president, the photos becoming more and more stock. Each Cold War president is driven to keep alive the country's myths—and yet, as Baudrillard suggests, in rendering these myths photographically concrete, their "mythic energy" is erased. Thus, the novel's structural inversions: the transformation of American culture—and American history—into the objects and images it has left behind, objects and images devoid of the mythic, demands that historiography become less a straight-forward telling of the story of history than a "counterhistory,"[6] an archeological project, breaking down the monoliths that the secularization (or media-driven reification) of history has created. In this sense *Underworld* is less a history than a reevaluation, not simply telling the story of the Cold War but, in some fundamental sense, untelling it.

Underworld is thus a two-sided novel. On the one hand, in its inextricable interconnections of narrative and history, the novel clearly becomes part of the literary genre Linda Hutcheon has famously described as "historiographic metafiction." This genre, which includes novels such as *Ragtime, V., The Public Burning, Midnight's Children*, and *Slaughterhouse-Five*, weaves together historical fact and fictional imagination, purposefully blurring the line between the two. As Hutcheon argues, "historiographic metafiction self-consciously reminds us that, while events did take place in the real empirical past, we name and constitute those events as historical facts by selection and narrative positioning. And, even more basically, we only know of those past events through their discursive inscription, through their traces in the present" (97). Historiographic metafiction suggests then that the past can be known through its historical traces; *Underworld*, by its interactions with those traces, similarly comments on the natures of both history and narrative. As I have already suggested, however, metafiction requires a certain continuing faith in the power of myth and particularly in the mythical power of history. In *Underworld* myth is lost; the novel instead acts to dismantle the genre of historiographic metafiction and its preconceptions, working not to create the past out of its narratives but instead to excavate and deconstruct the traces a reified history has left in the present. In so doing, the novel undermines all narrative processes, both the realist and the metafictional. Although Hutcheon claims for historiographic metafiction the "deliberate contamination of the historical with didactic and situational discursive elements, thereby challenging the implied assumptions of historical statements: objectivity, neutrality, impersonality, and transparency of representation" (92), DeLillo performs the same kind of contamination-and-challenging of *narrative* representation, calling the possibility of the accurate telling of any story into question.

This challenge to narrative leads to the novel's numerous structural and thematic reversals and inversions. About a third of the

way through *Underworld*, Nick Shay and Big Sims, his mentor in
the world of waste management, visit a landfill project in the company of Jesse Detwiler, a "garbage archaeologist" who had recently addressed their industry convention. Staring out at the
crater being filled with the detritus of Western civilization, Detwiler falls into what the narrator refers to as a sort of "talk-show"
patter, giving them his polished interpretation of the spectacle before them:

> Civilization did not rise and flourish as men hammered out hunting
> scenes on bronze gates and whispered philosophy under the stars,
> with garbage as a noisome offshoot, swept away and forgotten. No,
> garbage rose first, inciting people to build a civilization in response, in
> self-defense. (287)

The inversion implied in this theory—"Garbage comes first, then
we build a system to deal with it," as Detwiler later says (288)—is
one of the novel's central tropes. DeLillo, by pointing to garbage's
primacy, powerfully reverses our thinking about the relationship
between civilization and waste in our culture, highlighting the
dozens of instances of waste in the novel; waste both recyclable
and hazardous; organic, inorganic, and human. In this waste, and
particularly in its nuclear manifestations, we see that the mythic
structures of the Cold War itself—the epic battle between good and
evil—have crumbled in its aftermath, revealing the hidden costs of
maintaining those structures. In this sense, in the post-Cold War
period, the novel argues that the myths with which we protect ourselves—the myth of civilization's primacy, the myth of democra-
cy's triumph—are no longer the repositories of the sacred, the
transhistorical, but instead the ideological. Mythology has become
identical with reification; myths, or narratives, are all fated to be
lies. Through this repudiation of both myth and narrative, the
novel calls our attention to a powerful reconception of the self and
reevaluation of American individualism in the post-Cold War era.
The fate of the individual, as well as that of the narrative that must
be simultaneously told and untold, can be most clearly explored
through the character of Nick Shay.

UNMAKING

Timothy Morris has argued that "baseball fiction, and more generally the whole culture of baseball, is about assimilation to an

American way of life" (3); baseball fiction is also overwhelmingly about self-making, about the formation of the American individual. *Underworld*'s central plot line, that revolving around Nick Shay, bears much in common with this traditional narrative, except of course that the story is told backwards, with each successive episode receding in time, revealing a bit more of the submerged content of the episodes that have gone before. The only story told forward in time is the story of the baseball itself, the physical manifestation of the transformation of the mythic from the sacred to the reified. These two narratives are inextricably linked, not merely because Nick Shay comes to own the baseball but because the history of each, like that of the Cold War, is called into question. Each of these narratives begins in a moment of loss, and each becomes so reified throughout the novel that the work of understanding both personal and cultural history becomes, of necessity, an archaeological project, excavating the present in order to uncover the past. As the baseball's own archaeologist, the obsessive collector determined to learn the secret of its origins, thinks, "Strange how he was compiling a record of the object's recent forward motion while simultaneously tracking it backwards to the distant past" (318). This is precisely the path that DeLillo follows in exploring Nick Shay's character, introducing him at present, in the early 1990s, before tracking him backward to the early 1950s and the long-buried moment of destruction that changed his life.

This inversion of traditional narrative structures and the reversal of our thinking about civilization and waste come together in *Underworld* to produce a unified aesthetic of decomposition, of degradation, an aesthetic we come to suspect was always inherent in the Cold War itself, if buried by its mythology. As Ihab Hassan has noted, theories of postmodernism are surrounded by a discourse of unmaking: "decreation, disintegration, deconstruction, decenterment, difference, discontinuity, disjunction, disappearance, decomposition, de-definition, demystification, detotalization, delegitimization" (282). These terms are made literal throughout *Underworld*, as the novel's reversals allow us to witness both the decomposition of American culture into the garbage upon which it is founded and the regression of Nick Shay into genuine selfhood before that self was transformed into mythology.

Even the baseball story, ostensibly told in a traditional beginning-to-end structure, is undermined by that decay; in fact, that decay begins in the background of the game itself. As a torrent of

paper rains down onto the field from the upper deck in celebration
of the Giants' victory, a reproduction of Bruegel's *The Triumph of
Death*, ironically reproduced within the pages of *Life* magazine,
falls right onto J. Edgar Hoover's shoulder. The paper floating
down all around, the torrent of residues from purses and wallets
and bags, is described as "happy garbage now, the fans' intimate
wish to be connected to the event, unendably, in the form of pocket
litter, personal waste, a thing that carries a shadow identity" (45).
But this is only half of the story. Although the release of this cloud
of personal waste seems somehow a *creative* force—as Russ Hodges
thinks once it is all over, "this is another kind of history. He thinks
they will carry something out of here that joins them all in a rare
way, that binds them to a memory with protective power" (59)—
the happiness of this garbage, the protective nature of this history,
comes at the desperate cost of ignoring the other waste being released simultaneously, half a world away: the second Soviet atomic
test explosion. Only Edgar, *Life* and *Death* simultaneously in his
hands, sees both sides of the equation:

> The meatblood colors and the massed bodies, this is a census-taking of
> awful ways to die. He looks at the flaring sky in the deep distance out
> beyond the headlands on the left-hand page—Death elsewhere, Con-
> flagration in many places, Terror universal, the crows, the ravens in si-
> lent glide, the raven perched on the white nag's rump, black and white
> forever, and he thinks of a lonely tower standing on the Kazakh Test
> Site, the tower armed with the bomb, and he can almost hear the wind
> blowing across the Central Asian steppes, out where the enemy lives in
> long coats and fur caps, speaking that old weighted language of theirs,
> liturgical and grave. What secret history are they writing? There is the
> secret of the bomb and there are the secrets the bomb inspires, things
> even the Director cannot guess—a man whose own sequestered heart
> holds every festering secret in the Western world—because these plots
> are only now evolving. This is what he knows, that the genius of the
> bomb is printed not only in its physics of particles and rays but in the
> occasion it creates for new secrets. For every atmospheric blast, every
> glimpse we get of the bared force of nature, that weird peeled eyeball
> exploding over the desert—for every one of these he reckons a hundred
> plots go underground, to spawn and skein. (50–51)

The secret history being written in this blast is of course that of the
Cold War, a history based upon an inverted logic of death-in-life,
of loss-in-victory. As we have seen, Nick Shay much later describes

the triumphal baseball as being "all about losing"; the loss is inscribed in the home run itself. Thus, the Shot Heard 'Round the World, whether Thomson's homer, the Soviet test explosion, or Nick Shay's own shot, the dark basement room and the man he inadvertently kills—these three blasts, in announcing the opening of the Cold War, introduce a logic of destruction into American life. Only by working backward from the end result, by excavating the hundreds of plots gone underground, can the novel rescue history from its inevitable decay.

This emphasis on narrative reversal brings with it some moments of sickening revelation. There is a minor character in *Underworld* we first meet as a nuclear weapons test official, and a hundred pages later we are profoundly unnerved to glimpse during his masturbatory adolescence (403, 514). The seriousness of adulthood, particularly of a life devoted to defense work, is undermined by the change of direction, which reveals the teenage pornographic fantasies that always underwrite adult fantasies of destruction. Through the discomfort of this particular narrative's inversion, the novel uncovers the ways that Cold War mythology has fundamentally damaged its characters' self-perceptions. In accepting—or worse, valorizing—the logic of destruction, all of *Underworld*'s lives come to be, like the baseball, about losing. The only legitimate life-narrative that the novel can take on appears to be an antibildungsroman, a story of self-unmaking, breaking down the logic of destruction to find the self that preexists the bomb. Just as Jesse Detwiler debunks the myth of the primacy of civilization, revealing the invention of art and culture and philosophy as mere attempts to keep from being overrun by refuse, the novel suggests that the traditional story of self-making is equally mythic. Rather than being made, being self-determined in any sense, the individual is rather unmade, a tissue of lies constructed as a defense against the sludge in which the self is mired.

The only kind of self-making available within the novel is tied to a fundamental corruption, a dishonest reliance upon narratives one knows to be false. As Nick thinks, during spring 1978, not long after having joined the field of waste management,

> I've always been a country of one. There's a certain distance in my makeup, a measured separation like my old man's, I guess, that I've worked at times to reduce, or thought of working, or said the hell with it.

> I like to tell my wife. I say to my wife. I tell her not to give up on me. I tell her there's an Italian word, or a Latin word, that explains every-thing. Then I tell her the word.
>
> She says, What does this explain? And she answers, Nothing.
>
> The word that explains nothing in this case is *lontananza*. Distance or remoteness, sure. But as I use the word, as I interpret it, hard-edged and fine-grained, it's the perfected distance of the gangster, the syndi-cate mobster—the made man. (275)

This emphasis on "madeness" is key to understanding Nick. The early disappearance of his father, a small-time bookie, has been mythologized in Nick's mind, as legend replaces the man who abandoned his wife and two sons with the man hit by the mob for his inability to cover a debt. Nick clings to this self-created legend despite the overpowering evidence to the contrary, despite a known mob figure pointedly telling him:

> "Jimmy was not in a position where he could offend somebody so bad that they would go out of their way to do something. No disrespect but he was penny-ante. He had a very small operation he was running. Made the rounds of the small bettors. Mostly very small these bets. This is what he did. Factory sweepers and so forth. You have to understand. Jimmy was not in a position to be threatened by serious people." (765)

Nick walks away pleased by the made man's concern but ulti-mately unconvinced: "He was grateful for the time, genuinely, but he didn't think he had to accept the logic of the argument. The logic, he decided, did not impress him" (766). The only logic that does impress him, particularly later, after finding himself in a base-ment room with a shotgun in his hand, is destruction's own logic, in which violence must be meaningful rather than random.

After the shooting, in which he has been used as the agent of another man's suicide, Nick obsessively asks himself two ques-tions: "Why would the man say no if it was loaded? But first why would he point the gun at the man's head?" (781). The inverted progression implied by these questions, from secondary concerns to primary, from the role of the "victim" to the role of the self, re-veals the source of Nick's determination to place himself within the cultural mythology of the gangster, who is "made" rather than un-made through killing. In his later life, in the earlier sections of the novel, we have seen this mythology become a joke for Nick, but one he nonetheless expends tremendous amounts of energy cultivating: "They asked where I was from," he says in the early 1990s, "and I replied with a line I sometimes used. I live a quiet life in an unassuming house in a suburb of Phoenix. Pause. Like someone in the Witness Protection Program" (66). Or: "Think of a young man or woman, think of a young woman speaking a few words in a movie gangster's growl. This is something I used to do for pointed comic effect to get things done on time" (87). Despite this comic twist, Nick's reliance on the figure of the gangster nonetheless becomes a crucial part of his personal narrative; thus we can sense the irony involved when Nick tells us, near the beginning of the novel, that

> I lived responsibly in the real. I didn't accept this business of life as a fiction, or whatever Klara Sax had meant when she said that things had become unreal. History was not a matter of missing minutes on the tape. I did not stand helpless before it. . . . I believed that we could know what was happening to us. We were not excluded from our own lives. (82)

Nick's determined play with the mythology of violence, with the logic of destruction, reveals just how far he stands from "the real"; his life has in fact been constructed as a fiction, a narrative, one from which he is largely excluded. Nick's barely sublimated desire for the life of the gangster—the choice of waste management being only one aspect of that desire—is partly an attempt to build a more threatening alter ego, but it is also a desperate stab at rereading the violence in his past as something purposeful rather than random.

In the novel's Epilogue we follow Nick to Kazakhstan, the old Soviet test site, now being used for underground nuclear explosions designed, all too ironically, to rid the world of hazardous waste. Nick begins on the plane to draw the novel's many lines of destruction and disintegration together:

> I tell Viktor there is a curious connection between weapons and waste. I don't know exactly what. He smiles and puts his feet up on the bench, something of a gargoyle squat. He says maybe one is the mystical twin of the other. He likes this idea. He says waste is the devil twin. Because waste is the secret history, the underhistory, the way archaeologists dig out the history of early cultures, every sort of bone heap and broken tool, literally from under the ground. (791)

This is a connection that has been building throughout the novel, inextricably tying the Cold War's logic of destruction to the refuse and decay of American culture: just as Big Sims explains to Nick that "all waste defers to shit" (302), Nick's brother Matt posits that "all technology refers to the bomb" (467). Shit and the bomb come, in *Underworld*, to form a wholly secularized, dehistoricized, demythologized replacement for *Gravity's Rainbow*'s sacred triumvirate of American truths to be found in "shit, money, and the word" (28). The greatest loss in this demolition of the sacred is of course the loss of the word; the linear logic of linguistic communication has been undermined by the inversions the Cold War has produced.

In fact, before adopting the mythology of the gangster, Nick turned first to the word for a means to reconstruct the self he demolished in that basement room. "The minute I entered correction," he has by this point already told us, "I was a convert to the system" (502). Using his time in the correction system, Nick attempts to create a self:

> All that winter I shoveled snow and read books. The lines of print, the alphabetic characters, the strokes of a shovel when I cleared a walk, the linear arrangement of words on a page, the shovel strokes, the rote exercises in school texts, the novels I read, the dictionaries I found in the tiny library, the nature and shape of books, the routine of shovel strokes in deep snow—this was how I began to build an individual. (503)

By the novel's end, however, we have come to understand not only the impossibility of this kind of self-making but also the ways in which the traditional narrative materials of this self-making have themselves been unmade. Linear logic has given way to inversion, divergence, virtuality; text has become hypertext. "The real miracle is the web," Nick finally tells us, "the net, where everybody is everywhere at once" (808). But, the miracle of mystical union that the Web represents is itself described as "[a] fantasy in cyberspace and a way of seeing the other side and a settling of differences that have less to do with gender than with difference itself, all argument, all conflict programmed out" (826). This fantasy, of difference without differences, of union without contact, of place without space, reveals itself—as well as the novel's final invocation of "Peace"—to be another kind of narrative illusion, a new, luminous myth of wastelessness. As Nick theorizes,

> Maybe we feel a reverence for waste, for the redemptive qualities of the things we use and discard. Look how they come back to us, alight with

a kind of brave aging. The windows yield a strong broad desert and enormous sky. The landfill across the road is closed now, jammed to capacity, but gas keeps rising from the great earthen berm, methane, and it produces a wavering across the land and sky that deepens the aura of sacred work. It is like a fable in the writhing air of some ghost civilization, a shimmer of desert ruin. (809–10)

This ghost civilization is, of course, our own, written not in "bronze gates and whispered philosophy" (287) but in waste.

For J. H. Hexter there was liberation in arguing that history is composed not simply of facts but of narratives. In *The Universal Baseball Association* those narratives in fact *create* history. In *Underworld* DeLillo acknowledges the interconnections between narratives and history, while pointing out that many of those narratives are lies. The new locus of the sacred is in the landfill. History has been demoted to fable. And baseball? All but forgotten:

This is how I come across the baseball, rearranging books on the shelves. I look at it and squeeze it hard and put it back on the shelf, wedged between a slanted book and a straight-up book, an expensive and beautiful object that I keep half hidden, maybe because I tend to forget why I bought it. Sometimes I know exactly why I bought it and other times I don't, a beautiful thing smudged green near the Spalding trademark and bronzed with nearly half a century of earth and sweat and chemical change, and I put it back and forget it until next time. (809)

This artifact, half-hidden between books—some that might, by a slight stretch of the imagination, be thought of as telling a subset of the truth "straight-up"; others that tell all the truth but tell it slant—carries with it several imperfectly remembered histories. Far from recapitulating the whole history of the game, as Russ Hodges idealistically supposed such a baseball might, this ball is only its material form: green smudge, dirt, sweat, trademark. Buried along with this baseball, in among the jammed bookshelves, are the history of the game, the history of the Cold War, and the history of the individual. The lingering irony, of course, is that DeLillo's project of unmaking history creates new narratives, adding to that jammed bookshelf. But the power of history, as DeLillo reminds us in "The Power of History," is nonetheless given a "free veer from time and place and fate" in its reversal. Only in exhuming history's artifacts, in excavating these half-forgotten traces of the past, in untelling the already-told tales, can history be saved from its own "flat, thin, tight and relentless designs," the "stark pages" that reify myth into ideology.

Notes

An early version of this essay was presented at the 1999 MLA in Chicago. I would like to thank my co-panelists Mark Osteen and Arthur Saltzmann, as well as Timothy Morris and Tim Caron, for their insightful comments and questions, which provided useful contributions to this essay's development.

1. For a deeper exploration of Hexter's argument, as well as his own rhetoric, see Westbrook, 299–300. It should be noted that Hexter uses the term "history" to refer not to the past itself but rather to the disciplinary study of the past, thus inextricably tying history to the writing of history. My uses of this term should similarly evoke not events of the past but accounts of those events.

2. As well as being the only African-American fan present. For a reading of the dynamics of race in "Pafko," see Duvall's analysis.

3. Nonetheless, the readers of *Aethlon* voted *Underworld* number 16 in the journal's list of the 50 most influential sport-literature texts of the twentieth century. See Dewey, "*Aethlon*'s Fifty Most Influential Works Survey," 161–62.

4. A capitalization that carries obvious Christian overtones. For a reading of the novel as religious allegory, see Westbrook, 221–43.

5. See Westbrook: "The mythicity of baseball's texts emerges almost of necessity from a mythicity in the game itself — its rituals and roles, its characters, the tropological nature of its space and time, its 'plot' (the progress and rules of play), its object (to make the circular journey from home to home), its ground (a solid stage in a shifting cosmos), and its groundrules (the principles of order within this [con]text)" (10).

6. See DeLillo in "The Power of History": "Language can be a form of counter-history. The writer wants to construct a language that will be the book's life-giving force. He wants to submit to it. Let language shape the world. Let it break the faith of conventional re-creation." That conventional recreation is the form of mediated, reified history.

Underworld or: How I Learned to Keep Worrying and Live the Bomb

Thomas Myers

Man has, as it were, become a kind of prosthetic God. When he puts on all his auxiliary organs he is truly magnificent; but these organs have not grown on to him and they still give him much trouble at times. . . . Future ages will bring with them new and unimaginably great advances in the field of civilization and will increase man's likeness to God still more. But in the interests of our investigations, we will not forget that present-day man does not feel happy in his Godlike character.

—Sigmund Freud, *Civilization and Its Discontents*

Yes, gentlemen, they are on their way, and no one can bring them back. For the sake of our country and our way of life, I suggest you get the rest of SAC in after them. Otherwise we will be totally destroyed by Red retaliation. My boys will give you the best kind of start, fourteen hundred megatons worth, and you sure as hell won't stop them now. So let's get going; there's no other choice.

—General Jack D. Ripper, *Dr. Strangelove*

But the bombs were not released. I remember Klara Sax talking about the men who flew the strategic bombers as we all stood listening in the long low structure of sectioned concrete. The missiles remained in their rotary launchers. The men came back and the cities were not destroyed.

—Nick Shay, *Underworld*

So listen folks, for here's my thesis.
Peace in the world, or the world in pieces.
—"Old Man Atom," Sons of the Pioneers, 1947

We were born during the boom times, played house down in
the bomb shelter,
Suffered through the wonder years and silence at the dinner
hour.
But once upon a summertime, out behind the old garage,

161

We were buzzing on midnight, Luckys and Rolling Rock,
Thinking we were heroes in our own hometown.
Nothing less than heroes in that old hometown.
   —"Hero in Your Own Hometown," Mary-Chapin Carpenter, 1996

Imagine it. A movie premiere on a cold autumn New York evening early in the new millennium. The setting is Radio City Music Hall, and a giant crowd is present for an advance screening of a film that has been for years the subject of monumental media hype and conjecture. Critics from America and all over the world are in their seats, but most of the audience is composed of native New Yorkers, enthusiasts of American fiction and film who want to see what the two kids from the Bronx have put together. The theater darkens and the sound of knowledgeable, excited voices—the strong, cynical argot of Manhattan—drops to silence.

The Warner Brothers logo appears on the huge Radio City Music Hall screen and then fades to black as a cheerful civil defense ditty from the 1950s begins to play. Fade in to a long shot of contemporary, pastoral American farm country, then a medium shot of a Minuteman missile silo fenced off from languid Midwestern dairy cows and prairie-blown sweet corn. As Bert the Turtle sings, the massive lid of the silo blows off and the camera moves down into the underground tube as steam and the malevolent rumbling of the American missile come from the black hole.

The camera descends to reveal the purposeful tip of the nuclear missile vibrating within the steam, then pulls back out of the silo, which becomes the barrel of a sawed-off shotgun in the hands of young Nick Shay of the Bronx in the early 1950s. As the singing voice continues happily and confidently, the audience sees a close-up of Nick's eyes, his voice saying, "Is it loaded?" A voice off camera says, "No,"—then comes a close-up of George Manza, an odd smile on his face, looking at Nick. The audience sees Nick's eyes again, then a sustained close shot of his finger on the trigger. There is a quick cut back to the silo— American montage—and the camera rushes down the missile silo to reveal the Minuteman at the moment of ignition, then a cut back to Nick's finger pulling the trigger.

There comes a loud explosion—the mixed fury of the shotgun, the missile—and the screen goes to black. The happy 1950s voice offers a final musical exhortation to "Duck and cover" followed by silence. The audience hears crowd noise, then a Bronx street-wise voice say wistfully, "Longing on a large scale is what makes history." As the roar of the crowd rises to impossible levels, the camera fades in to reveal the face of young African-American Cotter Martin in Section 35 of the Polo Grounds on 3 October 1951. The audience hears the radio play-by-play of Russ Hodges in the ninth inning of the Giants-Dodgers game.

The screen goes to black again and in stark white letters comes the title: UNDERWORLD. *Hodges's voice continues as* A FILM BY

STANLEY KUBRICK *appears, then* THE POLO GROUNDS, 1951, *finally the inscription* THE TRIUMPH OF DEATH. *The audience sees the wide-eyed face of Cotter Martin, hears the crack of a bat, sees Cotter's eyes get wider as Hodges shouts, "There's a long drive," then a tighter close-up on Cotter's eyes as the announcer adds, "I believe." The baseball crashes with the sound of an incoming missile, of a shotgun blast, off the green metal stanchion of Section 35. The audience sees a medium shot of skinny Cotter straining and wriggling through bodies to get the ball, a close-up of the ball in his hand, then a long shot as he darts up the stairs, the sacred artifact clutched in his thin fingers, races into the black tunnel, and is gone. As the camera moves into the tunnel after him and the screen fades to black, the audience hears the radio voice of Russ Hodges yell again and again, "The Giants win the pennant! The Giants win the pennant!" Then it also fades into silence, into memory, arching toward the artistic-historical crossroad where fact and fiction meet—in short, into myth . . .*

I<small>F</small> *UNDERWORLD,* DON DELILLO'S EPIC MEDITATION ON FIVE DECADES OF Cold War culture in the United States, ever becomes a movie, Stanley Kubrick, of course, will not be its auteur. Kubrick died on 7 March 1999, two years after DeLillo's novel appeared, and weeks before *Eyes Wide Shut,* his dream-like swan song of obsession, guilt, and dark underground forces, was scheduled for release. But the impossible collaboration teases and intrigues—indeed, tickles the imagination—and what fan of the dark paranoia wing of the postmodern cultural funhouse would not smile in the darkened theater at the final credit SCREENPLAY BY STANLEY KUBRICK AND DON DELILLO? *Eyes Wide Shut,* released when Kubrick's own legend was already, as DeLillo writes in *Underworld,* "falling indelibly into the past" (60), features a hidden society of prominent personages who live in a world of twisted pleasures and ominous imperatives, a privileged secret network of sex and power that the protagonist, Dr. William Harford (Tom Cruise), glimpses, momentarily infiltrates, but never fully understands, even after it inhabits his imagination and threatens his very being. Kubrick had not made a film since 1987, when his hard-edged Vietnam film, *Full Metal Jacket,* appeared, but in 1994, three years before DeLillo's sweeping look backward at a half-century of nuclear paranoia, he rereleased *Dr. Strangelove or: How I Learned to Stop Worrying and Love the Bomb,* his biting satire of Cold War craziness and nuclear apocalypse that many critics and fans thought perhaps his best work. When it was originally released in 1964, America was still recovering from a near-miss in Cuba and a direct hit in Dallas as the quagmire in Vietnam was deepening, and many lauded *Dr. Strangelove* for its black comic vision of Doomsday Machines and MAD-ness (Mutually Assured Destruction) in high places, its Eros/Thanatos mix of hydrogen bombs and "precious bodily fluids." In his 1 March 1964 letter to *The New York Times* cultural historian and critic Lewis Mumford wrote, "The film is the first break in the catatonic cold war trance that has long held our country in its rigid grip." Overall, critics and viewers agreed that Kubrick had got it right, and *Dr. Strangelove* was a true if momentary catharsis of what had been building since the Soviet Union exploded its first atomic bomb in 1949 and the nuclear arms race and Cold War were on for real. From the Korean War to the death of John Kennedy, the world's two superpowers had twisted language and logic as effectively as they had boosted megatonnage and perfected delivery systems. Kubrick's response was to offer images of the American Cowboy (pre-Ronald Reagan) riding a bucking nuke onto Russian soil for the mandatory eight seconds, America's best and brightest configuring a survivable post-apocalypse underworld while worrying about a possible "mineshaft gap." Everyone laughed, took a breath, but the missiles on both sides remained operational and targeted through the next three decades, the central, fear-inducing cultural reality Don DeLillo uses as the atomic core (literally and figuratively) of *Underworld*. When *Dr. Strangelove* revisited American movie theaters in 1994, film critic Roger Ebert praised the film's vision and style all over again, concluding "if movies of this irreverence, intelligence, and savagery were still being made, the world would seem a younger place" (44).

Ebert and other critics seeking intelligence and cultural acuity in American art and expression at the end of the millennium would do well to look past Industrial Light and Magic and the suburban Cineplex to Don DeLillo, where they will find a mix more complex and troubling than the one Kubrick served up in the 1960s. The Cold War world of *Underworld* seems at once very young and very old, the innocent joy and communal celebration engendered by the Bobby Thomson 1951 home run inexorably transformed into a collective cultural experience manifesting, to employ Michael Herr's key phrases from *Dispatches* and the Vietnam War, only "noise, waste, and pain" and "epic enervation." Kubrick's 1964 nuclear comedy ends with a bang—several of them, in fact—as the world receives a "doomsday shroud" of something called Cobalt-Thorium G, becoming history's darkest joke with a hell (literally) of a punch line. Frank Lentricchia has noted that one of Don DeLillo's primary ongoing artistic victories has been "yoking together terror and wild humor as the essential American tone" (2). What Lentricchia identifies as DeLillo's dominant mode, "terrific comedy" (2), is discoverable in *Underworld* (consider Jackie Gleason's digestive travail at the Polo Grounds or Lenny Bruce's apocalyptic rim shots during the Cuban Missile Crisis), but there is a perhaps less comedy and more terror in the novel than in DeLillo's earlier works, combined with serious meditations on death and loss, Spirit and History, that animate a narrative more sprawling, probing, personal, and enigmatic than any of his previous books, including *Libra*.

Dr. *Strangelove* has more of the "terrific comedy" Lentricchia speaks of than does *Underworld*. Kubrick's Cold War ends in the blackest humor and brightest flash imaginable in ninety-three minutes of screen time and two hours of fictional time—the time it takes a B-52 to travel from its fail-safe point to its target inside Russia. DeLillo's story lasts 827 pages and nearly five decades and, like the very historical era it enfolds, transforms, and interprets, *Underworld* seems simultaneously to disperse before our eyes and continue to run on the power of its language and images—a story dead or dying, an epic that will not quit. *Underworld* concludes without either bang or whimper, if it can be said to end at all. Rather, it rolls to our Internet moment and hangs questions marks on it, empty clothes pins on the historical line. Stanley Kubrick in *Dr. Strangelove* had the most dramatic form of contemporary historical closure ever available to an artist, cinematic or literary—the literal End of History—and he used it to the greatest cultural advantage. In word and image, Kubrick was an American artist true to his personal vision, and to the possibilities and limitations of the material he chose. Indeed, of all his films, it is in *Dr. Strangelove* where he most seems to keep the faith as he confronts threatening, undeniable historical reality with the hopefulness and power of the individual creator. The same may be said of DeLillo and *Underworld*, but the epic, improvisatory, jazzy texture of the novel, its elaborate time structure, its plethora of characters real and imagined, and languorous, interwoven narrative strands make it a Cold War tale very different in aesthetic and cultural effect from Stanley Kubrick's tightly knotted piece of nuclear gallows humor. Why then play in the mind with an imaginary DeLillo-Kubrick collaboration, especially an impossible one, on *Underworld, the Movie*? Some of the reasons are matters of coincidence or serendipity, the small or personally intriguing ones, that is. The larger, more compelling ones have to do with history's unrelenting pressures and demands, with the role of the individual artist in a historical world increasingly devoted to mass thinking, blind consumption, and the substitution of tidy sound-bite closure for slow, deep thinking and crafted, elegant expression. The ultimate reason, however, has to do with the necessary aesthetic resolve and fortitude each cultural era needs if it is to be even mildly healthy, at all wise. One might imagine the DeLillo-Kubrick film of *Underworld* to be Wallace Stevens' "supreme fiction" as cinematic-literary epic, the shared nightmare of American Cold War history as the dream of art. Call it serious play (the most desired adult oxymoron). Call it something else perhaps, the small possibility that the demanding, faithful, historically engaged artist, both inside and outside the text, will be vigilant, resolute, and brave—the necessary hero in his old hometown.

This is heavy cultural baggage to ask two kids from the neighborhood to carry, but each is an artist prone naturally to significant aesthetic and historical volunteerism. Consider the backgrounds and personal legends of the two artists. Consummate, reclusive perfectionists, both suspicious or contemptuous of celebrity; both born in the Bronx—Kubrick in 1928, DeLillo in 1936 (on some cold, lost, black-and-white day in the borough, did an adolescent Stanley ever throw an iceball at little Donny or take his lunch money?). Two intellects fascinated by the power, beauty, and dangers of weaponry and high technology, by artificial intelligence and complex systems; obsessed with the potential in words and images to terrify and enchant the individual and the masses, to engender transcendent awe or holy hell in the individual imagination, in the heart and soul of the collective culture. Creators of elegant, complex fictions deeply and seriously engaged with real human history and culture; staunch defenders of the endangered individual up against the power or indifference of prodigious political, social, technological forces—some longstanding and discernible, others new, hidden, stylishly deadly and culturally surreal. A pair of fanatical craftsmen who in their chosen modes of artistic expression are students of what DeLillo in *Underworld* calls *dietrologia*—"the Science of what is behind an event. . . . The science of dark forces"

(280). Omnivorous Renaissance men who conform nicely in theory and practice to William Burroughs' definition of a paranoid—the guy who just found out what is really going on.

And surely DeLillo's description of Cotter Martin at the beginning of *Underworld* captures a great deal of himself and Kubrick also—"He speaks in your voice, American, and there's a shine in his eyes that's halfway hopeful" (11). Halfway, yes, for both artists in their respective novels and films assert the beauty, strangeness, mystery of existence as they trace in word and image the deadly odds and true dangers inherent in the human being's long walk through the dark corridors and stormy plains of history. Both men know the forest of contemporary culture can be a lovely, verdant paradise of enchanting, variegated color and texture—both insist as well that the beasts who live there may take you down merely to show they can do it. Both men are ascetics of their art, monks of the lens and the pen whose embattled, serious complex works are the demanding achievements of the pure aesthete as engaged cultural critic, as creative historical conscience. In his praising review of *Underworld* Vince Passaro made an overall assessment of DeLillo's literary mission that speaks just as strongly of the film art of Stanley Kubrick:

> The temptation will remain for the anti- and pro-DeLillo camps to read explicit political messages into his newest, largest, and best work. But a strong difference exists between writers with overarching political intention and those whose work is driven by a truly historical imagination. The latter group comprises the far greater artists—Shakespeare wrote in this way, as did Milton, Blake, Flaubert, George Eliot, Henry James, Joyce, and, perhaps most relevant in discussing DeLillo, Samuel Beckett and Joseph Conrad. This capacity to imagine the world in a woven language of the personal and intimate as well as the social, political, and historical—to give each its own reality as well as to enable each to function as a metaphor for the other—has been the highest measure of literary art in English. DeLillo has been able to do this with uncanny force; the fusion of the personal with the historical is, finally, the point of his fiction. (75)

That fusion of the personal with the historical permeates DeLillo's career: it is highly evident in early works such as *Americana* and *End Zone* but in more concentrated and elegant quotients in the more recent novels—*White Noise, Libra, Mao II*, and, of course, the greatest example, *Underworld*. But if one considers the filmography of Kubrick, a similar, deeply serious, exceedingly complex fusion of the personal, historical, and cultural is equally evident. Specifically, the prime theme that animates the personal-historical connections and collisions in the production of both artists repeats itself insistently like the bass line in a postmodern electronic musical composition: the struggle of the individual for recognition, definition, dignity, or mere survival in worlds dominated by collective alienation, mass death, the creation and application of antihuman categories of power and coercion in large organizations and systems. That theme is the main highway through the novels of Don DeLillo, but is also the artistic-historical Ho Chi Minh Trail through key Kubrick films: *Paths of Glory, Spartacus, Dr. Strangelove, 2001: A Space Odyssey, A Clockwork Orange, Full Metal Jacket, Eyes Wide Shut.*

In "The Power of History" DeLillo discussed *Underworld* and his larger beliefs on the relationship of the writer to history. In that essay DeLillo expressed concern about the increasing marginalization of the literary artist within contemporary culture and history, but he also asserted the significant, necessary mission of the writer to respond: "Language can be a form of counter history. . . . Language lives in everything it touches and can be an agent of redemption, the thing that delivers us, paradoxically from history's flat, thin, tight and relentless designs, its arrangements of stark pages, and that allows us to find an unconstraining otherness, a free veer from time and place and fate." Such a comment presents a Sphinxian riddle: how can the artist be both bound to and free of history, both inside and outside the ebb and flow? Paradoxically, DeLillo seems to believe, in theory and practice, that he is both, for in another response in *Newsweek* he said, "I'm always happier getting beyond politics and history and into language. This is what I do as a writer. I try to create clear and compelling sentences" (85). And in an earlier interview with Anthony DeCurtis, DeLillo argued, "I think fiction rescues history from its confusion. . . . the novel which is within history can also operate outside it—correcting, clearing up, and perhaps most important of all, finding rhythms and symmetries that we simply don't encounter elsewhere" (56). The artist has then the freedom and responsibility (and joy) to create as he will, but he is also pulled toward and obligated to history. In another key statement accompanying the publication of *Underworld*, DeLillo asserted, "I think the writer ought to be a bad citizen. The writer only has a responsibility to his own imagination. Fiction is always going to explore small, hidden, anonymous corners. And it should. But there is also the press of public events, and to writers, this becomes a kind of irresistible lure. The power of history" (Gillmor 68).

Therein lies the fascination with the imagined Kubrick-DeLillo film collaboration on *Underworld*—picturing in the eye, listening in the ear, to what the two historical-aesthetes would conjure. Both are expert creators and manipulators of the word and image. Indeed, Kubrick was one of the most literary of filmmakers in history, crafting images from books rather than original screenplays for most of his films. DeLillo is a writer obsessed with references to and representations of the celluloid and videotape image in his fictions, from *Americana* through *Underworld*. In movie after movie Kubrick was obsessively responsive to the subtleties and nuances of language and voice; in all of his novels DeLillo offers characters immersed in the beauty and mystery of the recorded image. In "The Power of History" DeLillo said that "the novel is the dream release, the suspension of reality that history needs to escape its own brutal confinements. . . . At its root level, fiction is a kind of religious fanaticism, with elements of obsession, superstition, and awe. Such qualities will soon or later state their adversarial relationship with history."

The phrase "adversarial relationship" is the key, taunting phrase—the tag that reveals finally that crucial artists such as DeLillo and Kubrick do not luxuriate in some Hall of Transcendent Fine Arts free of historical demand and threat, but as paradoxical historical-aesthetes always at battle in the center of a true (artistically) and real (historically) gladiatorial arena. *Underworld* has been discussed perhaps too reductively by many critics as a book about the negative effects of the Cold War, and it is a fiction rife with references to plutonium, B-52s, H-bomb tests, and radiation effects, but for as many creative sorties DeLillo makes toward "bombhead" technology and the cultural climate of death and fear that accompany it, the novel is also a veritable Wal-Mart of artist figures and art forms, the most important of whom are in clear adversarial relationship to the kinds of language, power, and logic that make five decades of waste and weaponry inevitable. Herman Kahn, the Grand Poobah of Bombthink, wrote a book appearing in 1962, the year of the Cuban Missile Crisis, with the very appropriate title *Thinking about the Unthinkable*. He began his elaborate discussion of the strategic permutations of thermonuclear war and civilian civil defense with an introductory chapter called "In Defense of Thinking" (who or what, one wonders, was attacking?) in which he made a striking cultural assertion:

> In our times, thermonuclear war may seem unthinkable, immoral, hideous, or highly unlikely, but it's not impossible. To act intelligently we must learn as much as we can about the risks. We may thereby be better able to avoid nuclear war. We may even be able to avoid the crises that bring us to the brink of war. But despite our efforts we may some day come face to face with a blunt choice between surrender or war. We may even have war thrust upon us without being given any kind of choice. We must appreciate the possibilities. We cannot wish them away. (19)

Published during the year humankind came closest in its bellicose history to species suicide, Kahn's book combined paradoxical arguments for both control and helplessness, choice and inevitability, but it also—fatefully if unintentionally perhaps—admitted thermonuclear war into the list of possible options for global conflict resolution at the very moment it suggested, incredibly, that Americans were not thinking seriously or specifically of the possibility of final war with the Soviet Union. Many critics have traced the long evolution of collective cultural response to nuclear weapons and war from Hiroshima to the present, and the overall discovery, small surprise, is that nuclear war was not only a prominent fear in the American imagination from the late 1940s through the early 1990s but the paramount historical nightmare. Paul Boyer, in *By the Bomb's Early Light: American Thought and Culture at the Dawn of the Atomic Age*, speaks for many cultural historians and millions of Americans who lived through the age of "Duck and Cover":

> So fully does the nuclear reality pervade my consciousness that it is hard to imagine what existence would have been like without it. It is as though the Bomb has become one of those categories of Being, like Space and Time, that, according to Kant, are built into the very structure of our minds, giving shape and meaning to all our perceptions. Am I alone in this feeling? (xviii)

Bad citizens and good artists—Kubrick in *Dr. Strangelove*, Tim O'Brien in *The Nuclear Age* (1985), DeLillo in *Underworld*, many others—answered, of course, "no." Boyer not only looked backward to *Dr. Strangelove*, then twenty years old, as a nuclear apocalyptic classic, but also unknowingly predicted a novel such as *Underworld* when he revealed his own cultural approach to the dawn of Cold War mentality in the United States: "Perhaps the best way to convey a sense of the earliest days of what almost immediately began to be called the 'Atomic Age' is not to impose too much order or coherence on them retrospectively. Out of the initial confusion of emotions and welter of voices, certain cultural themes would quickly emerge" (4).

Don DeLillo's achievement in *Underworld* is the masterful recreation, arrangement, and shaping of the confusion of emotions and welter of post-Hiroshima voices resistant to traditional narrative strategies in the shock-of-the-new nuclear age, and a recognition of that victory illuminates both the novel and the Cold War American culture it enfolds. It also places *Underworld* within a five-decade cultural project that was wildly diverse in mode, style, and tone on aesthetic levels; markedly consistent, determined, and often desperate in argument and mission on historical ones. A prime cultural response to the proliferation of official and unofficial attempts to make the possibility of nuclear war culturally logical and historically normative was for artists—musicians and poets, novelists and filmmakers—to undermine those premises, to "ban the bomb," with the counterhistory of imaginative words and images. With *Dr. Strangelove* Stanley Kubrick announced his nuclear politics as he used the essence of film art—storytelling in pictures—to overload the language of Cold War official thinking that made thermonuclear war ever more likely in 1964. Don DeLillo in *Underworld*, on the other hand, pushed the essence of literary art— storytelling in words—toward unprecedented reliance on a variety of nonlinguistic arts (jazz, painting, sculpture, architecture, of course, film) to make assaults no less aggressive or telling than Kubrick's on the established citadels of bomb culture. One turns off the VCR after viewing *Dr. Strangelove* and remembers the darkly ironic use of language—the President saying "There's no fighting in the War Room!"; a sign that reads "Peace Is Our Profession," the real slogan of the Strategic Air Command, as backdrop for a raging battle; the graffiti "Hi There" and "Dear John" on the noses of the nukes Major Kong (Slim Pickens) is about to deliver to Mother Russia; the reconstituted Nazi voice of Dr. Strangelove (Peter Sellers) rapturously writing a nightmarish vision of post-apocalypse America. A reader shuts the pages of *Underworld* and sees still and moving images in the mind—Nick and Marian floating over the

New Mexico desert and the decommissioned B-52s that have become Klara Sax's collective painted artwork, *Long Tall Sally*; the hundred television screens showing the Zapruder film at the party of the video artist; the photographic realism of Acey Greene rendering the Blackstone Rangers street gang; the mystical vision of Esmeralda on the Minute Maid orange juice billboard in the South Bronx.

What would finally attract Stanley Kubrick to DeLillo's American epic of nuclear weapons and burgeoning waste? Beyond filming works by canonized writers—Nabokov (*Lolita*), Burgess (*A Clockwork Orange*), Thackeray (*Barry Lyndon*)—the director was famous for choosing books that offered specific features: compelling images to his sensitive eye (Kubrick did still photography for *Look* magazine as a young man); sharp, multilayered language or dialogue to his ironic, educated ear; dark, mysterious, culturally complex themes to his intellect and imagination. He frequently found those combinations of odd, attractive, and ominous features in unexpected sources—Stephen King's *The Shining*, Peter George's *Red Alert* (*Dr. Strangelove*), Gustav Hasford's *The Short-Timers* (*Full Metal Jacket*), Arthur Schnitzler's *Traumnovelle* (*Eyes Wide Shut*). As Kubrick's career progressed, his films featured more and more visual imagery that was both luminous and alienating, language that was chiseled and poetic, tones and rhythms that were tough and tender. His unrealized dream was to create an epic film on the life of Napoleon—Kubrick had scouted locations in Europe and envisioned battle scenes with forty thousand costumed extras photographed in long helicopter tracking shots—and in his biography of the director, Vincent LoBrutto quotes Kubrick on the appeal Napoleon's story held for him: ". . . I find that all the issues with which it concerns itself are oddly contemporary—the responsibilities of power, the dynamics of social revolution, the relationship of the individual to the state, war, militarism, etc., so this will not just be a dusty historic pageant but a film about the basic questions of our own times, as well as Napoleon's" (322).

These are, of course, the issues of *Underworld* also as is the artist's response to them, both inside and outside the page and the frame. The novels of DeLillo and the films of Kubrick are in so many ways active contemporary responses to a key query by Napoleon—"What is history but a fable agreed upon?"—a question that carries within it the attractions and dangers of both creating world history and enfolding it in the features and contours of complex art. These are matters of power and responsibility, as both filmmaker and novelist demonstrate, and the linguistic, visual, and tonal features of *Underworld* announce it as rich and arable Kubrick artistic top-soil, cultural-historical acreage in which the director might have planted his own unique visions and made wondrous things grow.

What scenes and images in the novel would Kubrick have found most compelling? How would the director legendary for his per-fectionist's eye have composed, framed, and shot the strangest and most beautiful DeLillo moments in *Underworld*? Certainly many of those images would be of the artists and the art that reshapes, transmutes, or does battle with the economic, social, and techno-logical realities that foster death, fear, alienation, and inequity in Cold War America—the moments in the book when art most dra-matically engages history, when the inhuman is made at least par-tially human, when life rather than death transiently and tenuously triumphs. The choices in a novel as ambitious and rich as *Underworld* are numerous, but specific ones would seem irresist-ible to Stanley Kubrick: Klara Sax at the "jazz cathedral" of Sabato Rodia's Watts Towers; the guerrilla warfare and sexual politics of Truman Capote's Black & White Ball (shades of the masque in *Eyes Wide Shut*); Matt Shay's religious experience at Loew's Paradise where movie palace becomes cathedral; the ominous Cold War beauty of the painted B-52s of *Long Tall Sally* in the New Mexico desert; the mournful beauty of Ismael Muñoz's painted angels on The Wall in the Bronx and his wild designs on flashing New York City subway cars. In thematic, tonal, and symbolic counterpoint, certainly Kubrick would be attracted as well to the dark, ironic, and poetic cinematic possibilities within the proliferating images of vi-olence, waste, and war of *Underworld*, and one can begin to com-pose, light, and frame in the imagination keyed to DeLillo's cultural nightmares as Kubrick might: the adventures of the Texas Highway Killer; the "First we bomb them. . . . Then we fuck them" Vietnam run of Chuckie Wainwright (Kubrick back in the sym-bolic B-52 after four decades); the fateful final meeting of young Nick Shay and George the Waiter; the haunting, grotesque visit to the Museum of Misshapens in Kasakhstan.

Perhaps the chapter that most recommends the impossible but desired collaboration of novelist and filmmaker is also one where DeLillo's artist figures as engaged counterhistorians take center-stage in the most remarkable ways. Chapter 3 of Part 4—Cocksucker Blues, Summer 1974—is the epicenter of the book, both in regards to DeLillo's narrative structure and the real time-span of historical events. As a young filmmaker, Kubrick was heavily affected by the writings of Russian film masters Pudovkin and Eisenstein on the art of editing, and Chapter 3 of *Underworld* is not only an important confluence of artist figures in marked adversarial relationships to antihuman power and coercion but also a site where DeLillo's use of American montage as artistic-historical method is highly visible. The controlling persona of the chapter is not Nick Shay, the character most critics call the main character of the novel, but rather Klara Sax, who, in 1974, is an evolving artistic sensibility long removed from her brief tryst with Nick in the Bronx in the 1950s and almost equally far from the time she will perform her greatest artistic alchemy, the transformation of a group of deadly weapons of nuclear destruction into the collective, strangely beautiful technological mural called *Long Tall Sally* in the 1990s. The chapter is masterful and telling—how could Kubrick resist it?—as DeLillo gives the reader the imaginary Eisenstein film from the 1930s, *Unterwelt*, framed within the American kitsch of the Radio City Music Hall, complete with Rockettes in bondage collars forming the red star of the Soviet Union as prelude to the screening. The Eisenstein film-that-never-was is nonetheless a model of his real theories of montage and typage (editing and character development)—a symbolic underworld that speaks of the real Cold War it presages and in which it now resides—but the chapter, a dazzling show by DeLillo of theory wedded with practice, is itself a kind of cinematic montage.

Chapter 3 consists of three major scenes, the first and last offering the reactions of Klara Sax to the Eisenstein screening, the center scene devoted to the subway car graffiti master, Ismael Munoz—Moonman 157—whose bright kinetic designs have the same power to antagonize and transform political, social, and economic reality as did the Russian film master's in their time and place. Like the Russian director, Moonman 157 uses a team of craftsmen to create a personal art—Eisenstein's "moving pictures" are on black-and-white film stock; Moonman's are on speeding New York City transit cars—that speaks strongly to and about the individual and the masses. Like a master film editor, DeLillo in Chapter 3, indeed, throughout the entire 827 pages of *Underworld*, cuts elegantly from one artist and art form to the other, from one image of death and waste to another, creating and discovering new significance and relationship, constructing an epic American novel that consistently evokes thoughts of Eisenstein's montage of collision and attraction, the same editing techniques that so struck fledgling filmmaker Stanley Kubrick.

Perhaps it is not so strange that a great Russian film director is a significant influence and nexus for two key American artists: one a markedly bookish master of cinema, the other a distinctively movie-drenched writer, the Jewish and Italian odd couple from the Bronx. The two artists never met. Like the Dodgers and Giants, they left the old neighborhood for larger, different fields of play while only the imperial New Yankees, the Bronx Bombers, stayed home. But, as DeLillo reminds throughout his Cold War fictional epic, his compelling American montage, "Everything is connected in the end" (826). What would a full, real Kubrick-DeLillo collaboration of *Underworld, the Movie* be? A close associate of Kubrick's, Bob Gaffney, envisioned the director's dream film, the story of Napoleon, and surmised that "it would have been the epic to end all epics" (quoted in LoBrutto 321). Perhaps it would have been, but one can imagine a version of *Underworld, the Movie* that even the frame of Radio City Music Hall and a company of bombheaded, high-kicking Rockettes could not hold.

Perhaps closure offers a hint. In Kubrick's last film, *Eyes Wide Shut*, the final word uttered on screen—the great director's exit line—is "Fuck." After the spirit of Sister Edgar of the Bronx disappears into the cyberspace of *Underworld*, new American territory that offers the choice between the H-bomb home page and *dot com miraculum*, DeLillo's last word is "Peace." Put the two words together and they create a crude cultural imperative, one providing the strong likelihood, even the plutonium-filled promise, of Armageddon, the true enemy *Dr. Strangelove* and *Underworld* locate and target. If everything is connected in the end, even in the counterhistory of great art, then somewhere within its curved space and subjective time there is a screening room deep underground—one full of bright images, memorable voices, American dreams. Yes, imagine it.

The Baltimore Catechism;
or Comedy in *Underworld*

IRA NADEL

DRIVING TO THE WALL IN THE SOUTH BRONX AFTER LEARNING OF THE rape and murder of Esmeralda at the end of *Underworld*, Sister Edgar stabilizes her fear by reciting the Baltimore Catechism. Succumbing to its narcotic allure and incantatory nature, she recalls the confirmatory responses of her students to its questions and answers as "syllable-crisp, a panpipe reply that is the lucid music of her life" (815). She gets all the way to Lesson Twelve before they arrive at the projects, spots the freshly painted angel on The Wall commemorating the dead girl and gradually begins to lose her faith. Misspelled on the wall just below the image in running shoes is the message:

> Esmeralda Lopez
> 12 year
> Petected in Heven

> (816)

The comic irony and distortion of the spelling parallels the language and humor of the principal comic in the novel, Lenny Bruce, who played Baltimore one week after his 4 February 1961 success at Carnegie Hall in New York. But *his* Baltimore Catechism is the opposite of Sister Edgar's. Where she asks "who made us?" and answers "God made us," Bruce asks radical questions and offers unorthodox replies in routines such as "Christ and Moses Return" and "Religions Inc.," a Madison Avenue gathering of religious leaders including Oral Roberts, Billy Graham, Danny Thomas, and Pat O'Brien. It opens with the news that Dodge-Plymouth dealers have just raffled off a 1958 Catholic Church. [1]

Baltimore symbolically represents the cosmic order and comic disorder within the novel. Matt Shay, as a young Catholic student,

176

finds the Catechism a universal guide to living, but late in the novel Sister Edgar realizes that it paradoxically embodies both a received faith and a perilous condition expressed in the commercial warning, "Danger. Contents under pressure." The contents are violently released when she smashes the head of Michael Kalenka into the blackboard for his sarcastic answer to Lesson Five of the Catechism: who were the semi-nude male and female figures depicted in the Garden of Eden? "The original parents of us all [were] Tarzan and Jane," he smilingly answers (716). Lenny Bruce is the product of such release, the free-style, associative humor that indicts every supposed truth of the culture, although he also occasionally had his head smashed against a wall.

Comedy is resistance in *Underworld*, a way of striking back at the conformity, mediocrity, and uniformity of American life that is repeatedly shown to be duplicitous, questionable, and tricky. Comedy is a way of separating yourself from the position "they"—the government, society, domesticity—put you in: "The true edge is not where you choose to live but where they situate you against your will," Lenny Bruce cries in the novel (505). The only way to alter your position is through comedy expressed through satire, irony, or sarcasm, all three means of combating a society best defined by the pseudomagic of Jell-O, which displays remarkable powers of stability even when tilted at a 45-degree angle in the refrigerator of Erica Deming (514). Bruce's opening line, parodying Kennedy's opening line in his dramatic television address to the nation regarding the Cuban Missile Crisis—"Good evening, my fellow citizens"—deftly plays on the nature of comedy in the novel that simultaneously functions to celebrate and denigrate the patriotism of the country and its values (506). In *Underworld* comedy is Dantean, evoking the complex and subversive scenes and meanings of Dante's universe.

What few of the characters in the novel understand is that America constantly reinvents itself, turning waste into fuel. Nor do they grasp what DeLillo announced in *Libra*: that history is "the sum total of all the things they *aren't* telling us" (321 italics DeLillo's), a line more suited to Lenny Bruce than to the narrator of that novel. One measure of this uncertainty is the altered names in *Underworld*, a feature DeLillo introduced in *Libra*. In *Underworld* name changes are everywhere: Jackie Gleason was born Herbert John Gleason, although his mother called him Jackie, which stuck. Lenny Bruce was originally Leonard Alfred Schneider. Nick Shay was to be James Nicholas Costanza. J. Edgar Hoover was actually John, but when he found out that a John Edgar Hoover was running up bad debts and bounced checks around Washington, he quickly switched to the more formal J. Edgar Hoover.

People and history in the novel are not what they appear to be or named. Epithets frequently substitute for the real thing: Bobby Thomson's home run is known as the Shot Heard 'Round the World. Gleason's refrain, "You're goin' to the moon, Alice," becomes an American epithet for anger, frustration, and impatience. Even DeLillo's fabricated Eisenstein film is not what it seems: initially about revolt and release, its real theme is below the surface: "the contradictions of being" (444). America is a world of mystery and secrets where a young boy's father goes out to buy a pack of cigarettes and never returns. It is a world, DeLillo writes, where "the shadow facts [are] made real" and the real is made into shadows (17).

The dossiers of J. Edgar Hoover, where "paranoia and control" mingle, embody this falseness. An item placed there transcended "facts and actuality. . . . It was a truth without authority and therefore incontestable. . . . The file was everything, the life nothing" (559), underscored by Hoover's keeping in his personal file an 8 x 10 photo of the naked Lenny Bruce, dead from a drug overdose (574). What is real is the question asked by DeLillo in *Libra* and expanded endlessly in *Underworld*, epitomized in Klara Sax's question to Miles at Radio City Music Hall moments before the screening of the newly-discovered Eisenstein film, *Unterwelt*: "How do we know it's really the Rockettes and not a troupe of female impersonators?" (428).

I

You have to stay hip to stay connected.
—Lenny Bruce, *Underworld*

The two poles of comedy in the novel are Jackie Gleason and Lenny Bruce, the comedy of reassurance, domesticity, and the canned laughter of the situation comedy vs. the decentering, threatening, off-color humor of the satirist. The constant references to "The Honeymooners," replayed in Phoenix on the TV in the home of Nick Shay and watched nightly by his mother, contradict the acerbic, night-club satire of Lenny Bruce who gets his greatest pleasure from repeating the line, *"We're all gonna die,"* a message whose delivery masks its horror. Bruce speaks against the backdrop of the Cuban Missile Crisis, using Kennedy's speech as a leitmotif for his sardonic humor. Gleason does not even acknowledge the immediate nor the everyday, preferring the hermetic world of the Kramdens' Brooklyn apartment. Bruce dismantles the accepted; Gleason reasserts it, acting like Jell-O, able to remake himself and take new shapes that nevertheless reinforce continuity. Bruce's quip, "You have to be hip to stay connected" (505), means that only by being alert to current realities can you be connected to yourself and to your public. Without that knowledge, you will crack, fall away or, like Gleason at the Polo Grounds when he overconsumes (and overacts), throw it up, expelling the nutritious in the form of waste. Lenny Bruce is "the diamond cutter" (625), Jackie Gleason the cut-up. Bruce is spontaneous, Gleason rehearsed.

Lenny Bruce's history of comedy is brief: the older comedians did an act, telling the audience "this is my act" but "today's comic is not doing an act. The audience assumes he's telling the truth. [But] what is truth today may be a damn lie next week. The truth. When I'm interested in a truth, it's really a *truth* truth, one hundred percent. And that's a terrible kind of truth to be interested in" (quoted in Cohen 111). DeLillo presents Bruce as the voice of comic despair but also as the truthteller in the novel, the figure who courageously prosecutes the falsehood, shame, and false optimism of the age. Anticipating the blurring of distinctions that the novel will exhibit, Bruce ironically explains that "if the whole world were tranquil, without disease and violence, I'd be standing on the breadline right in back of J. Edgar Hoover . . ." (quoted in Cohen 112). The reference to Hoover is no accident. In 1958, Bruce sketched out a musical that included a small-time comic looking for work in the civil service. His application gets mixed up, and by mistake he is assigned to Hoover's office in Washington where he is to write speeches to be used by public officials in times of crisis. The problem is they all sound like the double-talk made famous by Sid Caesar. The comic also works as an undercover agent assigned to infiltrate the coffeehouses of San Francisco posing as a comic.[2]

II

And away we go.

—Jackie Gleason

Jackie Gleason identified with the humor of Jack Benny, Steve Allen, and Groucho Marx rather than with the burlesque house jokesters or the so-called sick humorists. He was an American comedian, a showman, often dressed in a recognizable uniform: that of a bus driver (he, of course, worked on the surface, while his neighbor Ed Norton worked underground, in the sewers of New York); he was a success with middle America because, as Nick realizes when he watches reruns of "The Honeymooners" with his mother in her room in his Phoenix home, "he gave us the line, gave us the sure laugh, the one we needed at the end of the day" (106). Gleason "was the joke that carried a missing history—the fat joke, the dumb joke . . . the punch line that survives long after the joke is forgotten." Gleason, he realizes, can make his audiences happy: "We felt better with Jackie in the room, transparent in his pain, alive and dead in Arizona" (106).

The pain of Bruce was never transparent. It lasted. As a comic, he was always on the edge, manic, putting his audiences in a similar position, never knowing what would come next. "They laughed, he bled" (629) DeLillo writes of the "mortician-comic" (546). Bruce indicted life, Gleason celebrated it and its easy solutions to its minor disruptions. Bruce faced its problems and lies. Through Gleason's use of television, he would be ever-present via reruns; Bruce was largely gone, present only through the few recordings he made; his autobiography, *How to Talk Dirty and Influence People* (its title a parody of American optimism and hope expressed in the work of Dale Carnegie and in millions of self-help books); his slim volume unabashedly titled *The Essential Lenny Bruce*; and the police photos of his naked body arranged with the props of a drug addict. Thus, whereas Gleason can be restored with a remote, Bruce remains shadowy, like a figure from Dante. A scene in the novel where he appears to disappear from the stage during a performance at Basin Street West in San Francisco on 24 October 1962 (ironically, during the Vatican Two Council in Rome and the Cuban Missile Crisis) represents this. Bruce slips into the darkness but never really leaves (548). Gleason's reception was positive, Bruce's negative: "The first show I met a lot of hostility to my left, if you call throwing up on my suit a bit of rejection, as I walked off" (quoted in Cohen 113).

We first see Gleason at the ballgame with Frank Sinatra, Toots Shor, and J. Edgar Hoover. He plays to the crowd and to his cronies and "sees nothing strange about missing a rehearsal to entertain fans in the stands" (24). Although he does not know it, he is playing to the backdrop of disaster: the just-exploded Russian atomic bomb. Bruce will also play against the backdrop of the bomb and the Cuban Missile Crisis, a similar threat to stability and peace, although he will know it and make sure others do as well.

Gleason's certified humor represented no more than the aggravations of a working man in a Brooklyn flat who "drove a vehicle licensed by society" (121). The rehearsed and insulated world of the Kramdens' apartment excludes the issues of the world. The childless Kramdens nevertheless deal directly with matters of domestic and urban disruptions, often introduced to them by their neighbor, Ed Norton. At the Polo Grounds, the public seeks similar reassurance, asking Gleason to do the familiar lines of dialogue from the popular *Jackie Gleason Show*. "The Honeymooners" was two days away from its first broadcast when Gleason missed rehearsal to attend the Dodgers-Giants game, 3 October 1951. His style of humor dissolves into the wisecracking, slightly risqué jokes of Charlie Wainwright.

But whereas Gleason's jokes and comedy reaffirmed the social fabric of domestic America, Lenny Bruce tore it apart. His invective, insults, and obscenity insured a negative reaction but a probing exposure of sham, deception, and deceit. He, like traditional Juvenilian satirists, needed to offend in order to correct the wrongs of the age. Nowhere was this more evident than in his frequent recitation of Thomas Merton's poem on Adolf Eichmann, which ends with these lines:

> I saw all the work that I did.
> I, Adolf Eichmann,
> vatched through the portholes.
> I saw every Jew burned
> *und* turned into soap.
> Do you people think yourselves better
> because you burned your enemies
> at long distances
> with missiles?

> Without ever seeing what you'd done to them?
> Hiroshima ... *Auf Wiedersehen* ...
>
> (quoted in Cohen 304)

Religion was his most notorious subject but DeLillo shows that Bruce is not far from the actual behavior of priests. When Bronzini meets Father Andrew Paulus to see if he would take on the chess tutoring of his prize student, Matt Shay, the conversation of the two close friends shifts at one moment to marriage. Bronzini asks the priest if he regretted not marrying. "I don't want to marry," he answers, "I just want to screw." In the tone and style of Bruce, he continues:

> "The verb to screw is so amazingly, subversively apt. But conjugating the word is not sufficient pastime. I would like to screw a movie star, Albert. The greatest, blondest, biggest-titted goddess Hollywood is able to produce. I want to screw her in the worst way possible and I mean that in every sense." (672)

A few pages later, in describing what is necessary to win at chess, the priest summarizes the very talents of Bruce: "He [the player] must enjoy the company of danger. He must have a killer instinct. He must be prideful, arrogant, aggressive, contemptuous and dominating. Willful in the extreme" (674). Interestingly, his own new idea of a new collegium reverts to a lost language—"we may teach Latin as a spoken language"—and a comedic technique Bruce exploits: "we may teach mathematics as an art form like poetry or music. We will teach subjects that people don't realize they need to know" (675). Later, Bronzini, the high school science teacher, tells his class that "we need numbers to make sense of the world. We think in numbers. We think in decades. Because we need organizing principles . . . to make us less muddled" (735). Ironically, one of the talents of Nick's missing father was his talent for remembering numbers.

Lenny Bruce incinerates his audiences, and walkouts were not uncommon. His repeated mantra, *"We're all gonna die,"* generates in the audience "the replacement of human isolation by massive and unvaried ruin" (507). For them, and for himself, he becomes "the hipster fink," the persecuted junkie,"the vengeance of the Lord" (507). Yet, the declaration of this line was "wondrously refreshing, it purified his fear and made it public at the same time—it was weak and sick and cowardly and powerless and pathetic and also noble somehow . . . [a] cry of grief and pain that had an element of sweet defiance" (547). Later in the novel, when the Cuban Missile Crisis passes, he considers altering his mantra, but not its manic delivery, to *"We're all gonna live"* (629). But, he does not because his need to recognize the unthinkable is still the same.

Lenny Bruce's cinematic method of the strung-out projectionist, cutting, interspersing, cutting again, and creating montage parallels the cinematic method of the novel and its recursive structure. (Jonathan Miller, at the time in *Beyond the Fringe*, noted that Bruce drew much of his style from films because Bruce realized that "the modern American Mind is nurtured on cineplasm and Disney-food, [and] John Hollander's B pictures which showed us shooting more real than singing or making love" [151].) Other "humorists" in DeLillo's novel, with the exception of the consoling humor of Jackie Gleason or the businessman Brian Glassic who repeats his pathetic "fastest lover *een Mayheeko*" story (796), reflect the stance of Lenny Bruce: caustic, critical, and inventive, using language as the medium of attack and celebration, exposing its contradictory meanings often through grenade-like, explosive deliveries. Even the young Matt Shay sensed the way language could breakdown and transform the solemn into the comic: *"Dominus vobiscum*, the priest used to say, and we'd push our way out of the vestibule, several kids chanting, Dominick go frisk 'em. What was Latin for if you couldn't reduce the formal codes to the jostled argot of the street?" (107). Here, the two worlds collide with the street triumphant over the church, comedy the solution to confusion or danger. The humor of the street with Nick and his youthful friends, or that of Moonman 157 and his gang, dominates the sense of the comedic in the novel, which is equally hip and angry, revealing in its energy falsehood and cover-ups.

Caught in the middle between the comic and cinematic extremes of the novel is grim-faced J. Edgar Hoover who understands history only as a dialectic in black and white. *Libra* introduced the FBI in various guises to DeLillo's work but excluded Hoover. In *Underworld* he takes on an important role, developing a dangerously simplistic view of "us vs. them." In his mind there is a constant battle between the United States and Russia, the patriots and the Communists, the moral and the immoral that imperils the purity of the country. Oblivious to his own contradictions, made clear in the opening scene where he is the grave presence among a set of enter-

tainers—Jackie Gleason, Frank Sinatra, and Toots Shor—Hoover
embodies contrast and contradiction.

Surprised to learn of the sudden detonation of an atomic weapon
by the Russians, Hoover returns to his seat at the ballgame only to
discover, in a torn magazine page blown onto his shoulder, an
image of Bruegel's *The Triumph of Death*. His eyes fixate on the
landscape of ruin just as he will later, behind a leather mask, fixate
on the figures at the Black & White Ball held by Truman Capote, an
ironic representation of his own hypocrisy and attempted cover-up
of his sexuality. Only after his death in 1972 was it discovered that
Hoover treasured a nude calendar of Marilyn Monroe he kept in
his basement rec room in Washington and that he, and select officials, often enjoyed watching pornographic films in the theater in
the basement of the Department of Justice Building. Virulently opposed to addiction in any form, Hoover banned coffee from all of
his agents when on duty; he also spoke in a staccato, rapid style,
not unlike Lenny Bruce. His personal files were notorious, and the
top secret "D" list (for destruct) was activated within an hour of
his death at age 77 on 2 May 1972.[3] Hoover's behavior is more Dantean than American, although in DeLillo the line between the two
always blurs. Contrasting images of historical joy, through the dramatic victory of the Giants, with historical despair, through the
dawn of the Russian nuclear age, establish the double vision of the
novel. The ironic witnesses to these conflicts are the paranoid FBI
Director and the cynical comic.

III

> But as the saying has it, one must go
> With boozers in the tavern and saints in church.
> —Dante, *The Inferno*, XXII

Lenny Bruce possesses a Dantean sense of comedy suitable for a
novel titled *Underworld*. Echoing Cantos XII–XXII of *The Inferno*, the
section known as the Malebolge, which deals with the barrators or
grafters (sellers of public office) and the sin of lying, Bruce annihi-
lates the public figures and government, as well as the church, for
their falseness and duplicity. He does so, of course, in vulgar and
offensive language, as Dante does in the corresponding section of
The Inferno. Indeed, as Robin Kirkpatrick has noted, "to Dante,

comic writing is writing cast in the lowest linguistic register," adding that in the Malebolge, there is "no vulgarism or obscenity which the poet will not willingly adopt in the interests of mimesis and linguistic realism" (227). Furthermore, the setting of this portion of *The Inferno* is not a landscape as in other portions of the poem but a cityscape: here, rock is cut into channels to resemble constructions of human design, notably alleys, sewers, and moats, whereas the sinners are represented as members of a community, degraded and self-punishing. This urban landscape is the essential world of Lenny Bruce.

The Malebolge concentrates, as do the sections in the novel representing Bruce, on fraud and deliberate deceit. As Bruce exposes the misleading nature of the Kennedy Administration and its Cabinet, Dante expresses realistic observations of deceptive behavior among various politicians, articulated in crude speech and vulgar behavior with Canto XXI ending with a fart and the next, XXII, impelled by a fart. Canto XXI also includes one of the favorite lines of Italian schoolboys: "And the leader made a trumpet of his ass" (XXI: 219). The language and action of these two cantos is direct and colloquial, the line on heavy drinkers (XXII: 223) epitomizing the outlook and technique of Bruce. Quarrel, rather than discussion or monologue, is the primary mode of discourse for him and Dante in this section of the poem.

The vicious comedy of this part of the poem draws furthermore on a lexicon of medieval not classical images, as DeLillo does throughout *Underworld*. Fire and heat are central references for DeLillo, whether it is Phoenix, where Nick chooses to live; the Pocket, where his brother works in a secret nuclear research center; or the desert, where Klara Sax paints. In the Eisenstein film the escaped prisoners find themselves moving across a barren landscape with fires in the distance, "the horizon line throbbing in smoke and ash" (442). Below the streets of New York, in an unused freight tunnel on the city's West Side, men exist who tried to live normally except they were below ground; knowledgeable about jazz, art, sex, and literature, these figures in their dark space became Moonman's teachers (435–36). Dante's recurrent images of desert and fire dominate Canto XIV of *The Inferno* and anticipate the devastation to the desert brought on by the atomic tests:

> All over the sand
> Distended flakes of fire drifted from aloft
> Slowly as mountains snow without a wind.

In this world, sand kindles "like tinder under flint" (XIV: 141, 143).

Mystical images appear in both works with the transfiguration of Beatrice who descends from heaven to appear to Dante in *Purgatorio* XXX, prefiguring Esmeralda who becomes a vision only after she also descends, thrown off a roof and killed. Preceded by blinding light and a mystical procession heralded by seven candlesticks, a veiled Beatrice appears to overwhelm Dante. In similarly blinding light, that of the elevated train soon to pass into the underground, Esmeralda is transformed into a vision on the billboard at the end of *Underworld*, appearing above a sea of orange juice as "Esmeralda on the Lake."

Dante's Hell, like Lenny Bruce's, is drawn from the hell of popular fantasy emphasizing humanity's deviation from God but with a focus on the actual and the dramatic, "the small round floor that makes us passionate" (Binyon XXII: 151) The satirical spirit of Cantos XXI and XXII with its knavish devils reflects the pattern of a corrupt society, although the heroes of *The Inferno* may be said to be those who rebel like Vanni Fucci, who proclaims "It was a bestial life, / Not human, that pleased me best" (XXIV: 253). This anticipates Lenny Bruce who announced, in one of his most Dantesque moments, "all my humor is based upon destruction and despair" (quoted in Cohen 112).

With a title like *Underworld*, it is no surprise that numerous parallels with Dante's epic exist, beginning with the scope and size of the two works—both crowded with human events—and extending to the structural and organizational levels of the two texts. Hierarchies exist in both works, from the formal levels of Hell, itemized and numbered in Dante, to the particularized places and time-line that are carefully rendered in DeLillo's novel. Dante also adopts actual historical figures for his text, from Count Ugolino of *The Inferno* to Caesar and Justinian in *Paradiso*, as DeLillo will do throughout *Underworld*. Landscapes in *Underworld* are redolent with Dantean images, from the massed crowds at the Polo Grounds to the images of death in Bruegel's *The Triumph of Death*. The flickering lives shooting past Klara and her mother as they ride the subway "up Manhattan and through the Bronx" (398), peering into tenement apartments, or the airport in Phoenix, which resembles Dante's crowded and tiered world of the Divine Comedy, are further examples of a modern, Dantean journey and spectacle.[4]

The bar under a bridge on the Lower East Side where Nick meets an old acquaintance from his Bronx neighborhood is another setting from Hell, a locale where the mystical and the grotesque meet. In the Bronx itself, Sister Edgar encounters figures who are more at home in the Malebolge than New York: matching "a man who'd cut his eyeball out of its socket because it contained a satanic symbol," an escapee from Dante's universe, is Nick's encounter with Donna, the swinger he meets and sleeps with at the hotel in the Mojave Desert. The act is intense, even grotesque, but performed with a mystical undertone, not unlike moments of desire and passion in *The Inferno* (247, 294–301). Other Dantean worlds in the novel include The Wall and its ruined South Bronx surroundings, the desolate waste management sites visited by Nick, the Arizona desert where Klara Sax repaints decommissioned Air Force bombers, Kazahkstan with its Museum of Misshapens, and the recovered Eisenstein film, *Unterwelt*.

The silent film fascinates because it documents the creation of a Dantean world, illustrating the destructive effect of science upon humans, turning the humans into grotesque victims of the atomic ray guns of the scientists. Deformed by blasts in a desolate landscape, the figures become cyclops, mouthless faces or cancerous bodies, escaped, it seems, from one of Dante's Circles of Hell. The very technique of the film echoes the technique of Dante with its "overcomposed close-ups, momentous gesturing, actors trailing their immense bended shadows" (429). Like the style of Bruce and the world of *The Inferno*, the film and its camera angle "is a kind of dialectic. Arguments are raised and made . . . there's a lot of opposition and conflict" (429). Deformed figures, possibly prisoners, "move through crude rooms in some underground space" and "scuttled through the shadows, hump-lurched with hands dragging" (429, 430).

The film reinforces the idea of shades or shadows, the repeated reference for the inhabitants of Dante's Hell. A viewer of *Unterwelt* appropriately remarks that "the theme deals on some level with people living in the shadows" (424), the condition of Dantean existence further suggested by Matt's belief that "there may have been an underworld of images known only to tribal priests, mediums between visible reality and the spirit world" (466). Reinforcing the underworld on the screen is the frequent shaking of the underground trains of the IND line on Sixth Avenue with their "cargo of human souls," one of whom is Moonman 157 (432–33). And in a statement that both links and separates the medieval and modern worlds, Matt thinks that "ideas used to come from below. Now they're everywhere above you, connecting things and grids universally" (466).

The inclusion of Italian in *Underworld*, the language consciously chosen by Dante to remove his text from the "tragic" language of Latin, justifying it as a "Comedy," is another link to the Renaissance epic. Throughout the novel, various Italian terms appear, confirming an ethnicity that is part of the book's ethos. Indeed, Italian, along with numbers, is the only way language or expression can be precise: characters rely on "dialect when an idea needed a push or shove into a more familiar place" often to summarize a situation as in *"Mannaggia l'America,"* the expression John the Super uses to explain the quality of garbage thrown away in America or *"Porca miseria"* for those kicked out on the street with their belongings (767, 768). Nick explains his distance from others to his wife through the word *lontananza* (275).

For Albert Bronzini, Italian is the language of memory, English of the present. In thinking about the corruptions of the dialect of southern Italy, Bronzini indirectly alludes to *The Inferno*. As he traces in his mind the origins of "Tizzoons," a slur and invective from *tizzo*—firebrand or smoldering coal and used by Dante in Canto XVI of *Paradiso*—, he traces its human dimension to *tizzone d'inferno*, a scoundrel or villain: "the word they used suggested a hellishness, a fiendishness that made it more unspeakable, in a way, than nigger." But they did use it in his neighborhood: "Tizzoons," a corruption, to suggest those on the fringes "who threaten society's peaceful sleep, who are always showing up and moving in. Tizzoon. . . . they narrowed their eyes and barely moved their lips. But they spoke it, they half hissed the word . . ."(768). Italian: it, too, can be corrupted.

The visual/cinematic imagination of DeLillo's encyclopedic writing further connects the two texts, although both concentrate on individuals—whether troubadors, prostitutes, popes, or pimps. Both works contain monsters and angels. Battling devils fighting in mid-air over the burning lake of pitch in Canto XXI or Dante walking the gauntlet of taunting demons are two dramatic and visual moments in the Malebolge section of *The Inferno* that equal descriptions of B-52 bomber flights over Vietnam guided by the navigator Chuckie Wainwright or the street fights in the Bronx involving Matt and Nick Shay (606–16).

One of the more fascinating geographic links between Dante and DeLillo is that of the pouch and the Pocket. The pouch refers to the fissures that separate various sections within certain levels of the circles of Hell, in Italian *bolgia*. The Pocket is a concrete underground space carved out of the gypsum hills of southern New Mexico where Matt Shay conducts his research into nuclear weapons with other "bombheads." The name derives from the "pocket gopher that lives in tunnels it frantically digs under the furrowed dunes" (402). This parallels the pouches in Dante, those rock slices that allow the characters to *descend* from one level to another in *The Inferno*. The nature that surrounds the Pocket is itself Dantesque: barren and white from the gypsum and alkali flats, a "whole white sea-bottomed world" where a six-thousand-year-old mummified baby was found in a cave. The wind comes from the Organ Mountains, reshaping the dunes and "turning the sky an odd dangerous gray that seemed a type of white gone mad" (402). On the edge of this world, in the towns downwind from the nuclear test site, are the malformed, the diseased, the disfigured.

Numerology is another link between the two texts. The fascination of Matt Shay with the number 13, found everywhere, echoes Dante. Cantos XXI and XXI of *The Inferno*, the satirical section dealing with the grafters, occurs in the Eighth Circle and Fifth Pouch or *bolgia* of Hell, which add up to 13, as do the digits of Moonman 157's name. The numerological absorption of *Underworld* is an extension of Dante's fascination with 3, from the three main divisions of his epic to the development of terza rime, the aba, bcb, cdc rhyme scheme of his three line stanzas or tercets. DeLillo merges Dante's fascination with 3's into his world, beginning with the publication date of the novel: 3 October 1997, alluding to 3 October 1951, the date of the dramatic Dodgers-Giants game that opens the novel. Three also shapes the structure of the novel: *Underworld* has six chapters (3 x 2) and 3 Manx Martin sections, the whole framed by a Prologue and Epilogue.

But in DeLillo, like Dante, numbers grow almost too large to fathom and possess a destructiveness that is incalculable: equations entered on a screen contain a mystery in that they might alter "the course of many lives" as "billion-bit data converted into images" (409, 415). Numbers are dangerous and some fear them, especially if they believe in a conspiracy theory where even the census hides the real numbers as Sims suggests to Nick (334–36). Everything, we soon learn, becomes a number; day after day, Matt translates "a dot on the film . . . into letters, numbers, coordinates, grids, and entire systems of knowledge" (463). Yet, numbers and names come together to form a narrative: the point of Moonman 157's name is "how the letters and numbers told a story of back-street life" (434); earlier, Russ Hodges, the voice of the Giants, remembers that "somebody hands you a piece of paper filled with letters and numbers and you have to make a ball game out of it" (25). Throughout the novel, the effort of uniting letters and numbers is constant as the 16-year old Moonman 157 understands. Traveling uptown on the Washington Heights local, he knows that each car "tagged with his own neon zoom" was the embodiment of

> the whole wildstyle thing of making your name and street number a kind of alphabet city where the colors lock and bleed and the letters connect and it's all live jive, it jumps and shouts—even the drips are intentional, painted supersharp to express how the letters sweat, how they live and breathe. . . . (433)

Both Aeneas and St. Paul descended into Hell according to Dante in Canto II of *The Inferno*; the poet follows but his descent downward is to make possible his ascent heavenwards. In *Underworld* Nick Shay's descent—from a Bronx roof top to the subterranean room of George Manza whom he accidentally kills (78–81)—makes possible a psychological, as well as physical, political as well as cultural ascent. Dante's descent is meant as a spiritual exercise *and* as a prelude to a political prophecy, the descent an inverted epic journey equal to the backward or reverse storytelling of *Underworld*. Both lead to a resolution that is complete and final: the circular motion that ends Dante's journey at the conclusion of *Paradiso* merges the individual will with the World-Will of God and the knowledge that "with our desert doth to our bliss belong" (*Paradiso* Canto VI: 119); at the end of *Underworld*, Nick navigates cyberspace and accepts the single, encompassing term, "Peace," on his screen. Earlier in the story, Matt Shay enacts a modern form of ascent to his *Paradiso* when he climbs to the heavens and the stars in mid-Manhattan at the Loew's Paradise movie theater. High in the balcony studying the firmament in the ceiling and the sky that seemed to move, Matt awaits a visitation from his missing father: all he sees, however, is a profusion of ornament and light.

The sense of loss and disappointment experienced by Nick and Matt in the novel, not only over the loss of their father but for the spiritual malaise of the country, recaptures the situation of Dante at the beginning of *The Inferno* who expresses his loss of purpose and direction:

> Midway on our life's journey, I found myself
> In dark woods, the right road lost. To tell
> About those woods is hard—so tangled and rough
>
> And savage that thinking of it now, I feel
> The old fear stirring: death is hardly more bitter.
> And yet, to treat the good I found there as well
>
> I'll tell what I saw, though how I came to enter
> I cannot well say, being so full of sleep
> Whatever moment it was I began to blunder
>
> Off the true path.

The mixture of retrospection, disorientation, and journey anticipates the quest and opening scene of *Underworld*: when we first see Nick, he has wandered "off the true path," skirting the desert in a rented Lexus, impetuously seeking out his one-time lover, Klara Sax, in the wilderness, returning, if only briefly, to the past before journeying onward (63–65).

Underworld possesses many Virgils, from Viktor Maltsev and Simeon Biggs to Marvin Lundy. Matt Shay is one of the more central, a guide to his brother's Dante. Matt had been to Vietnam, works in a world that mixes creativity with destruction, and acts as a kind of guide for his inquisitive, observing, but sometimes naive brother. A more likely Virgil, however, one experienced in the Underworld, is Lenny Bruce who has been to Hell and back and acts as society's rough-minded guide. Like Dante's counselor, he can speak to the beasts and escort us through the threatening landscape if we choose to follow. But, the novel lacks a Beatrice, substituting a kind of holy relic, pursued by many: the home run ball hit by Bobby Thomson, which Nick finally possesses in an effort to reclaim a moment of innocence before his Fall.

Narrative similarities between *The Divine Comedy* and *Underworld* include a reliance on dramatic fragments, stories that collectively rather than individually cohere. Although film may have been the immediate catalyst for this technique for DeLillo, Dante remains the primary model. In Canto II of *The Inferno*, for example, Dante has Virgil tell the story of his encounter with Beatrice who told him of her encounter with Lucy, who told her of her encounter with a gentle Lady in Paradise. So, also, at moments throughout the novel, there are stories-within-stories such as the details of those connected with the home run ball, the story of the recovered Eisenstein movie, or of Klara's many marriages and her intersection with Nick. And, as Nick and Matt Shay wander through the last half of the twentieth century, they parallel Dante and Virgil wandering in the fourteenth.

The medieval/ modern link between the two texts is heuristic; the traditional four levels of interpretation for *The Divine Comedy*, the literal, allegorical, moral, and the anagogic, apply with equal force to *Underworld*. The novel can be read in these terms as a record of the period between 1951 and 1992 (from the Dodgers-Giants game through the Cuban Missile Crisis to the end of the Cold War), as an extended metaphor of double signification where the figures and actions are equated to meanings outside the direct narrative (Klara, the artist, redefining the war machine as art, and showing that art connects the randomness of experience), as a representation of ethical principles (the choices Matt, the "bombhead," and Nick, as husband, father, and murderer, must face) and, finally, as a work possessing mystical or spiritual meaning (the theology of individual Christians, members of the clergy and that of the Church).

It can, however, be understood on another level, what is called in Italian the *dietrologica*, the science of "what is behind something. A suspicious event" (280), the science of dark forces that exist behind an event. The characters in the novel sense what Marvin Lundy, the baseball memorabilist racked with cancer, expresses: that there was "some terror working deep beneath the skin that made him gather up things, amass possessions and effects against the dark shape of some unshoulderable loss" (191–92). The characters in Dante share this anxiety.

IV

Satire is tragedy plus time.

—Lenny Bruce, *The Essential Lenny Bruce*

The Dantean world of the novel is the world of Lenny Bruce, embodying his nonconformist language and comic, corrosive morality. DeLillo argues that in a world of madness, only the posture of a Lenny Bruce, the "cool master of uncommon truth," the hipster drawing on a ghetto idiom who often speaks in code, abused by the law, harassed by the right, and attacked by his audiences can survive, speaking words never heard before, delivered in a hepped-up style akin to the black radar-bombardier Louis T. Bakey: "a staccato patter, a kind of hyperdrawl" (610; on Bruce's dialect 585). Yet, language maintains its medieval dimension to control reality expressed in the frequent acknowledgement of its origins and forgotten meanings in the novel. Even the terms used by children when they play possess this power. When you are "it," the term exhibits a "spectral genius" reflecting a part of childhood that "sees through the rhymes and nonsense words, past the hidings and seekings and pretendings to something old and dank, some medieval awe . . . that crawls beneath the midnight skin" (678). Sister Edgar realizes this when she stares at the orange juice billboard where the image of Esmeralda appears. In her mind she equates the lavish effort and technique to paint the detailed drops of juice splashing into a goblet with "medieval church architecture" (820). Whether it is Moonman 157, Sister Edgar, or the senior Italians like Albert Bronzini, the characters use ancient forms of language to be precise.

Father Paulus makes this clear to young Nick when he teaches him the language of a shoe. The welt, the vamp, the aglet, the grommet are particular, exact terms that transform the common into the arcane: "everyday things represent the most overlooked knowledge," Paulus tells him (542), a fact not lost on Nick who would explain to his own children the words for everyday objects: "the little ridged section at the bottom of the toothpaste tube. This is called the crimp" (105). This education is also what Bruce provides for his audiences, only the subjects are more controversial and hidden. As Nick thinks and Bruce enacts, "I wanted to look up velleity and quotidian and memorize the fuckers for all time, spell them, learn them, pronounce them syllable by syllable— vocalize, phonate, utter the sounds, say the words for all they're worth" (543). DeLillo adds that "this is the only way in the world you can escape the things that made you" (543). Lenny Bruce, one is not surprised to learn, traveled with, first, a *Webster's Dictionary* in his suitcase and, later, a copy of *Black's Law Dictionary* (cited in Goldman 401).

Bruce's attack on hypocrisy is the result of his commitment to

194 IRA NADEL

exact words and a reaction to his own run-ins with the law because of the directness of his own language. He shows how the confrontation with language is the confrontation with reality. Language for him is reality but a reality few want to accept as his repeated arrests for the use of obscenity throughout America confirmed. Just as Americans lack the attention span for normal wars, he quips, they prefer to avoid rather than confront language and its reality (544). Even Kennedy's appearance during the week of the Cuban Missile Crisis caused the public to respond to his image, not to his language: "'I saw his hair! Or, I saw his teeth! The spectacle is so dazzling they can't take it all in. I saw his hair!'" Bruce mimics (545). As Sister Edgar later remarks, "it's an epidemic of seeing. No conceivable recess goes unscanned" (812). Bruce, however, did respond to Kennedy's language, appropriating Kennedy's opening for his own, parodying it so that the comedic and the dangerous mixed through his words of welcome: "Good evening, my fellow citizens."

In the novel the use of language is corrupt but not its meaning. The misspelled words underneath the painted angel of Esmeralda Lopez can still be understood. The image of the girl appears through the picture of cascading Minute Maid orange juice framed at the bottom by one hundred cans identified by their typography. But as Moonman 157 expresses his frustration in not being able to find who killed the twelve-year old girl, he explains that "it's all I can do to get these kids so they spell a word correct when they spray their paint," proudly adding that "when I was writing we did subway cars in the dark without a letter misspell" (816). His own ungrammatical expressions, nevertheless, have meaning and are understandable. Ironically, language in the underworld, in the dark, is but above ground confused. After a few days of dangerously large crowds gathering before the mystical billboard, the image and its text disappears, replaced by two words: "*Space Available*" (824 italics DeLillo's).

But, when some individuals confront their reality, they are freed. When Nick realizes that his wife and his partner, Brian, have been having an affair, he is for one moment pleased because he was "relieved" of his "phony role as husband and father, high corporate officer. Because even the job is an artificial limb." He realizes something that Lenny Bruce long preached: none of it, the house, the cars, the children, the marriage, the job, ever belonged to him "except in the sense that I filled out the forms" (796). Appropriately, after this revelation, which occurs in the waste of Russia, Nick and Brian are taken to the Museum of Misshapens, the very embodiment of Dante and Lenny Bruce. There, they observe the shocking actual deformities brought about by radiation and nuclear disaster. This is an encounter with a world so far visible only through Dante's imagery or the comic distancing of Lenny Bruce's routines reconstructed in the novel. It is not the physical that is revealing, however: it is the ability to imagine such a reality in the first place. Or, as their Russian contact Viktor explains, "once they imagine in the beginning, it makes everything true. Nothing you can believe is not coming true" (801–2), he adds, equating himself with the power of J. Edgar Hoover's dossiers where "truth without authority" reigned (559). In sum, "it's all about lost information" where the "dot theory of reality" can be reengineered and restructured so that a dot can be translated into "entire systems of knowledge" (462–63).

One of these systems is, of course, waste, which is "the secret history, underhistory" (791). Part of Bruce's job in the novel is to reclaim language from waste, joining Father Paulus in his effort to show the young Nick that language *can* and *does* identify the parts—whether of shoes or life. And in the midst of the waste land of Russia, Nick imitates the very manner of a Lenny Bruce routine as he speaks to Brian, knowing of Brian's deception: "deep in the stink of a friend's falseheartedness . . . I started talking nonstop, manic and jaggy, babble-mouthing into the plane noise, hinting—I hinted insidiously, made clever references" (792). What was a routine, however, for Lenny Bruce becomes a reality: "all the banned words, the secrets kept in white-washed vaults, the half-forgotten plots—they're all out here now, seeping invisibly into the land and air, into the marrowed folds of the bone" (802–3).

Language used by others had been incapable of conveying meaning. It existed either as acronyms or empty phrases as Klara explained to an interviewer in the desert when relating that Oppenheimer and his cohorts did not even have a name for the bomb: "Oppenheimer said, It is merde. . . . He meant something that eludes naming is automatically relegated, he is saying, to the status of shit. You can't name it. It's too big or evil or outside your experience. It's also shit because it's garbage, it's waste material" (76–77). Bruce tries to name shit for what it is, through his use of obscenities and his riffs with off-color language, naming the ordinary and eliminating the hidden, eradicating the false. Shit, identified of course with garbage, is also slang for drugs but for Bruce it is also a source for his ideas: "he switched more or less in midsentence to a bit he'd been thinking about before all this missile shit, sitting on the can in LA because that's where his best ideas tended to drift into range" (629). The very sentence mixes military and bodily functions, synthesizing creativity and waste.

V

> I'll tell you what I long for, the days of disarray, when I didn't
> give a damn or a fuck or a farthing.
>
> —Nick Shay

Lenny Bruce paid a high price to prevent the waste of language. This meant not only his arrests—supposedly the first American to be seized for using obscene language in public—but his drug dependency and drinking. In the end he was "wasted," drug lingo for his own self-abuse. Paranoid, drug-dependent, on probation and overweight in his final months, Lenny Bruce finally overdosed. But the photos of his death, as it later came out, were staged. He was actually found keeled over in front of a toilet, his denims down around his ankles, with a needle sticking out of his right arm. A blue bathrobe sash was slung around his elbow. Mucus drained out of his nose. The two friends who discovered him got rid of the "spike," blotted away the blood from his needle-scarred arm, and threw the sash into a corner.

The police photos, presumably the ones in Hoover's personal file, show a slightly more dignified Lenny Bruce: he lies naked on his back with his feet pointing toward the toilet and his body laid out on the pantry floor. Coiled around his right wrist is the bathrobe sash and just beyond his right hand is a white box propped against the baseboard with the words "Aspeto Syringes" visible (Goldman 558; the photo appears in the prelims to the biography). The box was originally found by the police under the sink, and the sash was retrieved from the corner. Ironically the syringe that belonged in the box was not even a hypodermic needle; it was a large bulb device used to irrigate his arm when Lenny Bruce was recuperating from gangrene. "A photograph is a universe of dots," DeLillo declares in the novel, but, as we know, although being incriminating, it may not always be truthful (177). The actual cause of death, as stated in the coroner's autopsy, was acute morphine poisoning although those close to him deny his possession of the drug.

The Baltimore Catechism refers not only to the lessons Sister Edgar has drummed into her students but to Lenny Bruce. It was in Baltimore, in February, 1961, that his own "catechism" first appeared: *Stamp Help Out*, a 56-page concert brochure containing several early sections from the autobiography he was writing, the two longest sections in the booklet his reminiscences of vaudeville and a fictitious story of his first sexual encounter. The third topic of the booklet was marijuana, an extended riff on what became parodied as "reefer madness." Entertainment, sex, and drugs: Bruce's trinity and the catechism he would repeat for the remaining five years of his life.

Underworld begins with a voice but ends in silence. From "He speaks in your voice, American, and there's a shine in his eye that's halfway hopeful" to the silent pulses on the computer screen spelling "Peace," the novel moves from a rooted, particular experience to the "white space on map," to that of a blank computer screen, the cyber equal to the *"Space Available"* sign on the repainted billboard. "Cyber" in Greek means to navigate. Traveling from the regulated space of the Polo Grounds in New York to the limitless cyberspace of the computer screen proves what Lenny Bruce knew from the start: that "geography has moved inward and smallward" (788). The novel opens with a line that could apply with equal force to Bruce as to the narrator or to the young Cotter and ends with the sequence "of pulses on a dullish screen" (827). But in-between we learn what Bruce, our Virgil, knew all along and told us although we did not listen: that the "intersecting systems help pull us apart, leaving us vague, drained, docile, soft in our inner discourse, willing to be shaped, to be overwhelmed—easy retreats, half beliefs" (826). Our job is not only to acknowledge the "single seraphic word" (826) that silently stares at us out of the screen but to admit its weaknesses and that its meaning might be lost.

NOTES

1. Lenny Bruce, *The Essential Lenny Bruce*, ed. John Cohen, 61–62. Baltimore was also where Bruce met and fell in love with Honey Harlowe, a statuesque stripper, in 1951. He was playing, unsuccessfully, the Club Charles. The city was also the birthplace of Babe Ruth. The Baltimore Catechism, commissioned by the Third

Plenary Council of Baltimore in November, 1884, the principal synod of the Catholic Church in America, was intended for the instruction of children. It originally had 421 questions and answers, but a revision in 1941 enlarged the text to 499 questions and added an Appendix, "Why I Am a Catholic." The Catechism continued in general schoolroom use until the eve of the Vatican Two Council in 1962.

2. Albert Goldman from the journalism of Lawrence Schiller, *Ladies and Gentlemen, Lenny Bruce*, 218. Interestingly, DeLillo saw Bruce perform once, in New York at The Den in the Duane Hotel in Murray Hill. Kenneth Tynan, who wrote the Introduction to Bruce's autobiography, *How to Talk Dirty and Influence People*, also first caught Bruce's act there. See Gerald Howard, "The American Strangeness: An Interview with Don DeLillo," 3.

3. See Curt Gentry, *J. Edgar Hoover, The Man and The Secrets*, 31. Among Hoover's other peculiarities was the rumor concerning why Hoover always placed his hat behind the head of his companion, Clyde Tolson, when they traveled together each day to the Bureau in Hoover's limousine. Should an assassination attempt occur, the shooter would mistake Tolson for Hoover (22).

4. DeLillo's *Libra* opens with a similar scene: Lee Harvey Oswald riding "the subway to the ends of the city," shooting past the figures standing on the platforms, smashing through the dark. Riding in the front car, he realizes that "the subway held more compelling things than the famous city above," the tunnels holding a "purer form" of life "beneath the streets" (3–4). "The dark had a power" he realizes: "the beams picked out secret things," revealing the "secret force of the soul in the tunnels under New York" (13).

Works Cited

Amis, Martin. "An Excerpt from Martin Amis' Review of *Mao II*." Available online, http://martinamis.albion.edu.

———. "Survivors of the Cold War." *New York Times Book Review* (5 October 1997): 12–13.

Barthel, Manfred. *The Jesuits: History & Legend of the Society of Jesus*. Translated by Mark Howson. New York: Morrow, 1984.

Baudrillard, Jean. "History: A Retro Scenario." In *Simulcra and Simulation*. Translated by Sheila Faria Glaser. Ann Arbor: University of Michigan Press, 1994.

Begley, Adam. "Don DeLillo: The Art of Fiction." *Paris Review* 35 (Fall 1993): 274–306.

Benjamin, Walter. *The Arcades Project*. Translated by Howard Eiland, and Kevin McLaughlin. Cambridge: Harvard University Press, 1999.

Billen, Andrew. "Up from the Underworld." *London Evening Standard* (28 January 1998). Available online, http://www.thisislondon.co.uk.

Bizzell, Patricia. "Pecuniary Emulation of the Mediator in *The Great Gatsby*." *Modern Language Notes* 94 (1979): 774–83.

Boyer, Paul. *By the Dawn's Early Light: American Thought and Culture at the Dawn of the Atomic Age*. New York: Pantheon, 1985.

Brown, Gayle K. "'Into the Hands of the Papists': New England Captives in French Canada and the English Anti-Catholic Tradition, 1689–1763." *The Maryland Historian* 21:2 (1990): 1–11.

Cogliano, Francis D. *No King, No Popery: Anti-Catholicism in Revolutionary New England*. Westport, CT: Greenwood Press, 1995.

Cohen, John, ed. *The Essential Lenny Bruce*. New York: Ballantine, 1967.

Coover, Robert. *The Universal Baseball Association, Inc., J. Henry Waugh, Prop.* New York: Penguin, 1971.

Cowart, David. "The Luddite Vision: *Mason & Dixon*." *American Literature* 71:2 (1999): 341–63.

Dante. *The Inferno of Dante*. Translated by Robert Pinsky. New York: Farrar, Straus, and Giroux, 1994.

———. *The Portable Dante*. Translated by Laurence Binyon; edited by Paolo Milano. New York: Penguin, 1977.

DeCurtis, Anthony. "'An Outsider in This Society': An Interview with Don DeLillo." In *Introducing Don DeLillo*. Edited by Frank Lentricchia. Durham, NC: Duke University Press, 1991: 43–66.

DeLillo, Don. *Americana*. Boston: Houghton, 1971.

———. *The Body Artist.* New York: Scribner's, 2001.

———. *End Zone.* Boston: Houghton, 1972.

———. *Great Jones Street.* Boston: Houghton, 1973.

———. *Libra.* New York: Viking, 1988.

———. *Mao II.* New York: Viking, 1991.

———. *The Names.* New York: Knopf, 1982.

———. "Pafko at the Wall." *Harper's* (October 1992): 35–50.

———. *Players.* New York: Knopf, 1977.

———. "The Power of History." *New York Times Sunday Magazine* (7 September 1997). Available online, http:www.nytimes.com/library/books/090797article3.mtml.

———. *Ratner's Star.* New York: Knopf, 1976.

———. *Running Dog.* New York: Knopf, 1978.

———. *Underworld.* New York: Scribner's, 1997.

———. *Valparaiso.* New York: Scribner's, 1999.

———. *White Noise.* New York: Viking, 1985.

Dewey, Joseph, ed. "*Aethlon*'s Fifty Most Influential Works Survey." *Aethlon: Journal of Sport Literature* 16:2 (Summer 1999): 161–62.

Douglas, Mary. *Purity and Danger: An Analysis of the Concepts of Pollution and Taboo.* London: Routledge, 1984.

Duvall, John N. "Baseball as Aesthetic Ideology: Cold War History, Race, and DeLillo's 'Pafko at the Wall.'" *Modern Fiction Studies* 41 (1995): 285–313.

———. "Introduction: From Valparaiso to Jerusalem: DeLillo and the Moment of Canonization." *Modern Fiction Studies* 45 (1999): 559–68.

Ebert, Roger. "*Strangelove* Still a Mind-Blowing Treatise on Nuclear War." *Chicago Sun-Times* (28 October 1994): 44.

Eliot, T. S. "Portrait of a Lady." In *T. S. Eliot: Collected Poems, 1909–1962.* San Diego: Harcourt, 1964: 8.

———. "*Ulysses*, Order, and Myth." In *Selected Prose of T. S. Eliot.* Edited by Frank Kermode. New York: Harcourt, 1975.

———. *The Waste Land.* In *T. S. Eliot: Collected Poems, 1909–1962.* San Diego: Harcourt, 1964: 51–76.

Fitzgerald, F. Scott. *The Great Gatsby.* 1925. Edited by Matthew J. Bruccoli. New York: Scribner's, 1995.

Frazer, James George. *The New Golden Bough.* Edited by Theodor H. Gaster. New York: Criterion, 1959.

Gentry, Curt. *J. Edgar Hoover, The Man and The Secrets.* New York: Norton, 1991.

Gillmor, Don. "Baseballs and Bombs [Review of *Underworld*]." *Maclean's* (23 February 1998): 66, 68.

Goldman, Albert. *Ladies and Gentlemen, Lenny Bruce.* New York: Random House, 1974.

Hassan, Ihab. "Toward a Conception of Postmodernism." In *A Postmodern Reader.* Edited by Joseph Natoli, and Linda Hutcheon. Albany: State University of New York Press, 1993.

Heidegger, Martin. "The Origin of the Work of Art." In *Basic Writings*. Edited by David Krell; translated by Albert Hofstadter. New York: Harper, 1993. 143–212.

Helyer, Ruth. " 'Refuse Heaped Many Stories High': DeLillo, Dirt, and Disorder." *Modern Fiction Studies* 45 (1999): 987–1006.

Hexter, J. H. "The Rhetoric of History." In *Doing History*. Bloomington: Indiana University Press, 1971: 15–76.

Hofstadter, Richard. *The Paranoid Style in American Politics and Other Essays*. New York: Knopf, 1965.

Howard, Gerald. "The American Strangeness: An Interview with Don DeLillo." *Hungry Mind Review: An Independent Book Review* (1 September 1997). Available online, http://www.bookwire.com/hmr/hmrinterviews.article.

Hutcheon, Linda. *A Poetics of Postmodernism: History, Theory, Fiction*. New York: Routledge, 1988.

Johnston, Ian. "Does God Ride a Harley? And If He Does, Does He Wear a Helmet?" Lecture, 19 February 1997, Malaspina University-College, British Columbia, Canada.

Jones, Malcolm, Jr. "DeLillo Hits a Home Run [Review of *Underworld*]." *Newsweek* (22 September 1997): 84–85.

Joyce, James. *A Portrait of the Artist as a Young Man*. 1916. Edited by Chester G. Anderson. New York: Penguin, 1977.

Kahn, Herman. *Thinking about the Unthinkable*. New York: Horizon, 1962.

Kakutani, Michiko. "Of America as a Splendid Junk Heap [Review of *Underworld*]." *The New York Times* (16 Septemer 1997). Available online http://www.nytimes.com/books/97/09/14/daily.

Kavadlo, Jesse. "Celebration and Annihilation: The Balance of *Underworld*." *Undercurrent* 7 (Spring 1999). Available online, http://darkwing.uoregon.edu.

Kirkpatrick, Robin. *Dante's "Inferno": Difficulty and Dead Poetry*. Cambridge: Cambridge University Press, 1987.

Knight, Peter. "'Everything Is Connected': *Underworld's* Secret History of Paranoia." *Modern Fiction Studies* 45 (1999): 811–36.

Körte, Peter. "Sprache ise der Einzige Fluchtweg." *Der Standard* (30 October 1998): A1.

Leach, Marjorie. "Underworld Gods." In *Guide to the Gods*. Edited by Michael Owen-Jones, and Frances Cattermole-Tally. London: Gale Research, 1992.

LeClair, Tom. "An Underhistory of Mid-Century America [Review of *Underworld*]." *Atlantic* (October 1997). Available online, http://www/theatlantic.com/issues/97.

LeClair, Tom, and Larry McCaffery, eds. "Interview with Don DeLillo." In *Anything Can Happen*. Urbana: University of Illinois Press, 1983. 79–90.

Lentricchia, Frank. "The American Writer as Bad Citizen." In *Introducing Don DeLillo*. Edited by Lentricchia. Durham, NC: Duke University Press, 1991: 1–7.

Letson, Douglas, and Michael Higgins. *The Jesuit Mystique*. London: Harper, 1996.

Lewis, James R. " 'Mind-Forged Manacles': Anti-Catholic Convent Narratives in the Context of the American Captivity Tale Tradition." *Mid-America: An Historical Review* 72:3 (1990): 149–67.

Lewis, R. W. B. *The American Adam: Innocence, Tragedy, and Tradition in the Nineteenth Century*. Chicago: University of Chicago Press, 1955.

LoBrutto, Vincent. *Stanley Kubrick: A Biography*. New York: De Capo, 1999.

Mallon, Thomas. "The Bronx, with Thonx [Review of *Underworld*]." *GQ* (September 1997): 193–96.

Marotti, Arthur. "Southwell's Remains: Catholicism and Anti-Catholicism in Early Modern England." In *Texts and Cultural Change in Early Modern England*. Edited by Cedric C. Brown and Marotti. New York: St. Martin's Press, 1997: 37–65.

McClure, John A. "Postmodern/Post-Secular: Contemporary Fiction and Spirituality." *Modern Fiction Studies* 41 (1995): 141–63.

Melley, Timothy. *Empire of Conspiracy: The Culture of Paranoia in Postwar America*. Ithaca: Cornell University Press, 2000.

Miller, Jonathan. "The Sick White Negro." *Partisan Review* 30 (1963).

Morris, Timothy. *Making the Team: The Cultural Work of Baseball Fiction*. Urbana: University of Illinois Press, 1997.

Nel, Philip. "'A Small Incisive Shock': Modern Forms, Postmodern Politics, and the Role of the Avant-Garde in *Underworld*." *Modern Fiction Studies* 45 (1999): 724–52.

Noble, David. *The Eternal Adam and the New World Garden: The Central Myth in the American Novel since 1830*. New York: Braziller, 1968.

Osen, Diane. "A Conversation with Don DeLillo." *Publishers Weekly/National Book Foundation* (April 2001). Available online, http://www.pubweekly.com.

———. "Window on a Writing Life: A Conversation with National Book Award Winner Don DeLillo." *The BOMC Reading Room*. Available online, from http://www.bomc.com/ows-bin/owa/rrauthorinterviews.

Osteen, Mark. *American Magic and Dread: Don DeLillo's Dialogue with Culture*. Philadelphia: University of Pennsylvania Press, 2000.

Otto, Rudolf. *The Idea of the Holy*. Translated by John H. Harvey. London: Oxford University Press, 1950.

Ovid. *Metamorphoses*. Translated by Horace Gregory. New York: Viking, 1958.

Parrish, Timothy L. "From Hoover's FBI to Eisenstein's *Unterwelt*: DeLillo Directs the Postmodern Novel." *Modern Fiction Studies* 45 (1999): 696–723.

Passaro, Vince. "The Unsparing Vision of Don DeLillo." *Harper's* (November 1997): 72–75.

Pynchon, Thomas. *Gravity's Rainbow*. New York: Viking, 1973.

———. *Mason & Dixon*. New York: Holt, 1997.

Reynolds, David. *Beneath the American Renaissance: The Subversive Imagination in the Age of Emerson and Melville*. Cambridge: Harvard University Press, 1988.

Sanders, Scott. "Pynchon's Paranoid History." In *Mindful Pleasures: Essays on Thomas Pynchon*. Edited by George Levine, and David Levernz. Boston: Little, 1976: 139–59.

Serres, Michel. *The Parasite*. Translated by Lawrence R. Schehr. Baltimore: Johns Hopkins University Press, 1982.

Updike, John. "Hub Fans Bid Kid Adieu." In *Assorted Prose*. New York: Knopf, 1977: 127–47.

———. *Hub Fans Bid Kid Adieu*. Northridge: Lord John Press, 1977.

———. "Packed Dirt, Churchgoing, A Dying Cat, A Traded Car." In *Pigeon Feathers*. New York: Knopf, 1962: 246–79.

Vickery, John. *The Literary Impact of "The Golden Bough."* Princeton: Princeton University Press, 1973.

Walsh, James J. *American Jesuits*. 1934. New York: Library of America, 1984.

Westbrook, Deeanne. *Ground Rules: Baseball & Myth*. Urbana: University of Illinois Press, 1996.

Weston, Jessie L. *From Ritual to Romance*. 1920. Princeton: Princeton University Press, 1993.

Wiegand, David. "We Are What We Waste [Review of *Underworld*]." *San Francisco Chronicle* (21 September 1997). Available online, http://www.sfgate.com/cgi-bin/article.cgi?file = chronicle/archive/1997/0 9/21/RV14784.DTC.

Wills, Garry. *Witches and Jesuits: Shakespeare's "Macbeth."* New York: Oxford University Press, 1995.

Wood, James. "Black Noise [Review of *Underworld*.]" *The New Republic* (10 November 1997). Available online, http://magazines.enews.com/magazines/tnr/archive.html.

Wood, Michael. "Post-Paranoid [Review of *Underworld*]." *London Review of Books* (5 February 1998). Available online, http://www/lrb.co.uk/v20n03.

Underworld: A Bibliography

Marc Singer and Jackson R. Bryer

Listed below are all the materials related to *UNDERWORLD* that we could locate, including prepublication notices, reviews (marked with an asterisk), interviews, scholarly essays, and book sections. All items listed have been personally seen by the compilers. For significant assistance in giving us access to their files on DeLillo and *Underworld*, we wish to thank Brant Rumble and Nan Graham of Simon & Schuster.

I. Reviews, Interviews, and Features

* Alford, Steven E. "The Buried and the Lonely." *Ft. Lauderdale Sun-Sentinel* (28 September 1997): 9f.

* Amis, Martin. "Survivors of the Cold War." *New York Times Book Review* (5 October 1997): 12–13.

* Anderson, Don. " 'Cold War and Peace': The Hit That Should Be Read Around the World." *Sydney Morning Herald* (22 November 1997): 6:11.

* *Arena* (1 January 1998).

* Attwood, Alan. "DeLillo hits a homer." *Sydney Morning Herald* (25 October 1997): sec. 6, 11.

* Baker, Jeff. "DeLillo's grand slam." *Portland Oregonian* (5 October 1997): G1, G6.

* Barrett, Sharon. "Garbage." *Chicago Sun-Times* (21 September 1997): B23.

Battersby, Eileen. "Good stuff from the US." *Irish Times Weekend* (27 December 1997): 11. [*Underworld* listed as Battersby's top pick of American books]

* Beach, Patrick. "Peeling back *Underworld*." *Austin American-Statesman* (21 September 1997): D6.

* Begley, Adam. "In DeLillo's Hands, Waste Is a Beautiful Thing." *New York Observer* (15 September 1997): 38.

* Bell, Millicent. *Partisan Review* 65 (Spring 1998): 259.

"Best Books of 1997." *Library Journal* 123 (January 1998): 53.

* Billen, Andrew. "Up from the Underworld." *London Evening Standard* (28 January 1998): 25–26. [Interview]

Bing, Jonathan. "The Ascendance of Don DeLillo." *Publishers Weekly* (11 August 1997): 261–63. [Profile, focusing primarily on DeLillo's publication history]

* Birkerts, Sven. "Don DeLillo's Brave New World." *Double Take* 14 (Fall 1998): 126.

* Blythe, Will. "Oh, Beautiful." *Mirabella* 9 (September/October 1997): 50, 52.

Booklist 94 (1 January 1998): 730.

* Bowman, James. "History Beneath the Surface." *Wall Street Journal* (26 September 1997): A20.

* Boyd, William. "The course of true life." *The Observer Reviews* (11 January 1998): 15.

* Bradbury, Malcolm. "Not just a game of ball." *London Times* (1 January 1998): 30.

* Bradfield, Scott. "Secrets and Lies." *London Sunday Mail* (4 January 1998).

* Brezinski, Steve. *Antioch Review* 56 (Summer 1998): 378.

* Brown, Mick. "They're all out to get him." *Daily Telegraph Magazine* (3 January 1998): 30–35. [Review/Interview]

* Bukiet, Melvin Jules. "Below the surface." *Chicago Tribune Books* (21 September 1997): 1, 12.

* Burkman, Greg. "Life in America, Cold War-Style." *Seattle Times* (5 October 1997): M2.

Cahill, Timothy. "Author DeLillo Opens a Window on Himself." *Times Union* (15 November 1997): D4. [Interview/Profile, reports on a reading given at the New York State Writers' Institute]

* Caldwell, Gail. "Blasts from the Past." *Boston Globe* (28 September 1997): F1.

———. "Season's Readings: Critic's Choice: The Year's Best Fiction." *Boston Globe* (7 December 1997): G1, G6. [*Underworld* one of seven works of fiction selected]

* Campbell, McCoy. "*Underworld* is a tedious novel for the intellect." *Chattanooga Times* (23 October 1997).

* Case, Brian. *Time Out* (14–21 January 1998): 50.

* Cheuse, Alan. "Only in America." *Dallas Morning News* (28 September 1997): 8:J.

* Chinen, Nate. "Unnameable." *Philadelphia City Paper* (25 September–2 October 1997): 33. Available online, http://www.citypaper.net/articles/092597/bq.underworld.shtml.

* Clark, Lesley. "Touching base." *Scotland on Sunday* (28 December 1997).

* Clements, Denney. "*Underworld* is an uplifting masterwork." *Wichita Eagle* (5 October 1997).

* Conte, Joseph. "A masterful half-century mosaic of America's hybrid culture." *Buffalo News* (19 October 1997): F-6.

Cryer, Dan. "Low Profile." *Newsday* (28 October 1997): B6, B7.

* DeHaven, Tom. "High Anxiety." *Entertainment Weekly* (3 October 1997): 74–75.

* Deignan, Thomas. "Apocalypse, Then and Now." *The World & I* 13 (March 1998): 251–60.

"DeLillo Courts a Big Audience with a Big Novel." *Time* (8 September 1997): 71.

DeLillo, Don. "The Power of History." *New York Times Magazine* (7 September

1997): 60–63. [Short essay on the role of history in fiction and on the historical inspirations for *Underworld*]

* De Man, George. "Plumbing the Underworld." *Agni* (Web Issue 6, 1998). Available online, http://webdelsol.com/AGNI/asp98-gm.htm.

* Dibdin, Michael. "Out to get us." *London Sunday Times Books* (4 January 1998): 8.

* Dirda, Michael. "The Blast Felt Round the World." *Washington Post Book World* (28 September 1997): 1, 10.

* Docx, Edward. *London Express* (4 January 1998).

"Don DeLillo: the essential dinner-party guide." *New Statesman* (23 January 1998): 47.

* Downing, Ben. "Stalking the Elusive Zeitgeist." *New Leader* (22 September 1997): 17–18.

* Dugdale, John. "How Two Great Americans See One Garbage Dump." *Literary Review* (January 1998): 30–31.

* Dyer, Geoff. "Master of the mythic." *London Sunday Telegraph Books* (4 January 1998): 13.

* Eder, Richard. "Bard of the Bronx." *Newsday* (28 September 1997): B9, B11.

———. "Lost Souls." *Los Angeles Times Book Review* (28 September 1997): 2.

———. "Richard Eder's 10 Best Books of 1997." *Los Angeles Times Book Review* (14 December 1997): 11.

"Editor's Choice." *New York Times Book Review* (7 December 1997): 95. [*Underworld* selected as one of the best books of 1997]

"Editor's Choice: Best Bets of '97." *San Francisco Sunday Examiner & Chronicle Book Review* (23 November 1997): 2. [*Underworld* selected]

* Egerton, Ann. "Another Shot at History." *Norfolk Virginian-Pilot* (28 September 1997): J2.

* Elie, Paul. "DeLillo's surrogate believers." *Commonweal* (7 November 1997): 19–22.

———. "The Don of American novels." *Elle* (October 1997): 120.

* Ellenberg, Jordan. "A Waste of Games." *Boston Book Review* (4 October 1997): 36–37.

Feeney, Mark. "DeLillo's Dilemma." *Boston Globe* (30 September 1997): E1, E7. [Interview/Profile]

* Friend, Tad. "People are talking about: books." *Vogue* (October 1997): 266, 268. [A very light review]

Fry, Dann. "DeLillo's view: Where fiction and history intersect." *Seattle Times* (21 October 1997): F1, F2. [Interview/Profile]

Gardner, Curt. "UNDERWORLD Media Watch." *Don DeLillo's America: A Don DeLillo Page*. Available online, http://www.perival.com/delillo/underworld media.html. [Indexes reviews and other publications about *Underworld*]

* Gardner, James. "The Los Angeles of Novels." *National Review* (24 November 1997): 60–61.

* Gediman, Paul. "Visions of the American Berserk." *Boston Review* 22 (October/ November 1997): 46–48.

* Gerard, Philip. "Big Shots." Raleigh *News & Observer* (5 October 1997): 4G.

* Gillmor, Don. "Baseball and bombs: Don DeLillo prowls the shadows of America." *Maclean's* (23 February 1998): 66, 69.

* "Global overreach: A less-than-great American novel." *Economist* (8 November 1997): 94.

* Goddard, Dan R. "Is it a novel or a doorstop?" *San Antonio Express-News* (9 November 1997): 4J.

* Goetz, Thomas. "Future Shlock." *Village Voice* (26 August 1997): 43.

* Goldenberg, Judi. "Cold War Years: DeLillo Truly Depicts 1950s." *Richmond Times-Dispatch* (26 October 1997): K4.

* Gray, Paul. "How Did We Get Here?" *Time* (29 September 1997): 89–90.

* Green, Blake. "The Shot Heard 'Round the World." *San Francisco Chronicle* (14 October 1997): B1, B4.

* Hagen, W. M. *World Literature Today* 73 (Winter 1999): 145.

* Hannan, Brian R. "Rewinding History." *Dayton News* (3 October 1997).

* Hantke, Steffen. "Lessons in Latent History." *Electronic Book Review* 7 (Summer 1998). Available online, http://www.altx.com/ebr/reviews/rev7/r7han.htm.

* Harper, John. "DeLillo pursues refuse as he gets to heart of history." *Orlando Sentinel* (28 September 1997): F-8.

* Held, James. "We are the underworld." *Philadelphia Inquirer Books* (5 October 1997): Q1, Q6.

* Henderson, David W. *Library Journal* (1 September 1997): 216.

* Hensher, Philip. "Running wild with the ball." *Spectator* (3 January 1998): 22–23.

* Hitchens, Christopher. "Excuse-me-but-I-think-you-just-dropped-this-name." *Evening Standard* (11 December 1997): 11. [The article is highly critical of *Underworld's* prepublication hype but more appreciative of the novel than its title would suggest. Reprinted online as "*Underworld*: over-hyped and over here," at http://www.thisislondon.co.uk/dynamic/lifestyle/bottom_review.html?in_review_id=19888&in_review_text_id=15935]

Hoffert, Barbara, and Mark Annichiarico. "Prepublication Alert." *Library Journal* (1 June 1997): 78.

Jacobs, Alexandra. "The Best and Worst: Books." *Entertainment Weekly* (26 December 1997): 152. [Listed as one of the best books of 1997]

* Jones, Malcolm, Jr. "DeLillo Hits a Home Run." *Newsweek* (22 September 1997): 84–85.

* Kakutani, Michiko. "Of America as a Splendid Junk Heap." *New York Times* (16 September 1997): B1, B7.

Kamp, David. "DeLillo's Home Run." *Vanity Fair* (September 1997): 202, 204. [An extremely light review, sprinkled with a few quotes from DeLillo]

* Kendrick, Walter. "Fiction in Review." *Yale Review* 86 (April 1998): 143–52.

* Keough, Peter. "Innocence lost." *Providence* (RI) *Phoenix* (3 October 1997).

* Koster, Kim. *Anniston Star* (28 September 1997): 4F.

* Larson, Susan. "Perfect pitch." *New Orleans Times-Picayune* (28 September 1997): D6, D7.

* Lawson, Terry. "A great American novel." *Detroit Free Press* (28 September 1997): 7E.

* LeClair, Tom. "An Underhistory of Mid-Century America." *Atlantic Monthly* (October 1997): 113–216.

* Leonard, John. "American Jitters." *Nation* (3 November 1997): 18, 20, 22–24.

* Levy, Deborah. "Tested to destruction." *The Independent Magazine* (3 January 1998): 10

* Li, Victor. "Book Reviews." *Dalhousie Review* 76 (Autumn 1996): 445–49.

Lyman, Rick. "Finalists for Book Award Named." *New York Times* (16 November 1997): B3. [Reports *Underworld*'s nomination for the National Book Award]

* Malin, Irving. *Review of Contemporary Fiction* 17 (Fall 1997): 217.

* Mallon, Thomas. "The Bronx, With Thonx." *GQ* 67 (September 1997): 193–94, 196.

* Marchand, Philip. "When Garbage and Paranoia Rule." *Toronto Star* (4 October 1997): M17.

* Max, D. T. "Home runs, bombs, toxic waste, and thinking the unthinkable." *Miami Herald* (28 September 1997): 4L.

* McCracken, Henry Joy. "The aftermath of paranoia." *LM* 109 (April 1998). Available online, http://www.informinc.co.uk/LM/LM109/LM109_Books.html#3.

* McEnroe, Colin. "Don DeLillo's millenial masterpiece." *Rock Hill Herald* (12 October 1997): 4E, 6E.

* McKay, Peter. "A literary giant hits home with epic tale of America." *London Daily Mail* (9 January 1998).

* McManis, Sam. "The world that came in from the Cold War." *Ft. Worth Star-Telegram* (12 October 1997): Sec. E: 7. [Also printed in *San Ramon Valley* (CA) *Times* (21 September 1997).]

* Mellen, Joan. "*Underworld*—DeLillo's Triumph." *Baltimore Sun* (28 September 1997): 4E.

* Mewshaw, Michael. "The uses of junk." *New Statesman* (2 January 1998): 52.

* Miller, Sarah. "One nation, undercover." *Salon* (September 1997). Available online, http://www.salon.com/sept97/delillo970926.html.

Minzesheimer, Bob. "Author steps out of shadow with best seller." *USA Today* (23 October 1997): 3D, 4D. [Interview/Review]

* Morrison, Blake. "A big hit strikes it lucky." *Independent Sunday Review* (4 January 1998): 24–25.

Nel, Philip. "The Don DeLillo Society Bibliography." *The Don DeLillo Society.* Available online, http://www.ksu.edu/english/nelp/delillo/biblio.html. [Useful index of scholarly articles on all of DeLillo's writings, including *Underworld*]

* Norman, Geoffrey. "DeLillo's History of the Underworld." *Playboy* (November 1997): 31. [Very brief]

* Novak, Ralph. *People* (13 October 1997): 33.

O'Briant, Don. "Book Notes." *Atlanta Journal* (25 January 1998).

* O'Hagan, Andrew. "National Enquirer: Don DeLillo Gets under America's Skin." *Village Voice Literary Supplement* (16 September 1997): 8–10.

O'Toole, Fintan. "And quiet writes the Don." *Irish Times Weekend* (10 January 1998): 5. [Interview]

* Packer, George. "The Novel as Counterhistory." *Dissent* 45 (Winter 1998): 124–28.

* Passaro, Vince. "The Unsparing Vision of Don DeLillo." *Harper's* (November 1997): 72–75.

* Pearson, Allison. "Sermon on the scrapheap." *London Evening Standard* (12 January 1998): 45.

"Picks & Pans." *People* (13 October 1997): 33.

* Powe, B. W. "Don DeLillo takes on America." *Globe and Mail* (27 September 1997): D13.

* *Publishers Weekly* 244 (14 July 1997): 67.

"PW's Best Books 1997: Fiction." *Publishers Weekly* (3 November 1997): 51.

Quinn, Judy. "Scribner Nabs Next DeLillo." *Publishers Weekly* (11 November 1996): 24. [Prepublication notice for *Underworld*]

* Quinn, Paul. "Hitting the home run." *Times Literary Supplement* (26 December 1997): 21.

* Remnick, David. "Exile on Main Street." *New Yorker* (15 September 1997): 42–48. [Review/Interview]

Renzetti, Elizabeth. "*Underworld's* invisible man." Toronto *Globe and Mail* (25 November 1997): D1, D2. [Interview/Profile]

* Roberts, Rex. "Navigating the 'Underworld' of nuclear-age America." *Washington Times* (5 October 1997): B8.

* Salm, Arthur. "Analyzing the dots, DeLillo-style." *San Diego Union-Tribune Books* (5 October 1997): 2.

* Sante, Luc. "Between Hell and History." *New York Review of Books* 44 (6 November 1997): 4, 6–7.

* Seaman, Donna. *Booklist* 93 (August 1997): 1847.

* Shindler, Dorman T. "Flashbacks underscore modern America's ills." *Denver Post* (5 October 1997): 5F.

* Silleck, Sean. "*Underworld*: Novel brilliantly unearths 'underhistory.'" *Fayetteville* (NC) *Observer-Times* (12 October 1997).

* Silver, Daniel J. "Waste Management." *Commentary* (December 1997): 63.

Stern, Lorin. "The Crying of October 29." *Publishers Weekly* (11 August 1997): 263. [Blurb discussing the bidding for publication and screen rights]

Stillman, Rob. *Details* (November 1997): 98.

* Stonum, Gary Lee. "Seeking America's secret truths." *Cleveland Plain Dealer* (21 September 1997): 11-I.

* Strawson, Galen. "The Bomb and the baseball." *London Financial Times Weekend* (10/11 January 1998): 5.

Streitfield, David. "Don DeLillo's Hidden Truths." *Washington Post* (11 November 1997): D1-D2. [Interview/Profile]

Takahama, Valerie. "Musings on Writing, Art, and the Cold War." *Orange County Register* (26 October 1997): 23–24. [Interview/Profile]

* Tanner, Tony. "Afterthoughts on Don DeLillo's *Underworld.*" *Raritan* 17 (Spring 1998): 48–71.

Time (29 December 1997): 155. [*Underworld* listed as number two in "The Best Books of 1997"]

Trumm, James F. "The past explains the present." Toledo *Blade* (26 October 1997): G3.

Ulin, David L. "Secret history." *San Jose Mercury News Books* (12 October 1997): 3.

* "*Underworld.*" *Kirkus Reviews* 65 (1 July 1997): 967–68.

* Walsh, David. "The serious artist and the Cold War." *World Socialist Web Site* (November 1998). Available online, http://wsws.org/arts/1998/nov1998/und-n03.shtml.

* Walton, David. "A sprawling—maybe too sprawling—epic." *Star Tribune* (19 October 1997): F16. [Review also run in *Greensburg Tribune-Review* (28 September 1997); Louisville *Courier-Journal* (28 September 1997); *Trenton Times* (28 September 1997); *Arkansas Democrat-Gazette* (21 September 1997); and *St. Petersburg Times* (21 September 1997)]

* Ward, Nathan. "One Degree of Separation—Unearthing *Underworld*'s Bouncing Ball." *Village Voice* (23 September 1997): 141.

* Weisenburger, Steven. "*Underworld* on top of its game." *Lexington Herald-Leader* (28 September 1997): F6.

"What's Up This Fall." *Newsweek* (8 September 1997): 68. [Small preview of *Underworld*'s publication]

* Wiegand, David. "We Are What We Waste." *San Francisco Chronicle Book Review* (21 September 1997): 1, 6.

* Williams, Richard. "Everything under the bomb." *Manchester Guardian Weekend* (10 January 1998): 32–33, 35, 37. [Review/Interview]

Wolcott, James. "Blasts from the Past." *New Criterion* (December 1997): 65–70.

* Wood, James. "Black Noise." *New Republic* (10 November 1997): 38–44.

* Wood, Michael. "Post-Paranoid." *London Review of Books* 20 (5 February 1998): 3, 5.

* Wynn, Judith. "Underwhelming: DeLillo bites off more than we can chew." *Boston Sunday Herald* (5 October 1997): 61.

II. Scholarly Articles

Begley, Adam. "Don DeLillo: *Americana, Mao II,* and *Underworld.*" *Southwest Review* 82 (1997): 478–505.

Bérubé, Michael. "Endpaper." *Context: A Forum for Literary Arts and Culture* 5 (Fall 2000). Available online, http://www.centerforbookculture.org/context/no5/berube.html.

Castle, Robert. "DeLillo's *Underworld*: Everything that Descends Must Converge."

Undercurrents 7 (Spring 1999). Available online, http://darkwing. uoregon.edu/~ucurrent/uc7/7-cast.html.

Ford, Douglas Edward. "Waveforms Constantly Changing: Postmodernizing Electricity in American Fiction." Diss. 1998: Florida State University. *Dissertation Abstracts International* Section A 59.3 (September 1998): 821.

Green, Jeremy. "Disaster Footage: Spectacles of Violence in DeLillo's Fiction." *Modern Fiction Studies* 45 (1999): 571–99.

Helyer, Ruth. " 'Refuse Heaped Many Stories High': DeLillo, Dirt, and Disorder." *Modern Fiction Studies* 45 (1999): 987–1006.

Kavadlo, Jesse. "Celebration & Annihilation: The Balance of *Underworld.*" *Undercurrents* 7 (Spring 1999). Available online, http://darkwing.uoregon.edu/ ~ucurrent/uc7/7-kava.html.

Knight, Peter. "Everything Is Connected: *Underworld*'s Secret History of Paranoia." *Modern Fiction Studies* 45 (1999): 811–36. Revised and reprinted in Peter Knight, *Conspiracy Culture: From the Kennedy Assassination to "The X-Files."* London: Routledge, 2000.

Nel, Philip. "'A Small Incisive Shock': Modern Forms, Postmodern Politics, and the Role of the Avant-Garde in *Underworld.*" *Modern Fiction Studies* 45 (1999): 724–52.

O'Donnell, Patrick. "Under History, *Underworld.*" *Latent Destinies: Cultural Paranoia in Contemporary U.S. Narrative.* Durham, NC: Duke University Press, 2000.

Parrish, Timothy L. "From Hoover's FBI to Eisenstein's *Unterwelt*: DeLillo Directs the Postmodern Novel." *Modern Fiction Studies* 45 (1999): 696–723.

Pincott, Jennifer. "The Inner Workings: Technoscience, Self, and Society in DeLillo's *Underworld.*" *Undercurrents* 7 (Spring 1999). Available online, http:// darkwing.uoregon.edu/ucurrent/uc7/7-pin.html.

Ruppersburg, Hugh, and Tim Engles, eds. *Critical Essays on Don DeLillo.* New York: G. K. Hall, 2000.

Tanner, Tony. "Don DeLillo and 'the American mystery': *Underworld.*" *The American Mystery: American Literature from Emerson to DeLillo.* New York: Cambridge University Press, 2000. 201–21.

Walker, Joseph. "Criminality, the Real, and the Story of America: The Case of Don DeLillo." *Centennial Review* 43 (1999): 433–66.

Notes on Contributors

JACKSON R. BRYER is Professor of English at the University of Maryland, where he teaches courses in American drama and American fiction since 1920. His most recent publications are *The Actor's Art: Conversations with Contemporary American Stage Performers* and *F. Scott Fitzgerald: New Perspectives*.

DAVID COWART, Louise Fry Scudder Professor of American Literature at the University of South Carolina, has published widely in virtually every journal devoted to contemporary literature. His books include *Literary Symbiosis: The Reconfigured Text in Twentieth-Century Writing; Thomas Pynchon: The Art of Allusion; Arches and Light: The Fiction of John Gardner;* and *History and the Contemporary Novel*. His essay here is drawn from his recent work on DeLillo, *Don DeLillo: The Physics of Language*.

JOSEPH DEWEY, Associate Professor of American Literature for the University of Pittsburgh, is the author of *In a Dark Time: The Apocalyptic Temper of the American Novel in the Nuclear Age* and *Novels from Reagan's America: A New Realism*. He is completing work on a study on the fiction of Richard Powers. His essays and reviews have appeared in *The Review of Contemporary Fiction, Aethlon: The Journal of Sport Literature, The Hollins Critics, The Mississippi Quarterly, The Steinbeck Quarterly,* and *Modern Fiction Studies*.

KATHLEEN FITZPATRICK is an Assistant Professor of English and Media Studies at Pomona College. She has published essays on Edith Wharton and Thomas Pynchon and is currently finishing a book-length manuscript on representations of the electronic media in Pynchon and DeLillo.

JOANNE GASS is a Professor of English and Comparative Literature at California State University at Fullerton. Her specialization is the contemporary novel, and she has published articles on Angela Carter, Jamaica Kincaid, Joseph Conrad, Carlos Fuentes, and the Latin American novel.

PAUL GLEASON, who recently completed his doctoral studies at the University of Texas-Austin, has published essays and reviews in the *D. H. Lawrence Review* and *Joyce Studies Annual*.

DONALD J. GREINER holds the chair of Carolina Distinguished Professor of English at the University of South Carolina where he is also Associate Provost and Dean of Undergraduate Affairs. He has published books on Stephen Crane, Robert Frost, John Hawkes, John Updike, Frederick Busch, and the American novel in the 1980s. He serves as executive editor of *Critique: Studies in Contemporary American Fiction*.

STEVEN G. KELLMAN is the Ashbel Smith Professor of Comparative Literature at the University of Texas-San Antonio and is the author of *The Plague: Fiction and Resistance* and *The Self-Begetting Novel*. In addition, he has edited casebooks on topics that include Nabokov, William Gass' *The Tunnel*, and the film *Raging Bull*. His essays on a wide variety of topics in contemporary fiction and film have appeared in numerous casebooks, journals, and reviews.

IRVING MALIN, Professor Emeritus at City College in New York, as critic and editor, remains one of the most respected and widely published figures in American literary criticism. In addition to his regular review assignments for a variety of journals and magazines and his extensive work editing collections of essays on a wide range of topics in twentieth-century literature, he is the author of the seminal works *New American Gothic* and *Jews and Americans*.

ROBERT MCMINN's essay is taken from his doctoral dissertation from the University of Nottingham, "Don DeLillo, Events, and Local Gods." He has also published in *Henry Street* and *Borderlines*.

THOMAS MYERS is an Associate Professor of Humanities at St. Norbert College in De Pere, Wisconsin, where he teaches courses in literature, film, and American Studies. The author of *Walking Point: American Narratives of Vietnam*, he is presently working on a novel about American cinema.

IRA NADEL, Professor of English at the University of British Columbia, is the author of *Biography Fiction, Fact & Form*; *Joyce and the Jews*; and *Various Positions: A Life of Leonard Cohen*, winner of the 1996 Medal for Canadian Biography. He has also edited *The Cambridge Companion to Ezra Pound* and *The Education of Henry Adams*. His biography on Tom Stoppard appeared in 2001.

CARL OSTROWSKI is an Assistant Professor of English at Middle Tennessee State University in Murfreesboro. He has published articles on American literature and library history in *American Transcendental Quarterly*, *Literature and Medicine*, and *Libraries & Culture*. He is at work on a book treating the early history of the Library of Congress.

TIMOTHY L. PARRISH teaches American literature and culture at the University of North Texas. His essays have appeared in *Contemporary Literature*, *Modern Fiction Studies*, *Arizona Quarterly*, *Studies in American Fiction*, *Texas Studies in Literature and Language*, among others. He is the author of *Walking Blues: Making Americans from Emerson to Elvis*.

MARC SINGER recently completed his Ph.D. at the University of Maryland. He has published essays in *Journal of Narrative Theory*, *African American Review*, and the *International Journal of Comic Art*.

DAVID YETTER holds an MFA from the Warren Wilson MFA Program for Writers in North Carolina. He lives in San Francisco and is working on a novel.

Index

215